# PARTNERING
*with the*
# KING

**STUDY THE GOSPEL OF MATTHEW**

*and Become a Disciple of Jesus*

# PARTNERING
## *with the*
# KING

## JOHN L. HIIGEL

PARACLETE PRESS
BREWSTER, MASSACHUSETTS

2016 Second Printing (POD)
2013 First Printing

*Partnering with the King: Study the Gospel of Matthew and
Become a Disciple of Jesus*

Copyright © 2013 by John L. Hiigel

ISBN 978-1-55725-997-4

Library of Congress Cataloging-in-Publication Data

Hiigel, John L.
  Partnering with the King : study the Gospel of Matthew and become a
disciple of Jesus / John L. Hiigel
      pages cm
  Includes bibliographical references (pages      ).
  ISBN 978-1-55725-997-4 (trade pbk.)
  1.  Christian life. 2.  Bible. N.T. Matthew.—Commentaries.  I. Title.
  BS2545.C48H53 2013
  226.2'077—dc23                                    2012042075

10 9 8 7 6 5 4 3 2

Published by Paraclete Press
Brewster, Massachusetts
www.paracletepress.com
Printed in the United States of America

---

*Dedicated with gratitude to*

STEVE STUCKEY

HANK POTT

BRUCE MILLER

AND

SAMUEL CHETTI

*who discipled me to Jesus during my college years.*

# CONTENTS

# INTRODUCTION

When we turn to the Scriptures to ask how to live as Christians, we find not the word *Christian*, but *disciple*. When we ask about how to live as disciples, we find not a topical essay or a set of instructions, but a story.

The story is indispensable, because to be a disciple is to follow a living person: the Lord Jesus Christ. The Gospel of Matthew narrates Jesus' life so that we will join with him. It beckons us into the ongoing story of the one who fulfilled God's promises to redeem us, rose from the dead, and promised to be with us always. Discipleship is life with Jesus, for Jesus, in partnership with Jesus.

I invite you to read the Gospel of Matthew with me for a month. The book in your hands is not a commentary but a devotional study meant to be read straight through, a chapter a day, as you immerse yourself in the Gospel of Matthew. (By all means, read it at a different pace if that works better for you. Small groups or Sunday school classes may wish to read it a chapter a week from fall to spring.) For newcomers, the book can serve as an introduction to the Christian life. For more seasoned Christians, I hope that it will be a source of renewal and vision.

For readers who hesitate to begin a life of following Jesus due to questions about whether Matthew is reliable, I have added an appendix at the end that addresses this very question. You may want to read that foundational information before launching into Day 1 of the Gospel study.

*Please don't skip over reading the text of Matthew itself in order to get to what I have to say!* The entire Gospel is reproduced here in these pages to make it easy to integrate Scripture and explanation. In the end, my chapters are only here to illuminate what is already right there in your Bible.

# YOU GIVE THEM
# SOMETHING
# TO EAT

### Matthew 14:13-21

The Gospel of Matthew is more than a grand announcement of good news about Jesus the Messiah; it is a call to respond. At the beginning of Jesus' public ministry, as he announces God's kingdom, he calls some individuals to be his disciples. At the end, he commands them to go out and make more disciples all over the world. By narrating Jesus' story, this Gospel tells us what we need to know in order to follow him and to be involved with him in his merciful work. We get to see him in action, hear his voice, and watch what his on-the-scene disciples are learning and doing. As we do, we discover what Jesus intends for us.

One episode from the heart of Matthew's Gospel displays especially well what it means to enter into this sort of life.

### ■ Matthew 14:13-21

¹³ When Jesus heard what had happened, he withdrew by boat privately to a solitary place. Hearing of this, the crowds followed him on foot from the towns. ¹⁴ When Jesus landed and saw a large crowd, he had compassion on them and healed their sick.

¹⁵ As evening approached, the disciples came to him and said, "This is a remote place, and it's already getting late. Send the crowds away, so they can go to the villages and buy themselves some food."

¹⁶ Jesus replied, "They do not need to go away. You give them something to eat."

[17] "We have here only five loaves of bread and two fish," they answered.

[18] "Bring them here to me," he said. [19] And he directed the people to sit down on the grass. Taking the five loaves and the two fish and looking up to heaven, he gave thanks and broke the loaves. Then he gave them to the disciples, and the disciples gave them to the people. [20] They all ate and were satisfied, and the disciples picked up twelve basketfuls of broken pieces that were left over. [21] The number of those who ate was about five thousand men, besides women and children.

As the story begins, Jesus has received some disheartening news, and we find him traveling by boat across the small Sea of Galilee with his disciples, trying to find some solitude. By this point in the Gospel, Jesus is famous for his work of healing, and when word gets out where he is headed, large crowds pursue him and are waiting when the boat arrives at the shore. Rather than send them away, Jesus responds with compassion and enters into a sustained time of ministering to the people's ailments and needs.

We become aware of his inner group of disciples in verse 15, where, picking up on the healer's compassion, they too show sympathy for the people. The place is remote, far from anywhere the people could obtain food. The crowd is becoming hungry, and the hour is late. The disciples bring their concern to Jesus: "Send the crowds away, so they can go to the villages and buy themselves some food."

Jesus' response catches our attention: "They do not need to go away. *You* give them something to eat." The word *you* is emphatic. His command is apparently ludicrous, with the thousands of people present and the distance from any food source. The disciples respond with a protest, "We have here only five loaves of bread and two fish," as if to say, "You must be joking! This is all we have!"

Jesus, however, is quite serious. He tells them to bring him what little they have. He has the people sit down on the grass. He takes the precious food, looks to heaven in prayer and gratitude, and then breaks the loaves for distribution. Matthew says, "Then he gave them to the disciples, and the disciples gave them to the people." The whole crowd is fed until they are fully satisfied, with much more food left over than they had available in the first place.

The question, then, is who fed the people? Our first answer would have to be Jesus. There is simply no question of thousands of people being fed from what amounts to a sack lunch apart from Jesus' powerful action. In Matthew's Gospel, the story comes in the middle of a section which is designed to thrust before us the question, "Do you recognize who this remarkable man is who is doing these things?" The section culminates in 16:16 with Peter's acclamation: "You are the Messiah, the Son of the living God." The King has come (*Messiah* means "anointed king"), and his people have gathered to him. All glory and honor and credit belong to King Jesus. *He* has fed the multitude.

But the answer to the question of who fed the people is also the disciples. Jesus commanded them, "You give them something to eat," and that is what they did. They brought Jesus what they had, and he blessed it and enabled them to love the people effectively and to meet their needs. *This is the picture of discipleship.* To be a disciple is to enter into a surprising partnership with the King. We live with Jesus and learn from him what to care about. *He* then meets people's needs, but he does so in some significant way through us and with us. We play a decidedly subordinate role in the partnership—Jesus is the *King*—but he has given us an essential role. "You give them something to eat," he commands, and by his kingly power he makes it possible for us to do it.

Our experience is not identical to those disciples' face-to-face, in-the-flesh interaction with Jesus, but the pattern of action is quite similar. We draw our life and strength from the resurrected Jesus who has promised to be with us always, to live with us in his very personal spiritual presence (28:20). When we see people in need, it is by prayer that we bring the need to Jesus. Our "hearing" his command to feed them comes from reading his words and being part of the community of praying believers who collectively listen, seeking to discern Jesus' will in order to do it. As he did in Galilee, Jesus still does great things today, and he does them through us and with us who are his disciples, his apprentices, his assistant coworkers.

Many illustrations of this phenomenon are available in our world, but I will select the story of Habitat for Humanity. The movement began with three families living in the American South who had been thinking seriously about partnering with the Lord and each other. They had begun to share Jesus' compassion for the many people nearby who were living miserably in leaking shacks that they could not even afford to own. The three families pulled together a dozen friends to meet for intensive prayer, taking to Jesus the human need they perceived. They came to the conclusion that the Savior was directing them, "*You* build them homes." The three families together owned a patch of farmland. A couple of them knew some basics about building. The group of praying friends contacted some more friends, and the money came in to build the first houses. Followers of Jesus contributed their labor, joined by the grateful shack-dwellers themselves, whose new homes they were building. The houses were sold to them for no profit, with long-term payment schedules, at no interest. Those payments in turn went into building more houses. Within a few years (though not without some problems, including some persecution), twenty-seven houses had been built. Then the question arose, "Might the Lord bless a project like this among the poor in Africa?" Millard and Linda Fuller, two of the original partners in Georgia, were soon at work with new partners multiplying houses in a village in Zaire. Then the question was, "Could we build by this pattern wherever in the world people need housing?"[1] Over half a million houses have now been built worldwide, housing two and a half million people.

Who housed all these people? Clearly, Jesus did. Those involved with Habitat for Humanity from the beginning will testify that apart from Jesus, such results were unthinkable. The living Savior motivated, guided, empowered, and supplied his followers. At the same time, clearly, it was Jesus' modern-day disciples who housed all those people. They sensed his heart and opened themselves to partnering with him. In prayer, they pointed to the need and they brought him what they had—their equivalent of five loaves and two fish. Jesus blessed it, and before long, they provided abundantly for a multitude.

In Matthew's story about the feeding of the thousands, the role of a disciple is fundamentally *active*. It is true that the disciples in the story get to eat bread themselves, but they are fed as they are involved in feeding others. Theirs is not merely the essentially passive role of receiving and eating, but the active role of praying (bringing the problem to Jesus), obeying, and distributing. The kingdom of heaven that Jesus has come to inaugurate is dynamic and active, and the Christian life, the life of being Jesus' disciples, involves entering into that activity of God through cooperating with Jesus. The Gospel of Matthew as a whole serves as a guidebook in which Jesus teaches and demonstrates what disciples are to do. It would be hard to exaggerate the importance of the point for Christians today: the Christian life is intentional involvement with Jesus in what he is doing.

In both the story about Jesus' healing and feeding the crowds and the example of Habitat for Humanity, the acts of compassion focus on people's physical needs. I recently heard a public radio interview with a poor man about the dire circumstances in his country that sometimes prevent him from eating for days at a time. He said, "Our only hope is that Jesus of Nazareth will feed us." Jesus of Nazareth continues to rescue the hungry, and he does it most often by the hands of his disciples who see the need and bring to him what they have. The good news is that God loves human beings at the level of our bodies, and we distort the gospel if we limit the good news to spiritual realities. The life of discipleship is not an otherworldly spirituality that ignores the down-to-earth needs of people. Jesus' command to give the hungry people something to eat is, first of all, to be taken literally.

To make the opposite error would also distort the gospel. Jesus' concern is much broader than people's physical needs. It is interesting that the next mention of bread in Matthew treats the word metaphorically. In the story of the Canaanite woman whose daughter is tormented by a demon (15:21–28), Jesus speaks of bread and the woman speaks of bread crumbs. Both refer to what the daughter needs, which is a spiritual healing. Jesus has come to relieve everything in life that is dark and miserable. His mission is to overcome hunger and hurt of all kinds, and so in a comprehensive way, his saving action brings people the equivalent of a full and satisfied stomach. When Jesus says to his disciples, "You give them something to eat," he is drawing them into a partnership with him to bring relief and life to people at every level of what it means to be alive. In Matthew, Jesus says the kingdom of heaven (the active reign of God) has come on the scene where people live; that is, God is about to establish his good and beneficial will in a hurting world. Jesus saves people out of darkness in all its forms, and he employs disciples to help convey that salvation. We enter into this relationship of attachment to Jesus—living with him, conversing with him, imitating him, going with him where he goes, doing what he says to do—so that we can share in his mission. We have the opportunity as disciples to work out how every aspect of our lives, careers, and relationships will fit into this grand and good thing God is doing.

When we read the story of the feeding of the five thousand in its wider context in Matthew, we notice that at two other suppers Jesus similarly takes bread, blesses it, and breaks it for distribution: at the feeding of the four thousand in 15:36 and, significantly, at the Lord's Supper in 26:26. That last intimate supper with his disciples illuminates the other two meals, the feedings of the multitudes.

First, at the Lord's Supper Jesus refers to the bread as being himself: "Take and eat; this is my body." Ultimately, the bread of life that the world needs most—the bread that will most fully over-come the people's hunger—is *Jesus*. Back at the seaside, looking beyond the multitude's immediate situation, Jesus' command to his disciples, "You give them something to eat," means, give them Jesus—help people to know him and to live in nourishing, forti-fying relationship with him.

Second, the passage about the Lord's Supper shows that these extraordinary meals point forward to something greater. After giving his disciples the bread and the wine in anticipation of his body being broken and his blood poured out, he says, "I tell you, I will not drink of this fruit of the vine from now on until that day when I drink it new with you in my Father's kingdom" (26:29). Jesus joyously awaits the coming day—beyond his death and resurrection—when he will return in glory and host the Great Banquet anticipated by faithful Jews. Jesus has come to gather to himself God's people, Israel, and to fulfill the promises of blessing spoken to their ancestors. Those promises include blessings for the Gentiles as well, a multitude of whom will join in the end-of-time celebration (8:11; Isaiah 25:6).

For the thousands beside the sea, their moment of enjoying lim-itless bread and fish with Jesus anticipates that ultimate banquet. As the disciples serve food to the large gathering, they collaborate with Jesus in his mission to unite and bless God's people. Disciples, then, are not a scattering of disconnected individuals, but are always part of a community. Matthew's Gospel repeatedly stresses this indispensable "together" aspect of the Christian life.

We can say that this one episode encapsulates the Gospel's most important themes about discipleship. Jesus invites his followers to partner with him as he works to establish God's merciful reign on earth. It is a lopsided partnership, to be sure, for *all* the power and authority comes from him. Jesus is the King; we are the junior partners. But it is nonetheless a real partnership, and by making us his collaborators, Jesus validates us and makes our lives fruitful. It is an *intimate* collaboration: we live with Jesus, our source of life, watching and listening, learning and praying. It is an *active* collaboration: we do not sit by passively, merely waiting to receive blessings or to pass into an afterlife. It is a *cooperative* collaboration: we serve Jesus together with others who are the family of God. And it is a *world-changing* collaboration: through our discipleship, God compassionately satisfies the hunger of the world—physically, morally, and spiritually. This is truly good news. The Gospel of Matthew is a guidebook and invitation to this adventurous life of discipleship.

*As disciples, King Jesus makes us his partners in his work of compassion so that he meets people's needs, but he does so through us and with us.*

## DAY 2 | A PLACE IN GOD'S STORY

Matthew 1-2

■ Matthew 1:1-17

1 ¹ This is the genealogy of Jesus the Messiah the son of David, the son of Abraham:

² Abraham was the father of Isaac,

Isaac the father of Jacob,

Jacob the father of Judah and his brothers,

³ Judah the father of Perez and Zerah, whose mother was Tamar,

Perez the father of Hezron,
Hezron the father of Ram,
⁴ Ram the father of Amminadab,
Amminadab the father of Nahshon,
Nahshon the father of Salmon,
⁵ Salmon the father of Boaz, whose mother was Rahab,
Boaz the father of Obed, whose mother was Ruth,
Obed the father of Jesse,
⁶ and Jesse the father of King David.
David was the father of Solomon,
    whose mother had been Uriah's wife,
⁷ Solomon the father of Rehoboam,
Rehoboam the father of Abijah,
Abijah the father of Asa,
⁸ Asa the father of Jehoshaphat,
Jehoshaphat the father of Jehoram,
Jehoram the father of Uzziah,
⁹ Uzziah the father of Jotham,
Jotham the father of Ahaz,
Ahaz the father of Hezekiah,
¹⁰ Hezekiah the father of Manasseh,
Manasseh the father of Amon,
Amon the father of Josiah,
¹¹ and Josiah the father of Jeconiah and his brothers
    at the time of the exile to Babylon.
¹² After the exile to Babylon:
Jeconiah was the father of Shealtiel,
Shealtiel the father of Zerubbabel,
¹³ Zerubbabel the father of Abihud,
Abihud the father of Eliakim,
Eliakim the father of Azor,
¹⁴ Azor the father of Zadok,
Zadok the father of Akim,
Akim the father of Elihud,

<sup>15</sup> Elihud the father of Eleazar,

Eleazar the father of Matthan,

Matthan the father of Jacob,

<sup>16</sup> and Jacob the father of Joseph, the husband of Mary, and Mary was the mother of Jesus who is called the Messiah.

<sup>17</sup> Thus there were fourteen generations in all from Abraham to David, fourteen from David to the exile to Babylon, and fourteen from the exile to the Messiah.

It's not exactly a gripping beginning, is it? Today we are not very fond of genealogies. Even people who are interested in their own family tree become bored quickly when they have to read someone else's. This is because we find our public identity in things besides family—things such as job, rank, education. In the ancient Near East, though, people were known by their family ties. By means of this genealogy, Matthew identifies Jesus for us. Attaching ourselves to Jesus as his disciples is a little like getting married: we cannot fully know our partner without knowing our partner's family, and when we marry, we become part of that family.

Jesus' family is not just any family! God chose this family as his own people, gave them enduring promises, and vowed to bless all the other families of the earth through them. Jesus' family is Israel, and most of the family history that Matthew outlines was known and preserved in the Old Testament—the Hebrew Scriptures—whose authority Jesus and all the Jews trusted. Jesus' life is the most significant event in that special family's history.

Matthew is particularly interested in two ancestors, David and Abraham (verse 1). Abraham was significant because of the promises God made to him that reveal God's grand plan (Genesis 12:1–3). In order to save the world from the mess created by human sin, God's plan has been to bless Abraham and his descendants (the Jews) and then bless the rest of the world through them. This well-being that God continues to bestow on humanity includes equipping us to live righteously and justly (see Genesis 18:18–19). By tracing Jesus' family lineage back to Abraham, Matthew is saying that Jesus has come to fulfill God's grand plan to bless the world.

And within Abraham's lineage, Jesus is "son of David." David was Israel's greatest king, the man after God's own heart, chosen to lead Israel into faithfulness toward God. God promised to establish David and his heirs in a perpetual kingship over God's people: "Your house and your kingdom will endure forever before me" (2 Samuel 7:16). David's anointed descendant will bring blessing not just to Israel, but to the world. "May he rule . . . to the ends of the earth. . . . May his name endure forever. . . . Then all nations will be blessed through him" (Psalm 72:8, 17; see also Isaiah 55:3–5). Matthew announces that the King descended from David has come, the heir to God's promises, and blessings for the world are sure to follow.

The third key event in the family history, however, unlike God's heartening promises to Abraham and David, was a catastrophe. The "exile to Babylon" (verses 11, 12) was the deportation of the people of Israel from the Promised Land into slavery and misery, with Jerusalem and its temple destroyed. The Old Testament prophets' message was that the exile came because God's people had abandoned him and proved unfaithful to his *covenant* with them, the marriage-like bond he had established with them through Moses at Mount Sinai. Consequently, God had withdrawn his protection for a time. Invaders from the east took away the Israelites' security and political sovereignty, which they longed to recover. Those who did return from exile lived under the control of one foreign empire after another. But the same prophets who predicted the exile also spoke of a hopeful future under the kingship of a descendant of King David. In the centuries leading to Jesus' birth, the Jews waited and speculated and hoped, yearning for the Messiah (in Greek: *Christ*), the anointed King who would fulfill God's promises to Abraham and David. Matthew asserts from the very first verse that Jesus is the long-awaited Messiah.

So first of all, the genealogy tells us Jesus' identity: he is the promised King over God's people. The point for our discipleship is that everything revolves around him. Jesus will press the question, "Who do you say that I am?" and will say repeatedly, "Follow me; come to me." The decisive issue in every person's life will be to recognize who Jesus is and come to him.

This leads to the genealogy's second contribution: the idea that something long hoped for is being fulfilled. The technical term for this idea is *eschatology*, time arriving at its destination. Jesus' coming marks the decisive moment when God dramatically intervenes to fulfill his plans. Matthew symbolizes this idea of the fullness of time by the series of fourteens at the end of the genealogy (verse 17). The ancient Near Eastern peoples attributed meaning to certain numbers, particularly the number seven, which signified completion and fullness. The generations between Abraham and David were twice seven. The same interval of two sevens separates David and the exile, and after two more sevens comes Jesus. With him, the open-ended seventh seven has begun. Israel's long story has pointed forward to Jesus, and he is now on the scene to complete God's plan. One of the most important ideas for understanding discipleship is that every disciple is part of this grand unfolding story that is much bigger than our own individual life story. Whatever our own agenda may have been before encountering Jesus, it is now to find our place in God's plan. Instead of asking whether God fits into our story, we learn to ask where we fit in his.

This leads to a third emphasis, which a genealogy is ideally suited to express: Jesus comes to fulfill the destiny of a people, a family. He comes to gather Israel. His beloved people, scattered by exile, are to find home and family love in relationship with him. In the course of the Gospel, Jesus will often use family terminology to speak of his followers, describing disciples as brothers and sisters and mother and father and children. Being a disciple means finding our place in a community, a family, God's people.

With all of this emphasis on Jesus gathering his Jewish family, what are we to make of the eventual inclusion of Gentiles (non-Jews) in the community of Jesus? Matthew laments often in his Gospel that so many fellow Jews rejected Jesus. Nevertheless, Jesus attracted large crowds of Jews. The earliest Christian churches were made up almost entirely of Jews who believed that they were carrying the torch handed to them by the faithful Jews of all previous generations. But by the time Matthew wrote this Gospel, a fair number of Gentiles were included in the churches. The early believers opened their arms to Gentile members as Jesus instructed them to do (28:19; 24:14), confident that through their invitation Jesus was fulfilling God's promises to Abraham and David that he would bless the whole world. By emphasizing Abraham and David, to whom the global promises were made, and by including in Jesus' genealogy some Gentile women, Matthew points beyond the Jewish family to the Gentiles, whom God will bless, too.

The point is that the blessing comes to a community, an inclusive family. Nothing about Jesus' message or ministry is individualistic. Christian faith is not entirely or even mostly private, because we live it out alongside others as part of a community of faith. In Matthew, Jesus uses many images to portray his ministry of bringing people together: a shepherd gathering sheep, a farmer harvesting grain, a fisherman pulling in his fishnet, a mother hen gathering her chicks, a brother drawing together family members, and a builder assembling his church (a word that means "a gathering"). In coming to Jesus, we come into his family, whom we meet wherever we find his churches. We gain a long and venerable heritage, a common identity with men and women of faith going back well before Jesus and including all his followers since, with all their glory and all their imperfections. We belong. It is amazing to have a part in something so big and important.

### ■ Matthew 1:18–2:23

<sup></sup>18 This is how the birth of Jesus the Messiah came about: His mother Mary was pledged to be married to Joseph, but before they came together, she was found to be pregnant through the

Holy Spirit. [19] Because Joseph her husband was faithful to the law and yet did not want to expose her to public disgrace, he had in mind to divorce her quietly.

[20] But after he had considered this, an angel of the Lord appeared to him in a dream and said, "Joseph son of David, do not be afraid to take Mary home as your wife, because what is conceived in her is from the Holy Spirit. [21] She will give birth to a son, and you are to give him the name Jesus, because he will save his people from their sins."

[22] All this took place to fulfill what the Lord had said through the prophet: [23] "The virgin will conceive and give birth to a son, and they will call him Immanuel" (which means "God with us").

[24] When Joseph woke up, he did what the angel of the Lord had commanded him and took Mary home as his wife. [25] But he did not consummate their marriage until she gave birth to a son. And he gave him the name Jesus.

2 [1] After Jesus was born in Bethlehem in Judea, during the time of King Herod, Magi from the east came to Jerusalem [2] and asked, "Where is the one who has been born king of the Jews? We saw his star when it rose and have come to worship him."

[3] When King Herod heard this he was disturbed, and all Jerusalem with him. [4] When he had called together all the people's chief priests and teachers of the law, he asked them where the Messiah was to be born. [5] "In Bethlehem in Judea," they replied, "for this is what the prophet has written:

> [6] "'But you, Bethlehem, in the land of Judah,
>     are by no means least among the rulers of Judah;
> for out of you will come a ruler
>     who will shepherd my people Israel.'"

[7] Then Herod called the Magi secretly and found out from them the exact time the star had appeared. [8] He sent them to Bethlehem and said, "Go and search carefully for the child. As soon as you find him, report to me, so that I too may go and worship him."

⁹ After they had heard the king, they went on their way, and the star they had seen when it rose went ahead of them until it stopped over the place where the child was. ¹⁰ When they saw the star, they were overjoyed. ¹¹ On coming to the house, they saw the child with his mother Mary, and they bowed down and worshiped him. Then they opened their treasures and presented him with gifts of gold, frankincense and myrrh. ¹² And having been warned in a dream not to go back to Herod, they returned to their country by another route.

¹³ When they had gone, an angel of the Lord appeared to Joseph in a dream. "Get up," he said, "take the child and his mother and escape to Egypt. Stay there until I tell you, for Herod is going to search for the child to kill him."

¹⁴ So he got up, took the child and his mother during the night and left for Egypt, ¹⁵ where he stayed until the death of Herod. And so was fulfilled what the Lord had said through the prophet: "Out of Egypt I called my son."

¹⁶ When Herod realized that he had been outwitted by the Magi, he was furious, and he gave orders to kill all the boys in Bethlehem and its vicinity who were two years old and under, in accordance with the time he had learned from the Magi. ¹⁷ Then what was said through the prophet Jeremiah was fulfilled:

> ¹⁸ "A voice is heard in Ramah,
>      weeping and great mourning,
> Rachel weeping for her children
>      and refusing to be comforted,
>      because they are no more."

¹⁹ After Herod died, an angel of the Lord appeared in a dream to Joseph in Egypt ²⁰ and said, "Get up, take the child and his mother and go to the land of Israel, for those who were trying to take the child's life are dead."

²¹ So he got up, took the child and his mother and went to the land of Israel. ²² But when he heard that Archelaus was reigning

in Judea in place of his father Herod, he was afraid to go there. Having been warned in a dream, he withdrew to the district of Galilee, [23] and he went and lived in a town called Nazareth. So was fulfilled what was said through the prophets that he would be called a Nazarene.

The story of Jesus' birth and early childhood reinforces all three of the themes we observed in the genealogy: Jesus is identified as the great King; his birth signals God's anticipated moment for action; and his life fulfills God's plans for his people.

First, Matthew tells the story to say who Jesus is in as many ways as possible, beginning with his royal title, "This is how the birth of Jesus the Messiah came about." Jesus is conceived in a virgin's womb by the power of the Holy Spirit of God. His adoptive father, Joseph, provides the royal lineage—he is "Joseph, son of David." An angel declares the baby's name, Jesus, which means "the Lord saves," for he will save his people from their sins. Quotations from the prophets exalt him: he is the Messiah, the Shepherd of Israel, God's Son, "God with us." Gentiles from a distant country come to bow in worship before the child they call "King of the Jews." The final verse uses a play on the name of Jesus' hometown of Nazareth to speak of Jesus as the "branch" (Hebrew: *netzer*) of David's family on whom the Spirit of the Lord will rest (Isaiah 11:1–2). Could more declarations about who Jesus is possibly be packed into such a brief story?

Second, Matthew expresses Jesus' significance by saying repeatedly, "All this took place to fulfill what the Lord had said through the prophet." Jesus' coming is Israel's long-awaited event, the crucial moment in their family story. And third, the event is great because God is fulfilling his plans for his chosen people. Jesus relives the nation's pivotal episodes and personally embodies what it means to be God's chosen people. Like Israel of old, he goes down to Egypt and returns. Like exiled Israel, he is targeted for death by a hostile ruler. He has come to "save his people from their sins" and to shepherd his people Israel. All who become his followers (Jews first, but eventually Gentiles as well) are the sheep he gathers and serves.

So the decisive moment has arrived. Israel's long-awaited Shepherd King has come. How will the people respond? Matthew points to a sharp contrast. Jesus' coming is an intrusion to some but a joy to others. King Herod and the residents of Jerusalem are "disturbed"—troubled, upset, scared—by news about a king of the Jews. By contrast, some strangers from the east joyfully open their hearts and their treasures to the child born to be King and Savior. Ironically, it is these outsiders who model the right way to respond to Jesus' arrival. They recognize that something momentous is happening, and so they pursue him and kneel before him and offer him what they value most.

How much do these men really understand about God or Jesus? After all, they are pagan astrologers. Yet they sense that someone of surpassing importance has come, and they take action. They leave all that is familiar, all their comfort and safety, and press forward tenaciously to come to him and honor him. Their determination to pay tribute to the King of the Jews leads to a dramatic, thrilling venture with God, who guides them and fills them with joy.

We are drawn also to Joseph, a good man who responds admirably as his life is turned upside down by Jesus' coming. When he receives the angelic word regarding his fiancée, which shakes up his previous view of the world (a pregnant virgin!) and requires him to endure public embarrassment, he weds Mary, as the Lord commands him. Then, when living with Jesus forces ever more disruptions, detours, and dangers into his life, Joseph adjusts faithfully. (Luke tells us that Mary, too, adjusted admirably.) This capacity to change course in order to cooperate with what God is doing is one of the key marks of a disciple.

So even in Matthew's stories of Jesus' childhood we see models of how to respond to his arrival. Joseph and the Magi from the East recognize—they do not fully understand yet, but they recognize—that Jesus is the most important person they could possibly imagine. God's moment has arrived, so they adjust their lives, grasping that the time for action is now. They sense that a new future is dawning for God's people. Altogether, the first two chapters are a wake-up call for every reader of Matthew's Gospel. God is with us as never before. Jesus the Shepherd King has come to gather his people; get ready to respond!

> *Because the King has come, we adjust our lives,
> seeking our role in God's story and our
> roots in his family.*

<br>

**DAY 3** | # MORAL PREPARATION

Matthew 3

<br>

■ Matthew 3:1–12

**3**¹ In those days John the Baptist came, preaching in the wilderness of Judea ² and saying, "Repent, for the kingdom of heaven has come near." ³ This is he who was spoken of through the prophet Isaiah:

> "A voice of one calling in the wilderness,
> 'Prepare the way for the Lord,
>     make straight paths for him.'"

⁴ John's clothes were made of camel's hair, and he had a leather belt around his waist. His food was locusts and wild honey. ⁵ People went out to him from Jerusalem and all Judea and the whole region of the Jordan. ⁶ Confessing their sins, they were baptized by him in the Jordan River.

⁷ But when he saw many of the Pharisees and Sadducees coming to where he was baptizing, he said to them: "You brood of vipers! Who warned you to flee from the coming wrath? ⁸ Produce fruit in keeping with repentance. ⁹ And do not think you can say to yourselves, 'We have Abraham as our father.' I tell you that out of these stones God can raise up children for Abraham. ¹⁰ The ax is already at the root of the trees, and every tree that does not produce good fruit will be cut down and thrown into the fire.

¹¹ "I baptize you with water for repentance. But after me comes one who is more powerful than I, whose sandals I am not worthy to carry. He will baptize you with the Holy Spirit and fire. ¹² His winnowing fork is in his hand, and he will clear his threshing floor, gathering his wheat into the barn and burning up the chaff with unquenchable fire."

Matthew's call to be ready, sounded in his first two chapters, now intensifies. Centuries of waiting have come to an end, and God's moment for action has arrived. John the Baptist, the last of Israel's great prophets (11:13), comes on the scene to cry out, "Prepare the way of the Lord."

Dressed in rough clothes reminiscent of the prophet Elijah, John announces that the anticipated Day of the Lord has come (see 2 Kings 1:7–8; Malachi 4:5). God's appointed time to judge rebels and restore his people has arrived. John calls his audience to repent, to turn away from their sins, indeed to change their whole way of thinking and living in readiness for the any-day-now arrival of the one who baptizes with the Holy Spirit and fire.

John's announcement of the kingdom of heaven comes as good news. God had always been king—this is a recurring theme in the

Old Testament psalms and the prophets—but the Jews' hard experience seemed to suggest otherwise. *Human* kings appeared to be in charge century after century—oppressive foreigners with their fearsome armies: Assyrians, then Babylonians, then Persians, then Greeks, now Romans. The crowds likely understood John the Baptist's message to mean that God was about to overturn those worldly authorities and restore possession of the land to his people. John's choice of the Jordan River for his preaching and baptizing is full of symbolism. After their ancient Exodus from slavery in Egypt and wandering in the wilderness, the Israelites had entered the Promised Land by crossing the Jordan. Later, during the exile, Israel found itself back in the wilderness again. John now stations himself at the river, the gateway into the homeland, to announce an end to the gloom of being powerless and lost. As he preaches and baptizes, the people of Israel flow to him and open their hearts.

There is no more crucial idea in Matthew than John's phrase, "The kingdom of heaven has come near." John's message in 3:2 will be Jesus' message in 4:17, and then it will be Jesus' followers' message when he sends them out in 10:7. What does it mean? The key word is *kingdom*. God, who is heavenly (that is, a personal spiritual being), is truly the king of the world, and he is acting now to consolidate his kingship (his sovereignty, his reign) by overcoming all sources of evil and misery. The kingdom of heaven is *God's reign as king*. We misunderstand the phrase when we make *heaven* the key word and think that John and Jesus are talking about a place people go for life after death. Rather, the kingdom of heaven here refers to God's beneficial action in the world to take charge as king. The concluding phrase, "has come near," refers to the *now* of God's action. John is announcing that the crucial moment in God's grand story of salvation has arrived. The decisive phase in his enterprise to overcome evil with good has begun.

Precisely because God is about to combat evil in the world, John's message sounds scary and urgent: "Who warned you to flee from the coming wrath?" An ax is already poised to cut down the fruitless "trees." The one coming after John will baptize with the Holy Spirit and fire. John tells the crowds that God's great intervention will confront not only the evil "out there" in demonic political powers, but the evil "within" their own community. The people need to depart from sin in order to "prepare the way of the Lord" who is about to act on their behalf. John provocatively insists that even those with a reputation for piety need inner cleansing. Everyone will need to regroup in light of God's blazing holiness and his imminent action. A great sifting will soon separate the "wheat" from the "chaff." Now is the time to decide—to repent with a lasting repentance that yields a fruitful life.

John is not particularly diplomatic! "You brood of vipers!" His words sting, but his urgent call to repentance pinpoints the reason why many new believers today fail to get a solid start in the Christian life and why many long-time believers never go very deep. The obstacle is our resistance to coming clean about how we have lived before. What vices have we justified by persuading ourselves that everyone does it? When did we disregard good moral advice? What did we do out of selfishness or malice? What are we still defensive about? When did we ignore our conscience—or what have we done so many times that our conscience no longer troubles us about it? What did we participate in but shift the blame to others?

Through Jesus' death, God is certainly willing to forgive whatever he finds displeasing in our past or our present so that we can start fresh. But nothing can be off limits to God's scrutiny. John is saying that the only way to prepare for God's new action in our lives is to let go of those things. The point of repenting is that we want to cooperate with God instead of getting in his way. Only by giving God access to every corner of our hearts can we be free to partner with him.

Some may fear that if we face all those things in our personal story, we will begin to feel like a "bad person." Fortunately, we do not need to fear discovering that our moral deficiencies go deeper than we thought. As we will see in the Gospel of Matthew, Jesus is astonishingly willing to welcome people of all kinds, however bad their prior record has been, and to treat them as people of dignity and promise. It is a humbling but necessary step to realize that we truly need God's mercy and forgiveness.

Someone who has always had a reputation for being a "good person" may be especially reluctant to be inwardly honest. The Pharisees and Sadducees in this story are like that. So was I. I didn't want forgiveness; I wanted to get it right. I wanted to prove to myself that I could be a better man than those around me. Over the period of a year or so when I was a grad student, the Lord had to bring me through a series of failures in which I could no longer deny that I was becoming an irritating person. I needed forgiveness, and plenty of it, from God and the people in my life. I remember vividly the morning I just let go. "God, I'm sorry, deeply sorry, and I need all the help from you I can get." The relief was tremendous—like a huge load had been lifted from my shoulders! My whole future looked new.

The scene around John at the Jordan River is very encouraging. People with good reputations and bad are confessing their sins, receiving his baptism of restoration, and finding themselves open and ready for God's new action through Jesus.

## ■ Matthew 3:13–17

[13] Then Jesus came from Galilee to the Jordan to be baptized by John. [14] But John tried to deter him, saying, "I need to be baptized by you, and do you come to me?"

[15] Jesus replied, "Let it be so now; it is proper for us to do this to fulfill all righteousness." Then John consented.

[16] As soon as Jesus was baptized, he went up out of the water. At that moment heaven was opened, and he saw the Spirit of God descending like a dove and alighting on him. [17] And a voice from heaven said, "This is my Son, whom I love; with him I am well pleased."

John is an intriguing character, with his strange clothes and diet. He is the only person whose appearance Matthew describes; even Jesus is never described.

The Baptist's words are full of fireworks. He is a phenomenon, able to draw large crowds. His preaching penetrates their hearts and changes them. Yet as impressive as he is on his own merits, he persistently points to someone else who is yet to come and insists he is not in that man's league! From John's imagery we expect a fearsome person as Jesus enters the stage. This "more powerful one" comes with fire—with God's *Holy* Spirit. He wields an ax in wrath, a winnowing fork in judgment.

When we hear Jesus say later, "I am gentle and humble in heart, and you will find rest for your souls" (11:29), we do well to remember John's edgy advance description of Jesus. John is right. Jesus *does* require righteousness (5:18–20). He *does* come boldly to confront all the powers of evil in order to establish God's undisputed reign (12:28–29). He *will* one day sit in judgment over all humankind (25:31–32). The Savior has come "to fulfill all righteousness"—a great purifying work—and we all need his cleansing.

John is also right about Jesus' surpassing greatness. No wonder John hesitates to baptize Jesus, protesting that Jesus should instead be baptizing *him*. Jesus is peerless, far above John and everyone else. As he comes up out of the waters of baptism, the Holy Spirit descends on him, and the voice of God affirms, "This is my Son, whom I love; with him I am well pleased." The Spirit anoints him with power, and God acclaims him as Son. The multitude there at the river is in the very presence of God, three in one, Father, Son, and Holy Spirit. (Jesus will later command that followers be baptized into this threefold name of God [28:19].) Jesus is "God with us."

For all his greatness, what strikes us about Jesus in this passage is the opposite of what John has led us to expect. Jesus is not overwhelming. He comes without fanfare as part of the crowd, and he identifies with them. John has been calling the community of Israel to repentance, and though Jesus himself needs no repentance, he participates in baptism as part of that community. "Let it be so now; it is proper for us to do this to fulfill all righteousness," he says, not emphasizing his superiority, but rather his connection with the people. By submitting to baptism, Jesus begins to lead his people on the pathway of righteousness. As disciples, both Jew and Gentile, we can say that Jesus has not come to stand above us—though he most certainly is above us—but to live with us and identify with us and show us the way.

From the beginning of his public life, Jesus sets out, as the book of Hebrews puts it, to be the pioneer of our salvation (Hebrews 2:10; 12:2). In the life of faith, he is the trailblazer where others will follow. He does what his people must do. He will say to his first disciples, "Follow me," and he can say that because he is living the life he wants his followers to live.

Many have wondered about the time gap between Matthew 2 and 3. We hear nothing about Jesus after his early childhood until he emerges as an adult ready for leadership. What happened during those intervening years? Isn't it possible that nothing is recorded about those years because nothing noteworthy happened? The only hint Matthew gives us is in 13:55, where someone from Jesus' hometown identifies him as "the carpenter's son." The parallel passage in Mark calls Jesus simply "the carpenter." Jesus learned a trade. He worked with his hands and earned his daily bread. The beloved Son of God lived a normal human life in a small Galilean town. He went regularly to synagogue and learned the Scriptures (Luke 4:16), as any good Israelite young man would have done. Jesus identified with the people. He was baptized into solidarity with us, and he lived our life so we could learn to live his. God is well pleased with Jesus, and he has set out to form a whole people with whom he can be well pleased.

The kingdom of heaven has come near; that is, God is on the move to have his way on the human scene—right where we live and in the remotest parts of the globe. The loving God who opens the heavens and pours out his Spirit is ready to do something great in and through us. We have to re-imagine everything in light of this reality and prepare our hearts so we can cooperate with him in what he is doing. We will experience the meaningful life Jesus came to give us as we open within our hearts an unobstructed "straight path" for him.

*God is on the move to have his beneficial way on the human scene. We ready ourselves by opening the way for him in our hearts.*

# TEMPTED | DAY 4

## Matthew 4:1-11

■ Matthew 4:1-11

**4** ¹ Then Jesus was led by the Spirit into the wilderness to be tempted by the devil. ² After fasting forty days and forty nights, he was hungry. ³ The tempter came to him and said, "If you are the Son of God, tell these stones to become bread."

⁴ Jesus answered, "It is written: 'Man shall not live on bread alone, but on every word that comes from the mouth of God.'"

⁵ Then the devil took him to the holy city and had him stand on the highest point of the temple. ⁶ "If you are the Son of God," he said, "throw yourself down. For it is written:

"'He will command his angels concerning you,
> and they will lift you up in their hands,
>> so that you will not strike your foot against a stone.'"

[7] Jesus answered him, "It is also written: 'Do not put the Lord your God to the test.'"

[8] Again, the devil took him to a very high mountain and showed him all the kingdoms of the world and their splendor. [9] "All this I will give you," he said, "if you will bow down and worship me."

[10] Jesus said to him, "Away from me, Satan! For it is written: 'Worship the Lord your God, and serve him only.'"

[11] Then the devil left him, and angels came and attended him.

All people of faith, no matter how weak or how strong, experience temptation. To be tempted is to have our loyalty to God tested or strained, to be put at risk of falling away from God's path for us. It is reassuring to read that Jesus knows our experience of temptation firsthand.

He experienced it without being defeated by it. In his temptation, as in his upbringing and baptism, Jesus joins in the life of normal human beings. In particular, he identifies with his own people, reliving the family's story. His forty days in the wilderness recall Israel's forty years of wilderness trials before entering the Promised Land. With each temptation, Jesus keeps from stumbling by remembering what God told Moses during Israel's wilderness years (Deuteronomy 8:3; 6:16; and 6:13). Looking forward, Jesus also identifies with all who will become his disciples. Many who have begun the Christian life can attest to the experience of being strongly tempted right at the first. Just as Jesus' followers will face the possibility of being knocked out of action from the very beginning, so Jesus faces this trial right after his baptism.

Jesus has come to make God's merciful kingship the dominant force in the world, but he faces determined resistance from dark spiritual forces. In the desert he encounters the being called the devil or Satan, and many times in Matthew he confronts demons. They are malevolent spiritual beings, intelligent and organized, the negative counterpart to angels.[2] Though the days of fasting and prayer in the wilderness weaken Jesus' body, they strengthen his will. The devil attempts to derail Jesus before his ministry ever starts, but Jesus prevails, not because he has special power as the Son of God, but because he has disciplined himself in prayer and Scripture, and he receives moral strength from the Holy Spirit. By this early victory, he breaches the devil's defenses. The Savior is ready to launch his mission to establish God's reign. Hereafter, the demons will tremble in his presence.

Every generation of his followers will face the three temptations Jesus faces in the wilderness. At first glance, though, their meaning is obscure. They do not resemble the typical stumbling blocks of lust or greed or jealousy. So what is going on?

The devil's enticements make sense only because they target a man who intends to change the world. The devil, as portrayed in the New Testament, competes with God to control the world. He is by no means God's equal; he is a parasite. He latches on to people who rightfully belong to God and sucks the life out of them. By enticing people into what masquerades as real life, he draws them away from the Giver of life. Convincing them they will be free, he makes them his dupes and slaves. Many people are simple for the devil to manage. He easily keeps them from God by offering up naughty fun or selfish gain. Others try to be good, but they do little to hamper the devil's work as long as they don't consciously join up with God. Jesus, by contrast, has come to dismantle the devil's whole enterprise and to gather allies (disciples) to assist him in the task. The Savior's work to establish God's rightful authority on the human scene is a frontal assault on Satan's "kingdom" (12:25–26).

The devil is too shrewd to tempt Jesus to do anything obviously immoral. His real objective is to get him to claim what he is entitled to as God's man, as a worker on the side of good. If the devil can persuade Jesus to take charge of things for a moment, to grab a bit of advantage by asserting his rights, Jesus will be neutralized as a threat to the devil. His message to Jesus is this: "Don't wait for God to work things his way and in his time. Surely it is legitimate to take charge yourself and make good things happen." If the devil can get Jesus to assert his *own* will about something, even something worthy, he will undermine Jesus' entire mission to establish *God's* authority in the world. (Jesus expresses this point in his prayer, "Not as I will, but as you will" [26:39].) The three benefits the devil dangles before Jesus here in the wilderness are not evil in themselves. To the contrary, plenty, protection, and power (understood as influence) are basic benefits that God commonly provides to those who are faithful to him. But the devil offers Jesus shortcuts, ways to take charge for himself and leap impatiently ahead of God's own plans to provide.

First is the temptation to grab for plenty. Forty days of fasting is scarcely imaginable. The Spirit has led Jesus into the wilderness for intensive preparation. Jesus has no food and apparently no knowledge of when his fast is to end. The devil comes to him and suggests that food is at Jesus' very fingertips if he simply says the word. As the Son of God, Jesus could take care of himself on the spot. "God has withheld food from you out here; feed yourself. Turn these plentiful stones into bread."

Jesus responds that he has been receiving nourishment of another kind: life comes by the word of God. Moreover, even in his physical hunger, Jesus trusts that God will provide everything he needs as he needs it. He expresses both points by quoting Moses from memory, "[The LORD] humbled you, causing you to hunger and then feeding you with manna . . . to teach you that man shall not live on bread alone but on every word that comes from the mouth of the LORD" (Deuteronomy 8:3). Jesus trusts God with his time of humbling and hunger, reasoning that the God who provided for his ancestors will provide for him as well. He refuses to take untrusting, independent action.

In my days as a youth pastor, I took our church's youth from our home in Southern California to a poor village south of the

Mexican border for a week every year. Our ongoing project was to provide materials and labor to help men from a nearby town construct a church building and a pastor's residence for this village. Each evening during our visits, we built a campfire and sang and talked. Late one evening after the youth had all gone indoors and our Mexican team members had left for home, a half-dozen young men from the village came to the smoldering campfire and began to talk with me about plenty and want and what it might mean to trust God. These were vigorous men, and I presumed that they had been working all day. As we talked, they spoke respectfully, but they also had some pressing questions. Their leader asked me if I had given my wife a diamond when I married her. I said yes. I didn't say, "Of course," but he knew it was "of course." It is something most Americans do. He said that none of them would be able to do that. He asked me if I trusted God to provide food for my family. I said yes. He asked me why I thought God, rather than where I lived, was the reason I had enough food, because where he lived there were days when he did not have food. He asked why he should trust God rather than trust his own initiative (and cunning) to cross over to my side of the border, where eating every day could be an "of course" for him, as it is for me.

I have no identification with his experience of hunger, but Jesus does. Jesus grew up in a poor town much like that Mexican village, and now in the wilderness he goes without food for a very long time. The devil tempts Jesus to push the issue, to make bread an "of course" and do what it takes to get some. Instead, Jesus submits to being humbled through extreme want and trusts that God will meet his needs according to his wisdom. He does find God faithful—and soon he will call disciples to join him in feeding the hungry.

We in America believe we are entitled to food—and to a lot more than food—and we can be pretty intolerant of having to wait for it. We see people around us who have more of everything than we have, and advertising tells us relentlessly that we deserve to have more. (A recent ad chants, "I want it all, and I want it now.") The devil tempted Jesus to acquire plenty on his own terms rather than submit to God. Every believer today faces the same temptation. Matthew's Gospel will warn repeatedly about the enticements of material abundance.

The second temptation is for Jesus to assert his right to be protected. "If you are the Son of God, throw yourself down [from this very high place]." The devil even quotes Scripture to justify what he is suggesting to Jesus. He tempts Jesus to force God's hand: "Hurl yourself out there; God will protect you." Jesus' scriptural answer is instructive: "It is also written: 'Do not put the Lord your God to the test.'"

Today we put God to the test when we create our own peril through impulsiveness and pride. Students party unwisely and end up in trouble. Couples cohabitate disobediently or enter marriage without paying attention to God, and the relationship sours. Adults make risky career moves without patiently seeking him. Churches take grand initiatives out of spiritual valor and desire for reputation and wind up with a financial catastrophe. We bring on our own crisis, but then protest, "Where is God? How can I believe in God if he lets things like this happen to me? He should be protecting me." But Jesus is our model. He spends forty days in sustained listening, and he refuses to force God into an unnecessary rescue.

Likely, the devil does not expect Jesus to be impulsive, but rather to demand what he deserves as a good man. The Old Testament often says that God protects the righteous. The psalm the devil quotes is about God preserving his faithful ones from danger (Psalm 91:9–12). Similarly, the Proverbs say, "[The LORD] is a shield to those whose walk is blameless" (2:7), and "The righteous person is rescued from trouble" (11:8). Who is more righteous than the Son of God? The devil is saying, "You are about to launch out and do great things for God. Make God prove his support for you. Compel him to guarantee your mission by coming to your rescue."

Doesn't the Son of God have a right to personal security? By asking this question, the devil strikes at the heart of Jesus' mission. In 16:21 and several times again, Jesus will tell his disciples that he must be killed. The Son of Man has come "to give his life as a ransom for many" (20:28). Jesus speaks his most severe words ("Get behind me, Satan!") to his beloved disciple Peter when Peter tries to insist that God would surely not allow the Messiah to be killed. Jesus' death will not be the end—God will raise him from the dead—but nothing less than his sacrificial death will rescue sinners and break the devil's grip on power. Jesus must see it through.

Suffering and death await Jesus' followers, too. Jesus does not promise safety in this life. To the contrary, the students will be like their Teacher (10:25). Jesus commands his disciples to take up their cross and follow (16:24). The call to follow Jesus is potentially a call into harm's way. Safety is much to be desired, but not at the cost of faithfulness to God and his way.

With the third temptation, the one about power, the devil most clearly offers Jesus a shortcut. He shows him all the kingdoms of the world and their splendor and says, "All this I will give you, if you will bow down and worship me." This global authority the devil claims to offer is a counterfeit of the true authority God will give to Jesus after he dies on the cross and rises from the dead (28:18). Real power is God's plan for Jesus. The devil's temptation is merely, "What if you could take power from the start and gain it cheaply? Take a shortcut; get power quickly without the trials and suffering. Have what you are destined for on more favorable terms—your terms, rather than God's." But power achieved through selfish ambition competes with God. Jesus instead will serve God by waiting to receive power from God's hand.

With this third temptation, has the devil abandoned subtlety altogether? Surely he does not think Jesus would be attracted to the idea of worshiping *him*, no matter what the benefits. It is unlikely that he means anything as obvious as having Jesus fall on his knees and cry, "O great and mighty Satan!" Rather the devil is saying, "Get clout the way people of the world typically get it: compromise ethically; shade the truth; elbow aside someone unimportant. By operating that way you will be serving me and my objectives, but who will notice? You will gain power and prestige—just think of all the good you can do with your influence." It would be a fool's bargain. Gains from evil tend to vaporize. More important, though, ethical compromise destroys a person's moral core. The devil offers Jesus authority and status, and he entices us in the same way. No problem that disciples face will receive more attention in Matthew than the lure of power and prestige. Instead, we are called to "worship the Lord [our] God, and serve him only."

We have much to learn from Jesus' example about how to face temptation. First, Jesus lives in fellowship with God. God's Spirit leads Jesus into this intensive time with God, and God ministers to him at the end of it (4:1, 11). Jesus has learned by long practice during the noncrisis times what it is like to be with God, to listen to him, and to heed his guidance. If we have not yet accumulated years of walking with God, all we can do is start now cultivating that life with him, being led by his Spirit, and experiencing his help in each new situation.

Second, Jesus knows Scripture. He knows key passages so well that he can summon them to his aid in the moment of temptation. Bible learning is a valuable discipline (regular reading, study, and memorization). Additionally, much of Jesus' Scripture learning would have come in the assembly of God's people (see Luke 2:46; 4:16). Understanding comes through attentive fellowship with others who know God and his word.

Third, Jesus practices other disciplines—evident in this passage—including solitude, fasting, silence, and prayer. As we will see in the Gospel as a whole, Jesus made a point of getting away periodically from the busyness of life in order to spend concentrated time with God. For us, setting apart time for God will be a matter of working out a rhythm of engagement with the world and retreat from it. We are strengthened by quiet moments with God in a given day and by devotional hours or days in a given season.

Jesus faced temptation and prevailed. We face temptation and yearn to prevail. He focused on God's will and God's honor. He prepared through the spiritual disciplines of Bible learning and prayer, both alone and with others. He drew courage from God's ever-present Holy Spirit. If we follow his model, we too will discern God's will and will be strengthened more and more to do it.

*The devil attempts to derail Jesus, who aims to change the world. Jesus prevails, and so can we as we follow his example.*

# THE CALL TO DISCIPLESHIP

**DAY 5**

## Matthew 4:12-22

### Matthew 4:12-17

¹² When Jesus heard that John had been put in prison, he withdrew to Galilee. ¹³ Leaving Nazareth, he went and lived in Capernaum, which was by the lake in the area of Zebulun and Naphtali— ¹⁴ to fulfill what was said through the prophet Isaiah:

¹⁵ "Land of Zebulun and land of Naphtali,
   the Way of the Sea, beyond the Jordan,
   Galilee of the Gentiles—
¹⁶ the people living in darkness
   have seen a great light;

on those living in the land of the shadow of death
a light has dawned."

[17] From that time on Jesus began to preach, "Repent, for the kingdom of heaven has come near."

The preliminaries are completed. Jesus has been baptized in the Jordan and tested in the wilderness. The mission of John the forerunner has ended with imprisonment. It is time for the main event. Jesus emerges out of his desert solitude and the anonymity of his hometown into the arena of commerce and crowds, politics and racial tensions, demons and disease—the public life of Galilee.

His arrival is described as a light emerging in darkness. The new age dawns. The awaited moment comes present. "From that time on, Jesus began to preach, '. . . the kingdom of heaven has come near.'" Jesus announces that God is about to set his effective kingship in motion, and nothing will be the same again. Echoing John, Jesus calls out, "Repent"; rethink and revise everything about your lives in light of this new thing God is about to do.

In the first episode, we see how momentous the change will be in the lives of four fishermen.

## ◼ Matthew 4:18-22

[18] As Jesus was walking beside the Sea of Galilee, he saw two brothers, Simon called Peter and his brother Andrew. They were casting a net into the lake, for they were fishermen. [19] "Come, follow me," Jesus said, "and I will send you out to fish for people." [20] At once they left their nets and followed him.

[21] Going on from there, he saw two other brothers, James son of Zebedee and his brother John. They were in a boat with their father Zebedee, preparing their nets. Jesus called them, [22] and immediately they left the boat and their father and followed him.

J esus called them." We are struck by Jesus' authority. He comes up to these fishermen, tells them to follow him—to follow him apparently for the rest of their lives—and they get up immediately and do it. It is not that Jesus is unknown to them. They would have heard John the Baptist's testimony about him earlier (compare John 1:29–42) and would have known of his recent emergence as a preacher of the kingdom of God (Matthew 4:17). Luke adds that Jesus' call to follow him comes right after the fishermen see him perform a miracle (Luke 5:1–11). But Matthew, by telling the story so briefly, emphasizes not Jesus' reputation or miraculous achievements, but the impact of his presence. There is something compelling about Jesus himself—his face, his voice, his manner—that stirs the men to action.

It was not uncommon for a Jewish teacher to gather disciples, students who would accompany him, learn his ideas, and imitate his way of living. Most often, the potential disciple sought out the teacher, rather than vice versa (as, for example, in 8:19); but even among teachers who selected their own disciples, this narrative is unusual and startling. First of all, prior to encountering Jesus, in the fishermen's own minds the course of their lives is already set. They are not out fishing recreationally; this is their career. We see from the second pair of brothers working with their father that this is the family business. They decide to walk away from their nets and boats (their investment in equipment) and to leave their financial security behind in order to follow someone who offers them no assurances about income. It might occur to them to ask, "*Follow* you? Where are you going? What am I getting myself into?" Matthew reports no such questions. With both pairs of brothers, the decision to follow Jesus comes "at once," "immediately."

The last phrase in the report about James and John is positively scandalous: "immediately they left the boat *and their father* and followed him." In a culture that highly valued loyalty and respect toward parents, Jesus has the audacity to interrupt their activity so that the sons leave their father right in the middle of the day's labor.

We can only imagine Zebedee's stunned response. Jesus' call takes priority even over family expectations. Who is this guy who makes himself more important than a man's father?

Jesus' call of these four fishermen does not so much resemble the beginning of a typical rabbi-student relationship as it resembles the call of God himself to key persons in the Old Testament. Abraham is told, "Go from your country, your people, and your father's household . . ." because God has plans to redeem the world, and Abraham has a part in those plans (Genesis 12:1–3). Moses is told to leave his current life in order to be involved with God in rescuing his people (Exodus 3:1–10). God's call is authoritative. Abraham gets up and goes, not because he can make sense of it all practically, but because it is God who calls him. Moses goes only because God insists on it, and God is God. Similarly, the fishermen's response to Jesus is more about Jesus' authority than any thought of personal benefit or cost.

Jesus' call to the fishermen is also like God's call to Abraham or Moses in this way: whatever those men's lives had been about before the moment of the call, whatever their personal agendas might have been, from now on their lives are about something God is doing. The orientation of their minds shifts fundamentally. They used to live for themselves; now they live for God. Before, they made plans according to their ambition and common sense. Now they are following God's command and working out where they fit into God's plans. Their self-concept changes. Before, they could say, "I am my own man." Now they would say, "God has called me, and I belong to him."

Jesus points to their own line of work to illustrate what he has in mind for them. They have been fishermen, fishers of fish, but translated literally, verse 19 says, "I will make you fishers of people." Jesus is saying two things. First, he tells them, "I am going to *make* you into something." Jesus is promising to transform them as they walk with him and learn from him and imitate him. They are not yet equipped to be effective for God, but they will be. Second, they previously gathered and harvested fish, and now they will gather and "harvest" people. Jesus has come to bring together the renewed people of God, and these fishermen will partner with him in that endeavor. Many times Jesus pictures this assembling of his people unto himself, using images such as rounding up lost sheep or gathering chicks under a hen's wings or harvesting a crop of grain; here the image is gathering fish. The point is that Jesus will work to gather his people for blessed relationship with him, and disciples will join him in that work.

His wording as he calls them emphasizes how central Jesus himself is to their lives of discipleship: "Follow me." Jesus is not training them in a philosophy or a set of skills; he is calling them to be with *him*—to study and imitate him so they can draw people to him. He will never work himself out of a job, and his students will never graduate from his training or become independent. Their lives will always revolve around Jesus and what he is doing. Even after he dies and is raised from the dead, his disciples will live with him constantly, communicating with him and assisting him in his powerful work in the world. He will always be the main actor, and they will always be the supporting cast. Yes, Jesus is fully human, so he can show them how to live by his example; yet he is more than merely human, as they will discern in due time. Because of his divine status and authority, Jesus is worthy of becoming the focus of their whole lives.

The centrality of Jesus in the disciples' lives helps us see that "calling" is a bigger idea than "career." Our calling is to walk with Jesus and to cooperate with him in what he is doing. Along the way, our career may shift several times or stay the same. We may go long distances or stay put. We may serve in a "ministry" profession or something usually thought of as "secular." Or we may not do anything that looks like a "career" at all. Our calling is an enduring summons to follow Jesus—we never retire from it—and whatever he may guide us to do, we do it as part of our journey with him as his disciples. We are privileged in each new season of life to work out and discover where we fit into God's work.

Practically, how do we follow Jesus? How do we discover what he wants us to do? As we read Matthew's stories about Jesus in the flesh walking with his disciples, we can imagine how it will work for us who live with the risen Jesus, who promised to be with us always (28:20). The most helpful activity for learning his way is to converse with him. We *pray*—prayer will be a constant in the life of a disciple—and we *learn the Scriptures*. Jesus is our model here. As we saw in the temptation story, Jesus was a man of prayer, and he repeatedly quoted Scripture, taking his guidance from it. Scripture informs our praying and helps to generate a two-way conversation, so that we are hearing Jesus rather than just speaking to him. We further discern the Lord's will as we *reflect* about our journey with him thus far, asking, "What is he showing me about my strengths and weaknesses, my relationships and circumstances, my need to trust him more fully?" Additionally, we *ask advice* from others who know him. We are not alone: we walk with Jesus accompanied by others who are walking with him, too. Sometimes we will discern the Lord's will through counsel from the wisest Christians in our life. Most important, Jesus will guide us as we *obey* all we know of God's will. It does no good to seek to know God's will if we do not follow through and do it. As we do what we know God wants us to do, Jesus is free to show us our next steps. The fishermen did not know much yet about God's will for them, but they acted on what they did know: Jesus said to follow him, and they followed. As we heed Jesus' call to "follow me" and begin our lifelong journey with our risen Lord, we may be confident that he wants to make himself known and to guide us wisely and compassionately when we need it most.

The order of events in Matthew's narrative is significant. As Jesus begins to proclaim the good news (4:17), his first act of public ministry is to call these fishermen (4:19, 21). This shows that discipleship is central to Jesus' mission and method. Calling disciples is not just a means to something else—to gain assistants in order to do deeds of mercy out in the world. Making disciples and investing in their lives is the core of his ministry. We see this priority in his final command to his followers: "make disciples" (28:19).

Jesus is forming a community of partners whose hearts are adjusted to God's will. The Savior's public deeds of mercy, important as they are in their own right, are joined to his kingdom preaching in order to draw more and more people into the life of discipleship. There his mercy can be experienced most fully. These four men, a group that eventually becomes twelve (10:1), represent all disciples. The Gospels do not envision two categories of people in the community of Jesus—an especially committed minority called disciples by contrast to the majority who are "normal Christians." "Disciple" *is* the Gospels' word for "Christian," and committed discipleship is the way of life Jesus intends for us. Just as the fishermen submitted themselves to apprenticeship with Jesus, we who say yes to his call enter into lifelong training and fellowship with the Teacher.

*Jesus calls us to leave our previous lives to enter into the adventure of following him where he leads and doing what he does.*

# JOY INSTEAD OF MOURNING

**DAY 6**

Matthew 4:23-25; 8:1-34

## Matthew 4:23-25

23 Jesus went throughout Galilee, teaching in their synagogues, proclaiming the good news of the kingdom, and healing every disease and sickness among the people. 24 News about him spread all over Syria, and people brought to him all who were

ill with various diseases, those suffering severe pain, the demon-possessed, those having seizures, and the paralyzed; and he healed them. ²⁵ Large crowds from Galilee, the Decapolis, Jerusalem, Judea and the region across the Jordan followed him.

Jesus has begun his public ministry and has called disciples to join him. Now Matthew highlights two aspects of his activity among the Jews of Galilee: words and actions. He is teaching in their meeting places, the synagogues, proclaiming the good news of the kingdom. He is also active out in the villages and country-side "healing every disease and sickness among the people."

Jesus' twofold ministry of words and actions is then enacted for us in the following five chapters of Matthew. His teaching in the Sermon on the Mount, chapters 5–7, is supported by his public actions, chapters 8–9. The whole five-chapter portrayal is framed by two nearly identical verses, 4:23 and 9:35, whose uniting phrase is "the good news of the kingdom." Since the Jesus-in-action chapters help us understand what the kingdom is, I will present them first.

## ▨ Matthew 8:1–13

8 ¹ When Jesus came down from the mountainside, large crowds followed him. ² A man with leprosy came and knelt before him and said, "Lord, if you are willing, you can make me clean."

³ Jesus reached out his hand and touched the man. "I am willing," he said. "Be clean!" Immediately he was cleansed of his leprosy. ⁴ Then Jesus said to him, "See that you don't tell anyone. But go, show yourself to the priest and offer the gift Moses commanded, as a testimony to them."

⁵ When Jesus had entered Capernaum, a centurion came to him, asking for help. ⁶ "Lord," he said, "my servant lies at home para-lyzed, suffering terribly."

⁷ Jesus said to him, "Shall I come and heal him?"

⁸ The centurion replied, "Lord, I do not deserve to have you come under my roof. But just say the word, and my servant will

be healed. ⁹ For I myself am a man under authority, with soldiers under me. I tell this one, 'Go,' and he goes; and that one, 'Come,' and he comes. I say to my servant, 'Do this,' and he does it."

¹⁰ When Jesus heard this, he was amazed and said to those following him, "Truly I tell you, I have not found anyone in Israel with such great faith. ¹¹ I say to you that many will come from the east and the west, and will take their places at the feast with Abraham, Isaac and Jacob in the kingdom of heaven. ¹² But the subjects of the kingdom will be thrown outside, into the darkness, where there will be weeping and gnashing of teeth."

¹³ Then Jesus said to the centurion, "Go! Let it be done just as you believed it would." And his servant was healed at that moment.

No fate was more dreaded in Jesus' day than to become a leper. It is not just that leprosy horribly disfigures its victims and deteriorates their bodies; it makes them social outcasts. The Law of Moses required anyone who suffered with a serious skin disease to keep away from everyone else and to call out, "Unclean, unclean," to avoid exposing the community to defilement and contagion (Leviticus 13:45–46). Leprosy was a life sentence, impossible to cure. So until his encounter with Jesus, this leper is handicapped, ugly, alone, and apparently hopeless. In this one man we see a whole array of miseries.

Jesus' reputation as a healer is already well established by the time the leper finds him (see 4:24). Still, the man's boldness is remarkable. He defies social custom and scriptural law by bumping his way through the crowds to kneel before Jesus and assert, "Lord, if you are willing, you can make me clean." Not maybe—you *can* do this! Jesus is not a bit less confident: "I am willing. Be clean!"

Why does Matthew draw out the drama by saying, "Jesus reached out his hand and touched the man"? The next story sheds light on this one. There, the centurion says, "Just say the word, and my servant will be healed." Jesus could have healed the leper, too, merely by speaking. But how long has it been since someone lovingly touched him? Jesus recognizes the man's yearning for human contact. That compassionate touch may have meant as much to the man as having his body healed. We hear stories of early AIDS victims weeping in relief when someone finally esteemed them with a touch.

The centurion in the next story is a Gentile, a Roman officer, part of the foreign military force that kept the Jews under control. Though he is in a position to throw his weight around, he humbles himself before Jesus the Jew, imploring him to heal his servant's paralysis, and saying, "Lord, I do not deserve to have you come under my roof." Like the leper, he calls Jesus "Lord" and is absolutely confident that Jesus can perform the requested healing. The centurion says directly what the leper only implied: that the healing will be possible because of Jesus' authority. He says, "I salute my superiors, and lower-ranking soldiers snap to attention when I walk in the room. I know authority when I see it, and you, Lord, have authority! Just speak your command, and my servant will be healed." Each new phase of Matthew's narrative highlights Jesus' remarkable authority. Jesus calls, and the fishermen leave everything to follow him (4:18–22). He teaches, and the crowds marvel at his authority (7:28–29). He touches and speaks, and the incurable are cured. In the next story, he drives out demonic spirits with a word. In the one after that, he commands the wind and waves at sea, and they obey. God's kingdom is advancing, and Jesus has king-like authority to act with God's power and mercy.

These stories highlight a key characteristic of Jesus' work: he makes outsiders into insiders. The leper was an outsider because of his disease, and the centurion was an outsider by reason of his ethnicity and role. But now the leper's social isolation is over, and the Gentile centurion will be included at the great end-of-time "feast" that faithful Jews awaited. Jesus will embrace many more outsiders, but his work to establish God's kingdom will also have the reverse effect. Some who have the right heritage and insider status will despise Jesus' authority and will find themselves horribly on the outside. His warning to the descendants of Abraham, Isaac, and Jacob applies equally to modern Gentile Christians: elitist insiders may be kidding themselves ("Aren't we glad we're God's favorites!"). Contrast the humble new insiders, the kneeling leper and the centurion who reckons himself unworthy to have Jesus in his home.

## ■ Matthew 8:14–22

¹⁴ When Jesus came into Peter's house, he saw Peter's mother-in-law lying in bed with a fever. ¹⁵ He touched her hand and the fever left her, and she got up and began to wait on him.

¹⁶ When evening came, many who were demon-possessed were brought to him, and he drove out the spirits with a word and healed all the sick. ¹⁷ This was to fulfill what was spoken through the prophet Isaiah:

> "He took up our infirmities
> and bore our diseases."

¹⁸ When Jesus saw the crowd around him, he gave orders to cross to the other side of the lake. ¹⁹ Then a teacher of the law came to him and said, "Teacher, I will follow you wherever you go."

²⁰ Jesus replied, "Foxes have dens and birds have nests, but the Son of Man has no place to lay his head."

²¹ Another disciple said to him, "Lord, first let me go and bury my father."

²² But Jesus told him, "Follow me, and let the dead bury their own dead."

Two things catch our eye in this passage: Jesus' fulfillment of prophecy and his astonishing displays of authority.

In Jesus' ministry, Isaiah's prophecies are being fulfilled and God's kingdom is being established. Jesus can repeatedly speak to the crowds about the "kingdom of heaven" without pausing to explain what he means by it, because most of his listeners grew up attending the synagogues and learning the vision of God's reign contained in the Isaiah scroll (see Luke 4:16–19). Here in verse 17,

Matthew quotes Isaiah 53 to say that Jesus' work of healing marks the arrival of God's intervention to end Israel's misery: "He took up our infirmities and bore our diseases." Isaiah 53 speaks poignantly of an extraordinary servant of the Lord who will not only bear away their diseases, but suffer and die to reconcile his people to God.

When Matthew says in our pair of frame verses, 4:23 and 9:35, that Jesus was "proclaiming the good news," he is drawing another phrase from Isaiah—the sixty-first chapter—in which the prophet announces an end to exile by saying,

> The LORD has anointed me
> *to proclaim good news* to the poor.
> …
> to bind up the brokenhearted,
>     to proclaim freedom for the captives
>     and release from darkness for the prisoners,
> to proclaim the year of the LORD's favor
> …
> to comfort all who mourn,
>     and provide for those who grieve in Zion—
> to bestow on them a crown of beauty
>     instead of ashes,
> the oil of joy
>     instead of mourning,
> and a garment of praise
>     instead of a spirit of despair. (61:1–3)

As we will see, this passage is also behind the Beatitudes in Matthew 5. Because Jesus has come, the time of despair has ended and the time of joy has begun. This is the appointed moment, and God is taking charge. He is consolidating his kingship and setting his people free.

The compact narrative in Matthew 8:14–22 builds further on the theme of Jesus' divine authority. We see it first in his authority to heal. He cures all the sick who are brought to him, but more than that, he drives out demonic spirits with a word. Powerfully, Jesus brings "freedom for the captives and release from darkness." The Son of God who faced the devil's temptation in Matthew 4 now overwhelms the devil and liberates men and women from his oppression. The task of establishing God's reign in the world entails contending against spiritual forces of darkness, and Jesus has the power to do it.

The other aspect of Jesus' authority highlighted in these verses is his capacity to make demands. One among the teachers of the law comes to him seeking to be his disciple, "Teacher, I will follow you wherever you go." Jesus startles him by asking whether he knows what he is signing up for: "Foxes have dens and birds have nests, but the Son of Man [Jesus] has no place to lay his head." Following Jesus may require laying aside all comforts and ease.

In a second conversation (8:21–22), Jesus calls a man who hesitates because of obligation to his father. We wonder whether the father is already dead or whether he is still alive and the man is really saying, "Let me stay and take care of my father through his old age; and when he is dead and buried, I will come and follow you." Either way, Jesus' answer is blunt: "Follow me, and let the [spiritually] dead bury their own dead."

Repeatedly we see that Jesus expects his disciples to be loyal to him beyond all other loyalties, including loyalty to family. We observe it first when he calls the fishermen (4:18–22), whose obedience clearly inconveniences their families. James and John leave their father Zebedee sitting there in the boat. Peter follows Jesus without first consulting his wife (whom we learn about through the detail here in Matthew 8 that Peter has a mother-in-law). Even more audacious are Jesus' words in 10:37, "Anyone who loves their father or mother more than me is not worthy of me; anyone who loves their son or daughter more than me is not worthy of me."

It is not that Jesus despises family connections. To the contrary, home is a primary venue for learning discipleship. Jesus has called

Peter, and soon he is in Peter's home. The same will happen with Matthew the tax collector (9:9–10). While in their homes, Jesus makes a point of caring about their loved ones, healing Peter's mother-in-law and welcoming Matthew's friends. Moreover, Jesus uses his ties to his disciples to draw their loved ones into his ministry. The mother of James and John becomes a co-traveler with Jesus' disciples (20:17, 20) and cares for Jesus' needs all the way to the end (27:55–56). Peter's wife eventually becomes Peter's traveling companion in his missionary work (see 1 Corinthians 9:5, where Peter is called Cephas). Jesus further reveals his concern for disciples' families through his teaching. He strongly endorses God's commandment to honor father and mother (15:3–6); he stresses the importance of marriage (19:3–10); and he enthusiastically affirms parents who bring him their children (19:13–15).

But Jesus requires us to follow him whether our family is on board or not. Many have obeyed Jesus knowing that their families would ostracize them for abandoning family traditions or would condemn them for not staying close and available. Jesus makes these demands without apology, because the God whom he calls us to serve is surpassingly worthy. Jesus similarly had to disappoint his own family's expectations (12:46–50; compare Mark 3:20–21, 31–35).

## ■ Matthew 8:23-27

²³ Then he got into the boat and his disciples followed him. ²⁴ Suddenly a furious storm came up on the lake, so that the waves swept over the boat. But Jesus was sleeping. ²⁵ The disciples went and woke him, saying, "Lord, save us! We're going to drown!"

²⁶ He replied, "You of little faith, why are you so afraid?" Then he got up and rebuked the winds and the waves, and it was completely calm.

²⁷ The men were amazed and asked, "What kind of man is this? Even the winds and the waves obey him!"

J esus' authority can be underestimated, because he shares our human frailty. At the beginning of this story, he is utterly exhausted. How tired does a man have to be to remain asleep in a wildly tossing boat while cold waves splash in? The disciples believe they are going to drown. They wake him, apparently expecting little more than that Jesus would bail water or help them row to shore. But from this bone-tired man comes the voice of authority over nature itself, and suddenly the sea is glassy calm.

"Even the winds and the waves obey him!" *God* commands nature (Psalms 65:5–7; 89:8–9). "What kind of man is this?" The range of Jesus' authority expands with each new episode. He is master over afflictions and illness, demons and storms, and there is more to come. In these stories, we recognize that God's kingdom is present, because, in Isaiah's words, Jesus brings "joy instead of mourning . . . praise instead of a spirit of despair" (Isaiah 61:3).

## Matthew 8:28–34

28 When he arrived at the other side in the region of the Gadarenes, two demon-possessed men coming from the tombs met him. They were so violent that no one could pass that way. 29 "What do you want with us, Son of God?" they shouted. "Have you come here to torture us before the appointed time?"

30 Some distance from them a large herd of pigs was feeding. 31 The demons begged Jesus, "If you drive us out, send us into the herd of pigs."

32 He said to them, "Go!" So they came out and went into the pigs, and the whole herd rushed down the steep bank into the lake and died in the water. 33 Those tending the pigs ran off, went into the town and reported all this, including what had happened to the demon-possessed men. 34 Then the whole town went out to meet Jesus. And when they saw him, they pleaded with him to leave their region.

F reedom for the captives and release from darkness," says Isaiah. These two men are so captive to the powers of darkness that everyone hopes never to see them again. They are much like the people in today's maximum security prisons, so dark-hearted and violent that we shut them away. No one living near these two men imagines helping them, much less restoring them to full lives in the community. The enormity of the demonic power that has ruined their lives is vividly portrayed in the stampeding herd of pigs into which the demons flee. As terrifying as they are, we are struck by the demons' own terror in Jesus' presence: "What do you want with us, Son of God? Have you come here to torture us?" The powers of darkness tremble before Jesus.

The townspeople respond, amazingly, by asking Jesus to leave. He has restored two neighbors whom they had assumed were hopeless and in doing so has spared the town from their violent behavior. Thanks might have been in order. But Jesus has cost them a high-priced herd of pigs. What more disruption might he bring? Best to shun Jesus just as they had previously shunned the two violent demoniacs! He is too risky, too hard to control. What a tragedy! Who knows what benefits he could bring the townspeople if they would not drive him away?

Jesus turns "useless" people into useful, outsiders into insiders. Not all will welcome him—in relieving some, he disturbs others. He has come to shake things up, but that is good news for those who are not too attached to the way things have been. Discipleship is a calling into something wonderfully new: God's kingdom is present. We have joined up with Jesus, through whom God is intervening in the world to have his good and merciful way.

*Jesus displays the kingdom's presence,
transforming human misery into well-being—and
challenging disciples to join him unreservedly.*

# DEEP HEALING

Matthew 9:1-35

■ Matthew 9:1-8

9¹ Jesus stepped into a boat, crossed over and came to his own town. ² Some men brought to him a paralyzed man, lying on a mat. When Jesus saw their faith, he said to the man, "Take heart, son; your sins are forgiven."

³ At this, some of the teachers of the law said to themselves, "This fellow is blaspheming!"

⁴ Knowing their thoughts, Jesus said, "Why do you entertain evil thoughts in your hearts? ⁵ Which is easier: to say, 'Your sins are forgiven,' or to say, 'Get up and walk'? ⁶ But I want you to know that the Son of Man has authority on earth to forgive sins." So he said to the paralyzed man, "Get up, take your mat and go home."

⁷ Then the man got up and went home. ⁸ When the crowd saw this, they were filled with awe; and they praised God, who had given such authority to man.

With the paralytic, we encounter something new. Until this point, as Jesus has traveled around Galilee, he has delivered people from physical ailments and external threats, such as demons and a storm at sea. Here Jesus seems to look right past this man's obvious physical problem and into his inner life. He says, "Your sins are forgiven." Surely the man and the friends who carry him have come hoping for a physical healing. Jesus eventually provides it, but what he seems to say is, "Your need for healing goes deeper than you think—and I can heal you there, too." In order to overcome the human predicament and bring true well-being, Jesus must address our core sickness.

At the beginning of the Gospel, Joseph is told that Mary's baby "will save his people from their sins" (1:21). We are prone to think that sin only hurts the people who are sinned against. But sin hurts the sinner as well. Indulging in sin eats away at our character, dulls our moral sensitivity, and makes us less likely to do the right thing at our next temptation. As we persist in it, the people we most want to hold close lose trust in us, so that our relationships are unfulfilling and insecure. Worse, sin offends God and weighs us down with guilt so that we become alienated from him. Sin grinds us down and prevents us from experiencing the fullness of life that God wants to give us. Our sin certainly does hurt others—it does more damage than we grasp—but it makes *us* miserable, too. We need a rescue. "Take heart," says the Savior. He declares forgiveness here and then secures it by dying on the cross. By forgiving us, Jesus liberates us to enter confidently into God's embrace and begin the process of becoming good.

### ▧ Matthew 9:9-13

⁹ As Jesus went on from there, he saw a man named Matthew sitting at the tax collector's booth. "Follow me," he told him, and Matthew got up and followed him.

¹⁰ While Jesus was having dinner at Matthew's house, many tax collectors and sinners came and ate with him and his disciples. ¹¹ When the Pharisees saw this, they asked his disciples, "Why does your teacher eat with tax collectors and sinners?"

¹² On hearing this, Jesus said, "It is not the healthy who need a doctor, but the sick. ¹³ But go and learn what this means: 'I desire mercy, not sacrifice.' For I have not come to call the righteous, but sinners."

This story, too, is about forgiveness and inner healing. Matthew the tax collector is a compelling example of a sinner turned around by Jesus. It is hard to exaggerate how much the Jewish people despised the men who gathered taxes for the occupying Roman authorities. Not only were they traitors to their own people, they were notoriously corrupt. They lined their own pockets by cheating common folks whose wages barely kept up with the cost of daily bread. Jesus' call to such a man wondrously displays God's mercy. Matthew is not just forgiven; he will become a new man altogether. How immense are the possibilities for him now that Jesus has gotten hold of him! Assuming that he had a hand in writing this Gospel (see p. 312), we can say in retrospect that few people in all of history have had a greater impact for good than Matthew, the former villain.

It is too easy to write off people who have bad reputations—to see no hope or potential for them. I served for a couple of years in a Los Angeles drug rehabilitation program, and I followed up on a few of the residents afterward. One of the program's graduates ended up in a dreary multistory apartment building where the rent was cheap and where idleness, sex, and drugs were the way of life. In that unholy place, one young woman named Tutti had a particularly low reputation. One Sunday I went to pick up my drug program friend so we could go to church. To my surprise and delight, Tutti asked to come along. She had put on a colorful dress and had a smile on her face. It was an honor to have her with us in the car, because she wanted to go and meet with God. She had an inkling—and a yearning—that Jesus might welcome her and offer her a new life. To my horror, my drug program friend spent our whole drive commenting and chuckling about how absurd it was for Tutti, of all people, to be coming to church. Despite my best efforts, she took those painful words to heart, and I never saw her again.

It is hard to look past the reputations of people like Tutti and Matthew, but Jesus does. Matthew represents the utter outsider, the improbable, scandalous new friend of Jesus, whom he calls to be an insider in God's community. The Savior says, "You—yes, *you*, who never thought you would have anything to do with God—come follow me." Every reader can say, "If Jesus would welcome that man, I can come to him, too, confident that he wants me."

Jesus takes with him the fishermen he had called earlier and goes to Matthew's home, where they share a meal—apparently several meals—with him and his disreputable friends. *Many* tax collectors and sinners came and ate with Jesus and his disciples. These lively gatherings around Matthew's table are an enduring image of emerging disciples. Some of those engrossed in conversation with Jesus have followed him for some time and others are new. Many are misfits no one ever expected to see in such blessed company, and every person around the table is grateful to be included. Together they have entered into training with Jesus about how to live. We do well to think of every small group Bible study or Sunday school class, every prayer gathering or meeting for the Lord's Supper, as an opportunity for that kind of nurturing, healing time with Jesus. God's great world-changing endeavors start from such fellowship.

Some folks who are certain they belong to the club of God's insiders take offense at Jesus. The law teachers and Pharisees were disciplined members of Jewish society who sought to help their compatriots maintain righteous lives. Jesus' behavior scandalizes them. They are already outraged by his claim to forgive sins. Now Jesus is eating with the tax collector and his "sinner" friends. Sharing a meal in someone's home was a sign of friendship. The Pharisees charge that Jesus has made himself one of the sinners by associating with them.

Jesus responds by announcing his mission in the boldest way: "I have come . . . to call . . . sinners." His very purpose is to rescue lost, hurting people like Matthew. Jesus, the Great Physician, brings deep healing from God to people who recognize that they are sick. He has nothing to offer those who are "well," who are puffed up in pious self-sufficiency.

## ▦ Matthew 9:14-17

¹⁴ Then John's disciples came and asked him, "How is it that we and the Pharisees fast often, but your disciples do not fast?"

¹⁵ Jesus answered, "How can the guests of the bridegroom mourn while he is with them? The time will come when the bridegroom will be taken from them; then they will fast.

¹⁶ "No one sews a patch of unshrunk cloth on an old garment, for the patch will pull away from the garment, making the tear worse.

¹⁷ Neither do people pour new wine into old wineskins. If they do, the skins will burst; the wine will run out, and the wineskins will be ruined. No, they pour new wine into new wineskins, and both are preserved."

Again Jesus' leadership comes under scrutiny. "How is it that your disciples do not fast?" What they are really asking is, "What kind of sorry outfit are you running here?" John the Baptist's followers and the Pharisees fast on schedule (likely two days a week). By contrast, Jesus is feasting with his sinner friends. It's time to get serious!

Jesus answers John's disciples by reminding them why they fast: "Don't you see? Fasting to prepare for God's coming redemption is no longer appropriate. I have arrived!" The bridegroom is here; Jesus' presence marks the arrival of the kingdom joys. The event they were hoping for and preparing for has come, and it is time to celebrate. When his interrogators demand that Jesus should fast, they resemble a meticulous manager in charge of preparing a state dinner to honor a visiting dignitary. Failing to recognize the dignitary when he arrives, the manager treats him like one of the hired help: "Grab a polish cloth and help us get ready." Absurd!

Jesus is the main event: everything changes now. His activity to inaugurate God's kingdom brings joy and relief for many, but trouble is in store if people cannot adjust. To illustrate, he says, "No one sews a patch of unshrunk cloth on an old garment." Eventually the new patch shrinks and tugs at the ragged old garment until it tears worse than before it was patched. "Neither do people pour new wine into old wineskins." Soon the pressure of the new wine bursts the inflexible old leather bottle, and all is lost. Jesus brings something so new and dynamic that the old mindset simply cannot contain it.

It is not that Jesus is throwing out the past or devaluing their Jewish heritage. To the contrary, by saying, "Go and learn what this means: 'I desire mercy, not sacrifice,'" he is urging them to apply the ancient prophets' teaching. Moreover, those very prophets point forward to him, and so Jesus puts himself at the center of his message. His statements in Matthew 9 are full of *I* and *me*. "Follow me . . . I have come to call sinners . . . I, the Son of Man, have authority on earth to forgive sins . . . I, the bridegroom, am here, so let the celebration begin!" Jesus has come, and everything depends on receiving him. His audacious claims provoke such outrage that his critics will eventually crucify him. Anticipating his disciples' sorrow, he says, "The time will come when the bridegroom will be taken from them; then they will fast."

It seems obvious that Jesus would demand changes in someone like Matthew the tax collector. What we find, however, is that he demands change from all of us. Old people get stuck in "the way we have always done things," and young people become zealously certain they are doing things right because they are so committed and up-to-date. Feet-set-in-concrete certainty that we are living rightly toward God is the characteristic of the "righteous" people whom the Great Physician cannot help. Instead, disciples of Jesus need to become humbly adjustable people who are devoted neither to the traditional ways nor to the latest strategies, but to Jesus himself and to the real needs of people. Jesus' pronouncements about the bridegroom and patches and wineskins all repeat his fundamental message: "Repent—rethink everything! God's reign is breaking in, and it is happening through me. Follow me!" (4:17, 19).

## ■ Matthew 9:18–34

¹⁸ While he was saying this, a synagogue leader came and knelt before him and said, "My daughter has just died. But come and put your hand on her, and she will live." ¹⁹ Jesus got up and went with him, and so did his disciples.

²⁰ Just then a woman who had been subject to bleeding for twelve years came up behind him and touched the edge of his cloak. ²¹ She said to herself, "If I only touch his cloak, I will be healed."

²² Jesus turned and saw her. "Take heart, daughter," he said, "your faith has healed you." And the woman was healed at that moment.

²³ When Jesus entered the synagogue leader's house and saw the noisy crowd and people playing pipes, ²⁴ he said, "Go away. The girl is not dead but asleep." But they laughed at him. ²⁵ After the crowd had been put outside, he went in and took the girl by the hand, and she got up. ²⁶ News of this spread through all that region.

²⁷ As Jesus went on from there, two blind men followed him, calling out, "Have mercy on us, Son of David!"

²⁸ When he had gone indoors, the blind men came to him, and he asked them, "Do you believe that I am able to do this?"

"Yes, Lord," they replied.

²⁹ Then he touched their eyes and said, "According to your faith let it be done to you"; ³⁰ and their sight was restored. Jesus warned them sternly, "See that no one knows about this." ³¹ But they went out and spread the news about him all over that region.

³² While they were going out, a man who was demon-possessed and could not talk was brought to Jesus. ³³ And when the demon was driven out, the man who had been mute spoke. The crowd was amazed and said, "Nothing like this has ever been seen in Israel."

³⁴ But the Pharisees said, "It is by the prince of demons that he drives out demons."

Jesus has been circulating in Galilee and relieving human misery in episode after episode. Now we meet a woman who bears a whole collection of human miseries. Her stamina is drained by a flow of blood that has gone on for years. Her uniquely feminine disorder is humiliating. Moreover, such blood is labeled unclean by Hebrew law (Leviticus 15:19–33), so she has been a social and religious outcast. She comes to Jesus from behind, lacking the confidence to approach him directly, but trusting that Jesus is the one who can help her. She touches the edge of his cloak, and instantly she is "made well"—literally, in the Greek, she is "saved." Both his healing work and his rescuing people from sin belong to his mission to bring salvation to his people.

Jesus' pause to affirm the woman's faith interrupts his journey with a synagogue leader who is facing the ultimate misery: death. Every caring parent can imagine this man's anguish at losing his beloved child. We are amazed at his confidence that Jesus can restore his dead girl to life. More amazing still is that Jesus does not hesitate for a moment about undertaking such an assignment. Ignoring the ridicule from the gathered mourners, Jesus restores the man's daughter. The kingdom of heaven has come near. What can stop God's merciful advance into a hurting world if even death cannot?

Two brief stories complete the Jesus-in-action chapters. First, by giving sight to the two blind men (verses 27–31), Jesus vividly fulfills the prophecy that Matthew cited earlier: "The people living in darkness have seen a great light" (4:16). These men's years of darkness have come to an end because they have "seen" who Jesus is (Son of David, that is, Messiah) even before he heals them. Finally, Jesus overcomes satanic power by healing the mute demoniac. In the onlookers' responses, we see the contrast between those in the crowd who rejoice that God is at work through Jesus (verse 33) and those whose minds are so darkened (so blind!) that all they can see in Jesus is the devil (verse 34).

## ▓ Matthew 9:35

<sup>35</sup> Jesus went through all the towns and villages, teaching in their synagogues, proclaiming the good news of the kingdom and healing every disease and sickness.

This verse, the twin to 4:23, completes the frame for Matthew's first major section about Jesus' ministry. The five chapters in between highlight Jesus' "proclaiming the good news of the kingdom," teachings represented in the Sermon on the Mount, Matthew 5–7, and his "healing every disease and sickness," Matthew 8–9. I have presented his healing actions first, because by seeing Jesus in action we begin to grasp what he means when he teaches that "the kingdom of heaven has come near."

The kingdom of heaven is God's effective kingship. (It is not a place, but a reign. The other Gospels call it the "kingdom of *God*," without using the word *heaven* at all.³) In fulfillment of his promises to Israel, God's reign has become dynamically present—it has "come near." Through Jesus, God is intervening to enact his will on earth. His will is done as Jesus encounters human misery in each new circumstance and overcomes it. Jesus comes with authority and liberating power to challenge whatever is sick (leprosy, paralysis) and dark (demonic violence, habitual sin) and deadly (a storm at sea, a girl's death) and to bring restoration and blessing in its place. Through him, God's healing and his righteous authority are penetrating into every arena of human life.

As an essential part of Jesus' mission to establish God's reign, he has called the fishermen and the tax collector—and us—to be his disciples. Our missional Messiah is forming a missional people who are devoted to God's will being done in the world. We obey his call to "follow me," opening our hearts to his deep healing and making ourselves fully available to serve at his side in his transforming work.

We do still await something further, something worth anticipating with great yearning, a glorious final success of God's saving work, celebrated through the image of a great feast (8:11). For now, we live and serve in grateful submission to God's authority. Our eventual participation in the renewed world when Jesus returns in glory (19:28; 25:21) will be a brilliant new phase of enjoying his kingship.

*God's kingdom is present through Jesus, who heals human beings outwardly and inwardly. To serve with him, disciples need his healing and renewal.*

**DAY 8** | # GOOD NEWS OF THE KINGDOM

Matthew 5:1-16

### ▓ Matthew 5:1-2

5 ¹ Now when Jesus saw the crowds, he went up on a mountainside and sat down. His disciples came to him, ² and he began to teach them.

We have seen Jesus out among the people healing them in every way. Now we are ready to hear his words. Jesus sits on a hillside and surveys the crowds of hurting, needy people who have drawn near to him. From such common folk Jesus has summoned disciples whom he now teaches—people like the fishermen and the tax collector we have met, who have heard and obeyed his life-defining call to "follow me."

## Matthew 5:3–12

He said:

³ "Blessed are the poor in spirit,
   for theirs is the kingdom of heaven.

⁴ Blessed are those who mourn,
   for they will be comforted.

⁵ Blessed are the meek,
   for they will inherit the earth.

⁶ Blessed are those who hunger and thirst for righteousness,
   for they will be filled.

⁷ Blessed are the merciful,
   for they will be shown mercy.

⁸ Blessed are the pure in heart,
   for they will see God.

⁹ Blessed are the peacemakers,
   for they will be called children of God.

¹⁰ Blessed are those who are persecuted because of righteousness,
   for theirs is the kingdom of heaven.

¹¹ "Blessed are you when people insult you, persecute you and falsely say all kinds of evil against you because of me. ¹² Rejoice and be glad, because great is your reward in heaven, for in the same way they persecuted the prophets who were before you."

This is the famous Sermon on the Mount. It opens with what we call the Beatitudes, from the Latin word for "blessed." Blessed means "happy, fortunate, well off," so the Beatitudes are statements of good news. Jesus is announcing benefits that flow to disciples, a new well-being made possible by the presence of God's kingdom.

He speaks as the Messiah (Hebrew for "anointed one") who is "anointed to preach good news to the poor," in fulfillment of Isaiah 61. This is "the year of the Lord's favor." Jesus has *displayed* the "good news" by his healings, and now he *proclaims* it. The prophet had spoken of binding up the brokenhearted (the poor in spirit), of comfort for all who mourn, of the humble inheriting the land (earth), and of righteousness springing up before the nations—all phrases echoed by Jesus right here.

Despite an honorable tradition of interpreting the Beatitudes as demands that we should think and behave in a certain way (*be* poor in spirit, *be* mournful, *be* meek), we understand them more accurately if we recognize them as *announcements* of "the good news of the kingdom" (4:23) anticipated by Isaiah. The Beatitudes bring relief, not pressure to measure up. Jesus proclaims them not to spell out kingdom entrance requirements, but to assure disciples that God's kingdom is generously available, with all its benefits. He is declaring that people like those on the hillside, who are "harassed and helpless, like sheep without a shepherd" (9:36), now have bright prospects because the awaited shepherd has come for them (Isaiah 40:11; Ezekiel 34:23–24). The phrases that begin "blessed are" do not prescribe behavior; they describe people—those who have begun the journey of following Jesus.

The second phrase in each Beatitude, starting with "for," announces well-being bestowed on disciples now and in the future due to their attachment to the King. For example, Jesus declares his followers to be blessed, not *because* of being dispirited or persecuted, but because the kingdom now belongs to them (verses 3 and 10). Disciples of Jesus are a new community, many emerging from miserable circumstances, who are beginning to experience God's mercies. During the journey with Jesus, some characteristics will decrease (for example, being poor in spirit), and others will increase (mercy, purity of heart). The good news is that Jesus welcomes disciples from their position of weakness rather than achievement or strength. Strength and well-being will come in the course of time through relationship with him.

The Beatitudes are paradoxical, apparently self-contradictory. We see this especially if we translate the second one, "Happy are those who mourn." How different Jesus' list is from any normal list of people whom we would consider to be fortunate or well off! We usually list the popular, the wealthy, the good-looking, the well-connected, the powerful. Jesus turns it upside down. He points to the poor in spirit, the meek, and those who have experienced injustice. Think of today's social "losers," the ones whom popular people bully or reject or treat as invisible. *They* are in a position to rejoice, because God's kingdom action brings a welcome reversal of their fortunes. Those who are accustomed to being on the outside looking in will be insiders now.

In the first Beatitude, the phrase "poor in spirit" points to people who are desperate, depressed, humiliated. These people on the hillside are mostly poor, and many of them are sick (4:23–25). Now God is intervening to heal them, lift them up, and give them dignity and hope. But "poor in spirit" also refers to people who are "spiritually bankrupt,"[4] people who would say, "I have never been religious or spiritual, and I have always assumed that life with God is for others and not for me." Jesus says, "Good news for you: I bring you new possibilities. You are the very person who can become spiritually rich as you follow me."

The second Beatitude promises comfort for those who are saddened by tragedy and loss. God is present and active to restore mourners. The third and fourth Beatitudes signal that God is intervening to bring justice. The pushy and powerful are accustomed to having their way and controlling wealth. By contrast, people called "meek" in verse 5 are the humble, the politically powerless, the socially trampled upon. They will prevail because God is moving powerfully to put things right.

Verse 6 can be translated "hunger and thirst for *righteousness*" or "for *justice*." Both nuances are present. The yearning for justice when a person has been denied it can be overwhelming. Imagine the injustices some of the people on that hillside have experienced, living as they do under the domination of brutal Roman authorities. Now a far greater power than mighty Rome is stepping in to bring justice.

Jesus' genius, though, is to recognize that these people are not just victims of injustice, but sources of it. For God to establish right in place of wrongdoing, people's own hearts are going to have to change. In this sense, "those who hunger and thirst for righteousness" are people who long to be good—to be righteous people—but know they are not. I once overheard a fascinating conversation, in college, through the thin walls of my dorm room. The two guys in the next room were talking about my sister (!) so I felt justified in listening in. Out of the mouth of one of them came this: "You know what I would like? I would like to date Hiigel's sister, but it's never going to happen, because she is good and I'm not." What a remarkable statement! That guy wanted more than a beautiful girlfriend. He wanted to be a good man and to be the right match for a good woman, and he had concluded such a thing was beyond his reach. With poignant candor, he was expressing his hunger and thirst for righteousness. "Good news for you," says Jesus, "I can enable you to become good even down to the deep places in your heart through the spiritual resources of God's kingdom."

The kingdom of heaven has come with power, even miraculous power, as we saw in the Jesus-in-action chapters, and Jesus makes that power abundantly available to his followers so they can become better people than they ever dreamed they could be. Think of Matthew the tax collector: hopelessly corrupt, then thoroughly transformed through the process of cooperating with Jesus, the "physician" for our souls. Becoming righteous is an essential part of our calling as disciples and a major theme as the Sermon on the Mount unfolds. For all of us who have repeatedly disappointed ourselves by our own behavior, here is real hope. Jesus says those who hunger and thirst for righteousness will be satisfied. We really can become more and more deeply good persons as we cooperate with Jesus, because the power to do it comes from God. As Jesus lays out his high ethical requirements for disciples later in the sermon, he is building upon the foundation of this good news that God *empowers* us to become righteous as we depend on Jesus.

The last four Beatitudes (verses 7–10, before Jesus elaborates on the last one in verses 11–12) are just as much about good news and new possibilities as the first four. Jesus is forming a new courageous community commended by God, in continuity with the brave prophets of old (verse 12). As disciples experience this righteous fellowship with Jesus and one another, they are equipped to venture out counterculturally in mercy and purity of heart to make peace (verses 7–9). They will seem naïve and weak to the powerful, who will abuse them and try to make them afraid. But they will endure for Jesus' sake (verse 11), and they will succeed, because Jesus brings new kingdom power that disciples experience and exert as they increasingly see and know God (verses 8–9). They are destined for joy and triumph: "theirs is the kingdom of heaven" (verse 10).

## Matthew 5:13–16

13 "You are the salt of the earth. But if the salt loses its saltiness, how can it be made salty again? It is no longer good for anything, except to be thrown out and trampled underfoot.

14 "You are the light of the world. A town built on a hill cannot be hidden. 15 Neither do people light a lamp and put it under a bowl. Instead they put it on its stand, and it gives light to everyone in the house. 16 In the same way, let your light shine before others, that they may see your good deeds and glorify your Father in heaven."

In the Beatitudes, Jesus has announced that God's kingdom belongs to his disciples. This is good news—and it is also a call to take active ownership of the kingdom's agenda. They will not be "comforted" just to become comfortable or "satisfied" only to become complacent. They will not become the new insiders and then ignore those who remain impoverished in spirit.

Jesus uses two images to describe disciples' participation: "You are the salt of the earth," and, "You are the light of the world." The idea of light coming into a world of darkness expresses hope and relief (4:16; see also Isaiah 49:6). Salt, too, is an image of transformation. People use it to flavor food—or to preserve it from rotting. Priests used it to purify sacrifices in the temple. Speaking to the community of disciples, Jesus says, "You are the flavor in a dull, insipid world. Your lives will purify and reclaim a corrupt, rotting society."

Salt and light are images of penetration. Salt flavors and preserves meat by penetrating into it. Light dispels darkness by penetrating into places where it has been previously excluded. In the Jesus-in-action chapters, we see the penetrating action of God's kingdom in Jesus' ministry. Each new place he goes in Matthew 8–9, he encounters some aspect of human misery and replaces it with well-being. God's action through Jesus is to invade where God has been excluded, to penetrate with his blessings into places previously dominated by despair. Disease and paralysis, storms and demon possession, sin and death are all overcome, because in the person of Jesus, the reign of God is extending its reach.

The striking word in these verses is *you*. Considering Jesus' penetrating ministry among the people that brings healing and good news, we expect him to say, "*I* am the salt of the earth; *I* am the light of the world." In the Gospel of John, he says precisely that: "I am the light of the world," and in Matthew 4:13–17, Jesus' arrival marks the dawn of light among a people living in darkness. But here, Jesus says emphatically to his disciples, "*You* are the salt of the earth; *you* are the light of the world." He is saying, "The very kingdom action that I have begun among the people I will enable *you* to do." It is the same idea as his saying, "*You* give [the five thousand] something to eat" in Matthew 14. Jesus will empower their ministry, but his disciples will do the work. Jesus, as we observed him in Matthew 8–9, has begun to confront and reverse all that Isaiah 61 itemizes: oppression, brokenheartedness, darkness, captivity, mourning, shame, disgrace, and the spirit of despair. Our role is to join him in that merciful work. We are first of all *beneficiaries* of his transforming touch ("Blessed are you . . ."). He is a physician at work to heal our souls as we walk with him. But we also receive his adventurous call to be *agents* of transformation as salt and light—to be people *through* whom God renews a hurting world.

People of every generation ask, "What is the meaning of life?" Honestly, here it is: to live and serve with Jesus, who brings the reign of God. It is discipleship. As we live with and for him, he remakes our hearts and enables us to participate in his joyful, powerful, penetrating action to transform our world. This is worth living for. It is even worth dying for. Whatever else our lives were about before, now Jesus has called us to himself and to his healing project. Through Jesus, God moves to overcome every evil and to alleviate every misery—progressively for now through our involvement as disciples and decisively later when Jesus comes in glory and righteous judgment.

Jesus follows his declaration that we are salt and light with a command, "Let your light shine before others, that they may see your good deeds and glorify your Father in heaven." The full picture of our involvement with Jesus does not come clear all at once. We will be doing "good deeds," many of them small, some of them great. We will pray and care in the moments of each day but also in work that takes years to unfold. We will serve in ways that warm our hearts but also in tense, risky situations. We will seek the welfare of people right around us and people on the other side of the world. In all of it, we will honor God, and perceptive people will see his glory through us.

Prayerfully and attentively we ask God what it will mean for us to participate with Jesus as salt and light, penetrating into the world with God's goodness. How shall we alter our daily lives so that we care about people as Jesus does? How can our careers make a difference? Which of the world's many miseries especially moves our heart or comes to our mind when we pray? How can our wealth and possessions aid the cause? What actions could our church take? What relationships can we build outside the church that might help people to receive God's hope and healing? What words can we say to help our friends not only receive God's mercy, but become agents of it (as salt and light themselves) through the life of discipleship?

Jesus' embrace of us, and his call to be salt and light, makes our lives profoundly valuable and worthwhile, however insignificant they may seem to us at times. A return to the Beatitudes reassures us in our moments of doubt. When we ask, "Why would Jesus want me on his team?" or, "What possible impact can no-names like us have?" Jesus answers, "Blessed are you, for through such unlikely people as you, God is establishing his reign." Knowing that we were poor in spirit, meek, and far from righteous, nevertheless he drew us to himself to make us into lights shining in the world.

*We find our hope and our purpose as we join ourselves to Jesus, who brings the reign of God.*

# DAY 9 | NEW RIGHTEOUSNESS

Matthew 5:17-48

## ◼ Matthew 5:17-20

17 "Do not think that I have come to abolish the Law or the Prophets; I have not come to abolish them but to fulfill them. 18 For truly I tell you, until heaven and earth disappear, not the smallest letter, not the least stroke of a pen, will by any means disappear from the Law until everything is accomplished. 19 Therefore anyone who sets aside one of the least of these commands and teaches others accordingly will be called least in the kingdom of heaven, but

whoever practices and teaches these commands will be called great in the kingdom of heaven. [20] For I tell you that unless your righteousness surpasses that of the Pharisees and the teachers of the law, you will certainly not enter the kingdom of heaven."

Jesus' ethical teaching is different enough from the people's previous training that he has to defend himself from the Pharisees who charge that he is discarding the Law and the Prophets. "That's not true," Jesus says. He is training and empowering his disciples to *fulfill* God's Old Testament requirements. Jesus rejects the Pharisees' ostentatious rule keeping, because they still remain far from God in their hearts. He wants something better for his disciples.

In the verses that follow, Jesus neither eliminates the old laws nor adds new ones. Instead, he calls his disciples to live from a deep inner righteousness made possible by God. God's kingdom power is richly available now, so that just as we are to partner with him in doing works of mercy out in the world, we will also actively partner with him in transforming our own character. As we work out this righteousness with God's help, the Law and the Prophets will be fulfilled in our lives. In Matthew 5:21–48, Jesus describes the righteousness that is now possible and illustrates the actions by which we as disciples will adjust our hearts and change our world.

### ■ Matthew 5:21–26

[21] "You have heard that it was said to the people long ago, 'You shall not murder, and anyone who murders will be subject to judgment.' [22] But I tell you that anyone who is angry with a brother or sister will be subject to judgment. Again, anyone who says to a brother or sister, 'Raca,' is answerable to the court. And anyone who says, 'You fool!' will be in danger of the fire of hell.

[23] "Therefore, if you are offering your gift at the altar and there remember that your brother or sister has something against you,

<sup>24</sup> leave your gift there in front of the altar. First go and be reconciled to them; then come and offer your gift.

<sup>25</sup> "Settle matters quickly with your adversary who is taking you to court. Do it while you are still together on the way, or your adversary may hand you over to the judge, and the judge may hand you over to the officer, and you may be thrown into prison. <sup>26</sup> Truly I tell you, you will not get out until you have paid the last penny."

Jesus' pattern with each subject in 5:21–48 is to say: (1) You have heard the Law's commandment; (2) but by God's authority, I say to you that God intends for you to keep the commandment more thoroughly and from a changed heart; and (3) here are some creative "transforming initiatives" you could do as disciples to live out this greater righteousness in practical ways.[5]

This first section nicely follows the three-part pattern. In part one (verse 21), Jesus restates the commandment: "You shall not murder." In part two (verse 22), Jesus insists that true faithfulness to God is not just to refrain from actual murder, but to let go of everything in the heart that murder is made of. The act of murder begins in the heart, where resentments are savored and anger is fueled. If murder brings judgment, so does nursing anger and abusing people verbally and despising them as fools. His point is not to say that hating someone is "just as bad" as actually murdering the person—it isn't! His point is that all hatred is condemnable and does not belong in the life of a disciple. We are hardly virtuous if we refrain from physical murder but then harm people emotionally and socially through hatred. A true righteousness will mean valuing those people the way God does.

In part three (verses 23–26), Jesus gives two initiatives that a disciple could take to transform the situation. (Presumably there are many possible transforming initiatives, but Jesus proposes these two.) First, he says, "You want to worship God and present him offerings? Good. Offer him this first: be reconciled to the brother or sister whom you have offended and whom God loves. Go out of your way to bring peace in God's community. Do this, and the rest of your gifts and service to God will give him joy as well."

Jesus' second sample initiative is similar, this one presumably dealing with people outside the faith community: "Settle matters as quickly as possible with your adversary who is suing you. If you don't, the conflict will escalate, and your opponent's motivation to harm you will only increase." Jesus' advice extends far beyond legal actions. We are wise to stamp out the flames of conflict wherever they flare up. Our anger hurts us even though we may prefer that our opponent would feel the hurt. Some of the injustice and harm we experience from others may be devastating, and so anger is a natural response. Nevertheless, in both examples, Jesus instructs us to let go of anger rather than allow it to build up and control us. We will need spiritual power from God to be able to subdue our anger, and we need his healing touch to mend our wounds.

## Matthew 5:27-32

27 "You have heard that it was said, 'You shall not commit adultery.' 28 But I tell you that anyone who looks at a woman lustfully has already committed adultery with her in his heart. 29 If your right eye causes you to stumble, gouge it out and throw it away. It is better for you to lose one part of your body than for your whole body to be thrown into hell. 30 And if your right hand causes you to stumble, cut it off and throw it away. It is better for you to lose one part of your body than for your whole body to go into hell.

31 "It has been said, 'Anyone who divorces his wife must give her a certificate of divorce.' 32 But I tell you that anyone who divorces his wife, except for sexual immorality, makes her the victim of adultery, and anyone who marries a divorced woman commits adultery."6

Jesus cites another of the Ten Commandments, "You shall not commit adultery." Again he brings it down to a person's heart: "But I tell you that anyone who looks at a woman lustfully has already committed adultery with her in his heart."

Jesus actually intends for his disciples to do what he is saying. As the sermon ends, he says, "Everyone who hears these words of mine *and puts them into practice* is like a wise man who built his house on the rock" (7:24). One of the keys, then, for interpreting Jesus' teaching is not to read it as if he is being ridiculous. This principle applies both to the passage about lust and the one about gouging out eyeballs and cutting off body parts.

How many people have read Jesus' words, "I tell you that anyone who looks at a woman lustfully has already committed adultery with her in his heart," and said to themselves, "That is absurd; who can possibly avoid lusting?" If Jesus were saying that a married man commits adultery every time he notices that a woman is attractive, then it probably would be absurd—but that is hardly what he means. All sorts of thoughts enter our minds uninvited, some welcome and some unwelcome. These include sexual thoughts, and the mere appearance of a thought in our mind ("Wow, that person is attractive!") does not indicate our will or heart. Looking lustfully begins when we linger beyond that initial impulse of attraction and choose to sustain thoughts of the person as a mere object for our gratification.

To illustrate, consider the radio newsrooms you sometimes see in old movies. The news information arrives by means of ticker tape, a stream of half-inch-wide paper coming out of a slot in the wall. The news editor reads through stretches of the tape as it piles up, tossing aside much of it as being unworthy of attention, but tearing off and keeping some of it as worth focusing on for tonight's broadcast. Similarly, random thoughts enter our minds, but we can choose which thoughts to discard and which to pursue. That choice of what to retain in our mind is something we can discipline and control as God strengthens us. (It's not that we have *no* control over what enters our minds in the first place: where we go, how we behave, and what we watch and read does affect the quality of thoughts that come in.) What will we do with a sexual thought once it has entered our mind? Jesus is proposing a discipline of mind by which we habitually decide not to transition into lust. As we discipline our thoughts and turn to God, he fortifies us. In the life of discipleship, we constantly participate with God in forming our own character.

Again, when Jesus proposes transforming initiatives that we could take in order to fulfill the no-adultery commandment (verses 29–30), he is not being ridiculous. He employs a striking style of speech called hyperbole: he exaggerates to make a point. No eye plucking or hand amputations or self-castrations here, please! Jesus is saying to be serious about turning aside from things that influence us to sin. We have to be brutally honest about what tempts us and to say no to some things everyone around us is doing. As we do, some may tell us we are missing out on life (that we have maimed ourselves socially), but actually we are growing freer to be good. It is better to set aside any number of worldly "freedoms" than to harm our marriage or damage our fellowship with God. Too much is at stake.

### Matthew 5.33-37

33 "Again, you have heard that it was said to the people long ago, 'Do not break your oath, but fulfill to the Lord the vows you have made.' 34 But I tell you, do not swear an oath at all: either by heaven, for it is God's throne; 35 or by the earth, for it is his footstool; or by Jerusalem, for it is the city of the Great King. 36 And do not swear by your head, for you cannot make even one hair white or black. 37 All you need to say is simply 'Yes,' or 'No'; anything beyond this comes from the evil one."

The Pharisees had turned Moses' instruction to be honest and keep our promises into a whole system of fancy pledge making. "I swear by heaven!" (Now people say, "I swear to God.") "I swear by Jerusalem!" (Now it is, "I swear on a stack of Bibles.") "I swear by my head!" (Now we put our hand over our heart.) People resort to such conventions of language and ostentatious promise making because deceit is so common. The issue is not whether to take oaths or vows; the issue is our usual habit of hedging on the truth and making commitments with our fingers crossed. Jesus says, "Tell the truth all the time. Keep your word habitually." Being trustworthy is part of being light in a dark world.

## ■ Matthew 5:38–48

38 "You have heard that it was said, 'Eye for eye, and tooth for tooth.' 39 But I tell you, do not resist an evil person. If anyone slaps you on the right cheek, turn to them the other cheek also. 40 And if anyone wants to sue you and take your shirt, hand over your coat as well. 41 If anyone forces you to go one mile, go with them two miles. 42 Give to the one who asks you, and do not turn away from the one who wants to borrow from you.

43 "You have heard that it was said, 'Love your neighbor and hate your enemy.' 44 But I tell you, love your enemies and pray for those who persecute you, 45 that you may be children of your Father in heaven. He causes his sun to rise on the evil and the good, and sends rain on the righteous and the unrighteous. 46 If you love those who love you, what reward will you get? Are not even the tax collectors doing that? 47 And if you greet only your own people, what are you doing more than others? Do not even pagans do that? 48 Be perfect, therefore, as your heavenly Father is perfect."

In this passage we see vividly that the kingdom of heaven is breaking into a dark world. We will come up against evil persons who will attack and rob and demean us. Jesus wants us as disciples to do more than endure in such a world; he wants us to change it. In order to be light in the midst of such darkness, we will have to be different. Jesus' question, "What are you doing more than others?" shows that he expects us to excel beyond the usual standards for virtue.

Both of this section's paragraphs begin with a traditional saying used in Jesus' time to justify hurting and hating others: "Eye for eye, and tooth for tooth. . . . Love your neighbor and hate your enemy."[7] Both times Jesus authoritatively rejects the argument for hurting and hating by turning it upside down: "But I tell you, do not resist an evil person. . . . Love your enemies." Then he provides the fullest list yet of transforming initiatives: turn the other cheek; hand over your coat; go two miles; give to the one who asks from you; pray for those who persecute you.

When Jesus commands, "Do not resist an evil person," his point is, "Do not resist *by retaliating*." His goal is for opponents to reconcile. With a little imagination, we can see how Jesus' suggested transforming initiatives could change a tense situation. He says, "If anyone slaps you on the right cheek, turn to them the other cheek also." I remember an inner-city Los Angeles sixth grader's response to that verse: "My mama told me that any kid who's big enough to hit me is big enough to get hit back." I suspect his mother was urging him not to become known as a wimp, because then he would be picked on all the more. But Jesus is not saying that we should lack courage. There is something feisty about the person who, when insulted by a smack in the face, does not shrink away in fear or shame, but stands straight, looks the aggressor in the eye, and refuses to strike back. This courageous response says, "I will not yield to your intimidation; I will not hate you or be sucked into your violence." It changes the whole dynamic. The only way to break the cycle of violence is for someone to refuse to get even. Again we see Jesus' attempt to reduce tensions in his instruction to the victimized Jew that he could carry the occupying Roman soldier's pack not just the required first mile, but a second mile as an act of generosity. The whole relationship with the soldier changes during that second mile. Martin Luther King, Jr. latched on to these verses as he sought civil justice in the American South. He and unnamed hundreds, mostly from the local black churches, looked their oppressors in the eyes and refused to hate them. King was shot for it, and many who were less famous suffered, but the South was changed.

Jesus doesn't just say, "Love your enemy"; he says to be creative about it. Give abnormally. Love preposterously. Hand your coat to the fellow who is stealing your shirt. Ask God to heal the adversary who is trying to ruin you. Dream up ways to show more kindness than anyone would expect. Brainstorm with God and fellow disciples about how to bring peace, and then pursue it courageously.

Sometimes a disciple's transforming initiative will be to leave. Jesus did not always stay to face down his opponents (12:15; 14:13). His teaching about turning the other cheek should not be interpreted to mean, for example, that an abused wife should stay and take it some more. Getting out of there for a time may provide the shock the relationship needs if it is to have any future at all. Or for the healing of the victim and her children, the departure may have to be permanent. Disciples sometimes face violent situations in which the right and courageous act is to flee (for example, 24:16). What is never right is to get even.

In conclusion, Jesus says, "Be perfect, therefore, as your heavenly Father is perfect." Let us apply here, too, our principle that Jesus is not being ridiculous in what he says. True, perfect obedience will elude us. We will need God's forgiveness again and again. What Jesus is *not* saying, though, is, "Achieve abstract perfection or you will be excluded from the kingdom." Instead, he is giving positive guidance about how to love with a godly kind of love. The context is Jesus' command to love even our enemies and persecutors, so he is saying, "Place no limits on your loving, just as your heavenly Father loves without limit." The parallel verse in Luke reads not, "Be perfect," but, "Be *merciful*, just as your Father is merciful" (Luke 6:36). Both versions are saying not to limit our loving to the standards of the rest of the world, but to make God's complete love our standard. Then we will be "doing more than others." Then we will show ourselves to be "children of our Father in heaven." The command to imitate our heavenly Father brings us to our knees in worship: "Father, your love is amazing and unbounded." Then it makes us want to be like him, bearing his family likeness. With God helping us, our hearts will become more and more like his.

*We will be light in the world, far exceeding the usual standards for righteous living, as we cooperate with God in forming our character.*

# KINGDOM PRAYING | DAY 10

Matthew 6:7-15, 25-34, 7:7-12; review of 8-9

God has chosen to establish his reign in the world through collaboration with his people. If discipleship is living with Jesus and participating with him in what he is doing, then prayer will be our essential means of connecting with him.

## Matthew 6:7-15

[7] And when you pray, do not keep on babbling like pagans, for they think they will be heard because of their many words. [8] Do not be like them, for your Father knows what you need before you ask him. [9] "This, then, is how you should pray:

"'Our Father in heaven,
hallowed be your name,

<sup></sup>[10] your kingdom come,
your will be done,
> on earth as it is in heaven.
[11] Give us today our daily bread.
[12] And forgive us our debts,
> as we also have forgiven our debtors.
[13] And lead us not into temptation,
> but deliver us from the evil one.'

[14] For if you forgive other people when they sin against you, your heavenly Father will also forgive you. [15] But if you do not forgive others their sins, your Father will not forgive your sins."

Jesus introduces his model prayer by assuring us as disciples that God hears us and knows us. God is our heavenly *Father*, who tenderly embraces us; and he is our *heavenly* Father, transcendent in majesty and power. He cares enough to hear our prayers and is powerful enough to answer them. As we pray, we are entering into the eternal Father's life and thoughts.

Jesus then invites us to make requests to God. The first three requests, verses 9–10, concern God's emerging reign in the world. "Hallowed be your name" means "may you be honored as holy." These words express praise and affirm that God is worthy to receive honor. We pause to enjoy God, awed by his greatness. At the same time, "hallowed be your name" is a request that God would so move in people's hearts that all will esteem God and hold him in awe. We can request this worshipful heart first for ourselves and then for others. "God, help my thoughts, words, and actions to honor you as holy. Help the thoughts, words, and actions of my family members and close friends to honor you as holy. Touch the hearts of people in my church and my city and to the ends of the earth so they begin to worship and adore you."

The paired phrases "Your kingdom come, your will be done" work together in a way that is common in Hebrew poetry: the second line clarifies the first. "Your kingdom come," means, "God, please take charge and complete the saving work you have begun," and the indicator that his saving work is succeeding is that God's "will [is] done, on earth as it is in heaven." The request picks up both the "already" and the "yet to come" of God's kingdom: "May your way take hold progressively here and now in our world [already], until you intervene finally to end all evil and reign unopposed as King and Lord of all [yet to come]." By praying for his reign to take hold we acknowledge that he works in small places, such as our own circumstances, as well as in the wider world. Thus we may focus our petitions first on ourselves and then on others: "May you reign as king in the details of my life; may you reign in my loved ones' hearts and in our church and our city and in every corner of the world" (naming places and situations that have been on our hearts). The double request, "your kingdom come, your will be done," says in a general way what we will pray for in a variety of specific ways. The Lord's Prayer is an outline for our creative praying as we unite our hearts to God's heart.

The second half of the prayer supports the first half. Beginning with, "Give us today our daily bread," we ask God to meet all of our needs so we can pursue his reign and his will. We need food, and "daily bread" stands for our other daily necessities as well. We need release from guilt ("debts" refers to our moral obligation toward those we have hurt). We need to be reconciled with those who have sinned against us ("our debtors")—otherwise bitterness will hinder our efforts to serve. We need guidance and strength ("lead us not into temptation") so we will not fall away from God. And we need deliverance from all forms of evil, including accident or disease, as well as human or demonic attack. So in this second half of the prayer, we are asking God to take care of us so we can focus on the primary thing, which is to collaborate with God so that his will is done on earth.

Eight times in the prayer Jesus uses the pronouns *we* and *our* and *us*. Whether we pray alone or with others, we are members of a team of people who have adopted God's agenda as our own agenda. To illustrate, I recall asking a student named John about his career direction. He told me that just two weeks earlier he had taken a job with a regional insurance company. As he talked, I was struck by how frequently he referred to the company as "we." "We are a growing company. We have added this product. We have expanded to new cities." In a short time, he had so identified himself with the company's personnel and mission that to him it was obvious to say "we." Similarly, disciples belong to a team, a family. When we pray that God would be honored and that his will would be done, we embrace the Christian team's mission and identity as our own. When we ask him to meet our daily needs and forgive us and protect us, we depend upon God together as a family.

### ■ Matthew 6:25–34

25 "Therefore I tell you, do not worry about your life, what you will eat or drink; or about your body, what you will wear. Is not life more than food, and the body more than clothes? 26 Look at the birds of the air; they do not sow or reap or store away in barns, and yet your heavenly Father feeds them. Are you not much more valuable than they? 27 Can any one of you by worrying add a single hour to your life?

28 "And why do you worry about clothes? See how the flowers of the field grow. They do not labor or spin. 29 Yet I tell you that not even Solomon in all his splendor was dressed like one of these. 30 If that is how God clothes the grass of the field, which is here today and tomorrow is thrown into the fire, will he not much more clothe you—you of little faith? 31 So do not worry, saying, 'What shall we eat?' or 'What shall we drink?' or 'What shall we wear?' 32 For the pagans run after all these things, and your heavenly Father knows that you need them. 33 But seek first his kingdom and his righteousness, and all these things will be given to you as well. 34 Therefore do not worry about tomorrow, for tomorrow will worry about itself. Each day has enough trouble of its own."

These are some of Jesus' most beautiful words of assurance. Nature surrounds us with evidence of God's caring and attentiveness—see how he feeds the birds and dresses the flowers—and so we know we can trust him with our needs. The opposite of trust is fear and worry. By fretting, we gain nothing; by praying, we draw upon God's loving provision. With each new difficulty, we choose whether to turn inward in anxiety or toward God in trust.

Jesus coaxes us, "Do not worry," not meaning we should take no responsibility for planning or making a living. Rather, as we live responsibly according to our calling (as best we understand it), we can trust God daily to meet our needs. We build a habit of consciously leaning on God rather than anxiously running after all these things as nonbelievers do. This passage lays out the same pattern as the Lord's Prayer. To pray wholeheartedly "your kingdom come, your will be done," *is* to "seek first his kingdom and his righteousness." We will pursue as our surpassing passion that God's will would be done in the world and in our own lives, and we can pursue that passion unhindered as we trust him to meet our needs along the way.

### ■ Matthew 7:7–12

7 "Ask and it will be given to you; seek and you will find; knock and the door will be opened to you. 8 For everyone who asks receives; the one who seeks finds; and to the one who knocks, the door will be opened.

9 "Which of you, if your son asks for bread, will give him a stone? 10 Or if he asks for a fish, will give him a snake? 11 If you, then, though you are evil, know how to give good gifts to your children, how much more will your Father in heaven give good gifts to those who ask him! 12 So in everything, do to others what you would have them do to you, for this sums up the Law and the Prophets."

We seek God's kingdom and his righteousness by asking, seeking, and knocking. When Jesus says, "For everyone who asks receives; the one who seeks finds; and to the one who knocks, the door will be opened," he is describing the very nature of kingdom living. God welcomes the kind of initiative and energy inherent in the words *ask*, *seek*, and *knock*, and he makes things happen when we do them. As disciples, we link prayer and action in our striving that God's will would be done in our world and that his righteousness would govern our character.

The famous Golden Rule culminates this section about prayer. What would we want others to do for us if we were thinking about it most clearly? We would want them to seek God's very best blessings and well-being for us. So doing for others what we would have them do for us includes praying for them (including for our enemies) that God's generous will would be done in their lives.

Making requests to God through prayer has the effect of releasing spiritual power. *Ask, and you will receive.* God changes our world as we collaborate with him through prayer. This is no cliché. By teaching us to pray, Jesus involves us in his transformative work. The results of our praying are as real as any of Jesus' acts of power—as real as a blind man receiving sight or a tax collector becoming righteous.

We welcome his promises—it will be given to you; you will find; the door will be opened to you—but we invite frustration if we detach those promises from their purpose, which is to help us pursue God's reign. We miss the point if our praying is consumed only with what we immediately need or would like to have. God *does* meet our needs and often adds abundant benefits, apparently for no more profound reason than that it pleases him to give them. But we are tempted to live out our own agendas instead of God's and to treat God like a vending machine where we insert requests and receive prizes. We say, "God is there for me," when sometimes we really mean, "It's all about me." That approach is foreign to

Jesus' teaching here. Praying from self-absorption can leave us disillusioned and bitter: "I prayed for what I wanted and it didn't happen, so I don't trust God anymore."

Instead, Jesus' kind of praying is designed to bring us into a respectful encounter with our heavenly Father and to make our hearts like his. God answers prayer—in his own time and way—not just to meet our needs, but to prompt us to know him better so we will trust him and savor his love. "If you, then, though you are evil, know how to give good gifts to your children, *how much more* will your Father in heaven give . . . !" Every time Jesus says "much more" (6:26, 30; 7:11), he stresses God's bigheartedness. God is far more generous to us than even the best human parents are to their children, and he gives us nothing but good gifts. As we pray for God's will to be done and trust him for what we need, we discover his heart and venture into the unexplored vastness of his generosity.

[The biblical text for Matthew 8-9 is printed with Days 6 and 7.]

We return now briefly to what I have called the Jesus-in-action chapters. In Matthew 8–9, we see Jesus circulating among the people and encountering their real-life troubles. By his presence in each new scene, the kingdom of God is penetrating into people's lives with goodness and relief. In practical ways, Jesus is establishing God's kingship and doing his will among the people. Prayer plays an essential part.

Prayer takes a distinctive form here. People ask *Jesus* for help in the way we would expect them to ask God. Without sorting it all out theologically, they recognize that God is with them in the presence of Jesus, and so they come to him with their requests. He repeatedly affirms them for doing so. In the early chapters about Jesus' childhood, baptism, and temptation, we glimpsed Jesus' humanity, his full identification with our experience. At the same time, this man born of a virgin is one of a kind, so that Isaiah's prophecy about "God with us" is fulfilled uniquely in him. In 8:23–27, Jesus is so human that he sleeps, exhausted, in the tossing boat, yet he is so astonishingly powerful that his disciples ask, "What kind of man is this? Even the wind and the waves obey him!" Who but God can dominate creation like that? Jesus expects them to count on *him* for such things. We see Jesus' divine identity, then, when he answers what amount to prayers ("Cleanse my leprosy; heal my servant; raise my daughter from the dead"). Repeatedly, the people bring their needs to Jesus as if to God, and he provides for them.

As Jesus does his works of power, he often points to the people's own role in the miracles. After declaring the centurion's servant healed, Jesus praises the centurion's "great faith." After healing a woman's chronic flow of blood, he says, "Your faith has healed you." As he opens the eyes of the two blind men, he says, "According to your faith let it be done to you." They display faith by bringing their actual problems to Jesus, trusting that he can and will act. They are not disappointed!

Jesus is collaborating with the people of faith. He explicitly connects his acts of power to their decisions to trust him. The power comes entirely from him, yet their act of coming to him is essential. By praying, they are effectively partnering with the King. Hear their confidence! "If you are willing, you can make me clean." "Just say the word and my servant will be healed." "Come put your hands on my daughter, and she will live." "If I even so much as touch his cloak, I will be healed." Notice, too, that several of these prayers of trust are for someone else. The centurion intercedes for his servant. The synagogue leader appeals for his daughter. The men whose faith Jesus notices bring him their paralyzed friend. As these intercessors come to Jesus, his compassion unites with their compassion for the servant, the daughter, the paralytic.

In these chapters, the disciples whom Jesus called are traveling with him, watching him as apprentices in his kingdom work. When he praises the needy petitioners one by one for their faith,

Jesus is teaching his circle of disciples to entrust their own difficulties to him. If they are going to participate with him in kingdom work, they not only need to commit to him in trusting obedience, but turn to him in trusting prayer. Jesus' one comment about the disciples' own faith comes when they have failed to entrust their dilemma to him. During the storm at sea, he says, "You of little faith, why are you so afraid?" (8:26). They have panicked and believe they will drown instead of trusting that Jesus could do something to help them. Having seen Jesus act to relieve others, could they not trust him with their own problem now?

In so many of the stories in Matthew 8–9, the person making a request shows faith immediately and Jesus answers the request immediately. It would be tempting to expect such immediacy all the time in our own praying. The miracle stories in these chapters display by quick results the kind of power that Jesus often exerts more slowly as we pray. God wants not so much to solve every problem hurriedly, but to draw us into a sustained trusting relationship with him as he works. Seeing the first disciples' "little faith" out on the sea, we recognize that our own faith will not emerge fully grown all at once. The Twelve are still learning how to trust Jesus. Faith accumulates over time as his followers have more and more experience with him. We too can expect a long journey toward mature faith. Through our praying, Jesus builds up our store of experiences of his power and mercy so that our faith grows. As we seek first God's kingdom and entrust our needs and dilemmas to him, we will see his power, and his world-changing work will be done.

*By prayer, we collaborate with God, committing ourselves to his kingdom work and opening the way for his power to meet the challenges we face.*

**DAY 11** | # BEWARE

Matthew 6:1-6, 16-24; 7:1-6, 13-29

I was a student at UCLA in the glory days of its basketball program under the legendary coach John Wooden. I played in the band for the home games and the championship tournaments, and I lived in the dorm with players who told me about the team practices. It was a great opportunity to observe how a successful team works. Coach Wooden had no tolerance for showing off, or "hotdogging." A player who dazzled the crowds for personal glory got benched immediately. To promote unselfishness, whenever a player scored a basket with a teammate's assist, the player was to make a visible gesture to credit that teammate as they ran back down the court. He also taught them to play aggressively without accumulating fouls. A player in foul trouble is unproductive, because he has to sit out for much of the game and play too cautiously the rest of the time. It is all very well to wear the team jersey and play eagerly, but Wooden taught his players to be *effective* through smart, selfless play.

Jesus wants his disciples to be effective through smart, selfless participation—to be salty salt and shining light. "Beware," he says. "Disciples who lose saltiness are not good for much" (5:13). He is concerned that we may wear the team colors, but become dim and ineffective in the contest against darkness. We may have our guard up against the common vices Jesus itemized earlier in his sermon (hatred, lust, dishonesty, and the like) but still be sidelined. Three perils can make disciples fruitless and spiritually impotent: the love of applause, the lure of wealth, and the pitfalls of being naïve.

## ▪ Matthew 6:1–6, 16–18

6 [1] "Be careful not to practice your righteousness in front of others to be seen by them. If you do, you will have no reward from your Father in heaven.

[2] "So when you give to the needy, do not announce it with trumpets, as the hypocrites do in the synagogues and on the streets, to be honored by others. Truly I tell you, they have received their reward in full. [3] But when you give to the needy, do not let your left hand know what your right hand is doing, [4] so that your giving may be in secret. Then your Father, who sees what is done in secret, will reward you.

[5] "And when you pray, do not be like the hypocrites, for they love to pray standing in the synagogues and on the street corners to be seen by others. Truly I tell you, they have received their reward in full. [6] But when you pray, go into your room, close the door and pray to your Father, who is unseen. Then your Father, who sees what is done in secret, will reward you."

. . .

[16] "When you fast, do not look somber as the hypocrites do, for they disfigure their faces to show others they are fasting. Truly I tell you, they have received their reward in full. [17] But when you fast, put oil on your head and wash your face, [18] so that it will not be obvious to others that you are fasting, but only to your Father, who is unseen; and your Father, who sees what is done in secret, will reward you."

Don't show off," Jesus warns us. "Don't dramatize your piety to impress people." The danger comes not from something evil, but something good: practicing your righteousness. What could be more laudable than giving money to the poor or praying or fasting? But precisely because these spiritual disciplines are praiseworthy, disciples will be tempted to do them in order to be praised by others. To do that would be to replace "hallowed be your name" with "praised be *my* name."

Jesus takes a word from the arts to make his point. In his day, *hypocrite* meant play actor, a performer seeking applause. Great actors disguise their true identity by convincingly portraying fictional characters. In three scenes in this farce—giving, praying, fasting—the actor plays a devout character and skillfully masks his own true self: an egotist yearning for people's praise. Trumpets call for attention as he gives to the poor. Grandiose monologues substitute for prayer. He spends hours in makeup to look properly pitiful while fasting. As the curtain comes down on his performance, he is exhilarated by the crowd's applause.

But Jesus says the crowd is the wrong audience and their praise is a meager reward. Applause from others is like an addictive drug that leaves us craving more. How rich, by contrast, is praise from God: "Well done, good and faithful servant" (25:21), or "Come, you who are blessed by my Father; take your inheritance, the kingdom prepared for you since the creation of the world" (25:34). Disciples have to choose over and over whether to live for empty human praise or for God's "well done." Jesus warns crowd pleasers ominously, "Truly I tell you, they have received their reward in full."

Living to impress others—especially living *religiously* to impress others—is so hazardous that Jesus overstates the needed counter-measures. "Rather than impress an admirer or even yourself," he says, "be sneaky in your giving, so that even your left hand doesn't know that your right hand has done it. Do your praying in a closet, if necessary, to avoid being admired. Put on your most glowing look, lest anyone might be impressed that you are fasting." As with the other hyperbole in the sermon, we miss his point if we make rules out of these comments. Jesus, who said earlier, "Let your light shine before others, that they may see your good deeds and glorify your Father in heaven," has no intention for us to hide in closets. We cannot fully pray "*Our* Father" without praying sometimes in the presence of others. We *are* to do acts of righteousness—some-times publicly—but with our focus on glorifying our God rather than ourselves.

## ▓ Matthew 6:19-24

¹⁹ "Do not store up for yourselves treasures on earth, where moths and vermin destroy, and where thieves break in and steal. ²⁰ But store up for yourselves treasures in heaven, where moths and vermin do not destroy, and where thieves do not break in and steal. ²¹ For where your treasure is, there your heart will be also.

²² "The eye is the lamp of the body. If your eyes are healthy, your whole body will be full of light. ²³ But if your eyes are unhealthy, your whole body will be full of darkness. If then the light within you is darkness, how great is that darkness!

²⁴ "No one can serve two masters. Either you will hate the one and love the other, or you will be devoted to the one and despise the other. You cannot serve both God and money."

A second peril that can ruin our effectiveness for Jesus is to love money. Or is loving money just another version of loving attention? Wealth and status go hand in hand. Our culture esteems those who accumulate the most. In Matthew 4, the devil tempted Jesus to pursue both plenty and prestige, and Jesus now warns us as disciples not to stumble. We will stumble if we cannot see clearly. In 6:22–23, Jesus says, "If your eyes are healthy, your whole body will be full of light." Healthy eyes enable us to see what is valuable so we can go after it. The most valuable treasure is not money, but life with God, which disciples enjoy already in this life and will receive even more fully in the next.

Is it possible to be rich and serve Jesus? It would be foolish to underestimate the power of wealth to enslave a person's heart. I officiated at a funeral once for a wealthy suicide victim whose widow asked me to read from Matthew 6, because her husband's Bible bookmark happened to be at that passage. The service was conducted at one of the wealthiest clubs in Los Angeles. After explaining about the bookmark, I calmly read verses 19–21 about storing up treasure in heaven, where moths and vermin do not destroy, and where thieves do not break in and steal, and verses

25–26 about God generously feeding the birds of the air and splendidly clothing the lilies of the field. Jesus' gentle words landed like hammer blows. "Where your treasure is, there your heart will be also." All around the room jaws clenched and eyes narrowed. At the end of the ceremony, few greeted me with the typical, "Nice service, pastor." The man's suicide punctuates Jesus' warning: "What good will it be for someone to gain the whole world, yet forfeit their soul?" (16:26).

When Jesus says, "Store up for yourselves treasures in heaven," he is not saying, "The only thing that matters is the afterlife." He is urging us to become rich now in life toward our heavenly Father. Then we will be effectively salt and light in the world. People who seek instead to be wealthy and well thought of have no saltiness; they conform to the morally gray world around them. The only way we can make a difference is to be different. To fulfill Jesus' vision for disciples, we need to discipline ourselves to live for our heavenly Father's approval and set our hearts on the wealth that is truly wealth.

■ Matthew 7:1-6, 15-23

7 ¹ "Do not judge, or you too will be judged. ² For in the same way you judge others, you will be judged, and with the measure you use, it will be measured to you.

³ "Why do you look at the speck of sawdust in your brother's eye and pay no attention to the plank in your own eye? ⁴ How can you say to your brother, 'Let me take the speck out of your eye,' when all the time there is a plank in your own eye? ⁵ You hypocrite, first take the plank out of your own eye, and then you will see clearly to remove the speck from your brother's eye.

⁶ "Do not give dogs what is sacred; do not throw your pearls to pigs. If you do, they may trample them under their feet, and then turn and tear you to pieces."

. . .

¹⁵ "Watch out for false prophets. They come to you in sheep's clothing, but inwardly they are ferocious wolves. ¹⁶ By their fruit

you will recognize them. Do people pick grapes from thorn bushes, or figs from thistles? [17] Likewise, every good tree bears good fruit, but a bad tree bears bad fruit. [18] A good tree cannot bear bad fruit, and a bad tree cannot bear good fruit. [19] Every tree that does not bear good fruit is cut down and thrown into the fire. [20] Thus, by their fruit you will recognize them.

[21] "Not everyone who says to me, 'Lord, Lord,' will enter[8] the kingdom of heaven, but only the one who does the will of my Father who is in heaven. [22] Many will say to me on that day, 'Lord, Lord, did we not prophesy in your name and in your name drive out demons and in your name perform many miracles?' [23] Then I will tell them plainly, 'I never knew you. Away from me, you evildoers!'"

Jesus now lays bare a more subtle maneuver that we use to puff up our reputation: we spoil someone else's reputation by finding fault. Jesus lampoons the sanctimonious examiner, tweezers in hand, bent over his victim's eye, oblivious to the slab of lumber everyone else can see protruding from his own eye. He paints this ludicrous picture so we will be embarrassed about our arrogance. If God grants us to see some fault in a friend, we can first thank God for the opportunity to examine ourselves. As we recognize our own failures before a holy God, we can become more charitable and patient toward our friend. On the other hand, if we scold and slander and condemn, we have something to fear: "In the same way you judge others, you will be judged, and with the measure you use, it will be measured to you" (7:2).

Jesus' point is often lost. Some non-Christians (or even fellow Christians) may throw this passage in our faces. "You're being judgmental," they say, missing the irony that by declaring this, they are likely being judgmental themselves. Obviously, when we have been overbearing and condescending, we deserve to be scolded. But often our accusers quote "judge not" as if it means "make no distinctions between right and wrong—don't ever recognize that anyone's behavior, ideas, or motivations are wrong or harmful."

Such interpretations grow out of our culture's prevailing idea that no universally binding moral principles exist—that morality is relative and personal and none of anyone else's business.

That is clearly not what Jesus means. First, as he lays out his imagery of the speck and the plank, he assumes that we *will* eventually help remove the speck we have noticed in our partner's eye. We will remove our own plank first—that is, we will admit and remedy our own faults—a process that requires humility, prayer, and effort. Then we can have the right attitude and discernment to assist our friend.

Second, in the very next verse Jesus requires disciples to make some assessments about people—to consider which ones might be "dogs" and "pigs" so we can avoid being attacked by them. Being easily fooled can damage our usefulness to God just as severely as being vain or greedy. Jesus himself was not the slightest bit naïve, and he counsels his disciples to be "shrewd as snakes," not just "innocent as doves" (10:16). Some people are malicious, and disciples can be harmed or even killed by trusting the wrong person. Before we make ourselves vulnerable by sharing our personal story with someone, we have to consider whether the hearer will welcome it as compassionate ministry or will seize on it as an opportunity to betray us.

In 7:15–23, Jesus warns further, "Watch out for false prophets. They come to you in sheep's clothing, but inwardly they are ferocious wolves." Again, we have to make assessments about people's character. Jesus is cautioning the community of believers to be smart about whom we follow and whom we trust to speak on God's behalf. We have to look beneath the "sheep's clothing" of stirring preaching and sensational achievements. "Watch out," he says. "You will know them by their fruits"—by their behavior and their character. Providing we have first repented of our own sins and prayerfully sought God's guidance, it is not "judgmental" to hold a manipulative, self-absorbed, or hurtful leader accountable. To the contrary, doing so may be essential, both to protect the church's members and to prevent public scandal. God rejects such leaders' posturing (7:22–23), and the church is wise to do the same.

Third, Jesus' command, "Do not judge," comes only two verses after his command to "seek first God's kingdom and his righteousness." Jesus would firmly reject today's notion that one person's idea of morality is just as good as another's. God's kingdom is his rule, his moral dominion. Through Moses and the prophets, and especially through Jesus' life and teaching, God has revealed his will for humanity. The test of anyone's idea of morality is its conformity to that merciful, authoritative will of God. We as disciples cannot begin to help in the world until we can discern that some behaviors and ideas grieve God's heart.

## ▓ Matthew 7:13-14, 24-29

[13] "Enter through the narrow gate. For wide is the gate and broad is the road that leads to destruction, and many enter through it. [14] But small is the gate and narrow the road that leads to life, and only a few find it."

. . .

[24] "Therefore everyone who hears these words of mine and puts them into practice is like a wise man who built his house on the rock. [25] The rain came down, the streams rose, and the winds blew and beat against that house; yet it did not fall, because it had its foundation on the rock. [26] But everyone who hears these words of mine and does not put them into practice is like a foolish man who built his house on sand. [27] The rain came down, the streams rose, and the winds blew and beat against that house, and it fell with a great crash."

[28] When Jesus had finished saying these things, the crowds were amazed at his teaching, [29] because he taught as one who had authority, and not as their teachers of the law.

Jesus, the amazing, authoritative teacher of wisdom, closes his sermon by warning about the worst kind of naïveté: self-delusion. He is saying, "Don't kid yourselves into thinking that you belong to me if you really belong to the world. If you are on the path everyone else is on, it is probably the wide road that leads to destruction. If you praise me and do impressive things [verses 21–23] but don't actually do what I am teaching you to do, you are hardly mine."

Kingdom people are set apart by this: they hear Jesus' words and put them into practice. To obey Jesus consistently is to be strong; to ignore him is to put ourselves in jeopardy. He talks of rains pouring down, streams rising, winds blowing. "Don't be lulled into false confidence by the sunny times in life, because turbulent events are coming that will strip away all pretense." In the big picture, he refers to the earth-shaking Day of Judgment. More immediately, he refers to the severe storms that disciples will face during the journey of discipleship: the death of a loved one, financial crisis or job loss, physical suffering or disability, tragedies of war or natural disaster, religious persecution, or betrayal by a friend or spouse. The discipline of doing what Jesus says to do day by day in our uneventful times is our only adequate way to prepare for the crisis that could otherwise knock us off our feet. We will build our house either on rock or sand. Generally, those who collapse emotionally and morally in a crisis have been drifting along in the flow of life without ever *deciding*: "I will seriously live for God; with his help, I will discipline myself to do as Jesus commands."

When Jesus challenges us to put his teachings into practice, he is not requiring the impossible. He is the power behind the kingdom righteousness, and he will enable us. As we cooperate with him, he reshapes our heart and satisfies our hunger and thirst to live his way (5:6). His Sermon on the Mount brings consummate good news: everyone who desires to can live with God, receive the kingdom blessings, and be empowered to serve as salt and light in the world.

*To prevent us from being ineffective as we participate in God's world-changing endeavor, Jesus cautions us about applause, money, and naïveté.*

# GATHERING PEOPLE TO JESUS

## DAY 12

Matthew 9:35 – 10:42

### Matthew 9:35 – 10:8

35 Jesus went through all the towns and villages, teaching in their synagogues, proclaiming the good news of the kingdom and healing every disease and sickness. 36 When he saw the crowds, he had compassion on them, because they were harassed and helpless, like sheep without a shepherd. 37 Then he said to his disciples, "The harvest is plentiful but the workers are few. 38 Ask the Lord of the harvest, therefore, to send out workers into his harvest field."

10 1 Jesus called his twelve disciples to him and gave them authority to drive out impure spirits and to heal every disease and sickness.

2 These are the names of the twelve apostles: first, Simon (who is called Peter) and his brother Andrew; James son of Zebedee, and his brother John; 3 Philip and Bartholomew; Thomas and Matthew the tax collector; James son of Alphaeus, and Thaddaeus; 4 Simon the Zealot and Judas Iscariot, who betrayed him.

5 These twelve Jesus sent out with the following instructions: "Do not go among the Gentiles or enter any town of the Samaritans.

⁶ Go rather to the lost sheep of Israel. ⁷ As you go, proclaim this message: 'The kingdom of heaven has come near.' ⁸ Heal the sick, raise the dead, cleanse those who have leprosy, drive out demons. Freely you have received; freely give."

The Sermon on the Mount ends with Jesus demanding that his disciples act on what he has taught them (7:24). Now with his second major speech (beginning in 10:5), he sends them into action.

Two vivid metaphors set the stage. First is the image of Jesus as the shepherd to lost sheep. The milling crowds were "harassed and helpless, like sheep without a shepherd," and Jesus, full of compassion, has come to gather them—to guide, heal, and protect them, reflecting God the Shepherd in the Twenty-third Psalm. The second metaphor is the harvest. Like shepherding, the harvest is about gathering: the shepherd gathers lost sheep; the farmer gathers ripe grain. Both images have an air of urgency. The sheep are in danger; the harvest opportunity must not be missed. The lost sheep and the ripe grain represent human lives.

Our paramount goal, then, is to gather people to Jesus. In the twentieth century, leaders debated about whether Christian mission should focus on freeing people from hunger, disease, and oppression or on preaching the good news of eternal life with God through Christ. In the twenty-first century, visionary leaders are reuniting those twin objectives, just as we find them united in 9:35 and again in 10:6–8.[9] The goal of both the healing and the proclaiming is to gather people to Jesus himself. We go out and give and serve freely, asking nothing in return. Nevertheless, we meet the deepest needs we find "out there" by bringing the people "in here," into the church community where Jesus dwells. We help them to become deliberate partners, giving and receiving along with us.

Our first step is to pray (9:38). Prayer empowers our work and helps us see the big picture. It will be a large harvest! By asking God to send out more workers into the harvest, we begin to envision ourselves as part of a grand team endeavor.

Jesus shows us our ministry by calling and instructing the Twelve. Who are these representative disciples whom Jesus calls and sends? First, they are all Jews, corresponding to the twelve sons of Jacob, who fathered the tribes of Israel (19:28). For now, Jesus is sending them exclusively to fellow Jews (10:5–6), for in God's grand plan, salvation comes to the world through the Jews (Genesis 28:10–14). Second, like Jacob's sons, the twelve disciples are all men. Jesus may have additional reasons for choosing only men. He would thereby prevent public rumors about an inner circle that was together night and day. Moreover, in his culture, the public trusted only men as witnesses, and men would be less vulnerable to harm as Jesus sent them out on unprotected roads and into the homes of strangers. Jesus initiates a new phase after he rises from the dead. Then he includes Gentiles among the sheep to be gathered (28:19; 10:18), and he sends women to be the first ones to proclaim his resurrection (28:10).

Perhaps the most telling observation about the Twelve is that they are nobody special. They are Galileans, folks from the cultural backwater. They are not prominent or sophisticated, just fishermen and other commoners. They are diverse, including a former collaborator with the Romans (Matthew) alongside a patriotic Zealot dedicated to overthrowing the Romans (Simon). Included, too, is a cranky fellow named Judas. Jesus is going to build his church and change the world through such an unlikely group as these twelve. Any time we look out over our own church and think we only see unpromising people, we can envision new possibilities by remembering how effective the Twelve ultimately became.

As Jesus sends out his novice evangelists, he instructs them to preach about the kingdom and gives them astonishing authority "to drive out evil spirits and to heal every disease and sickness." That is, they will be doing things that Jesus was doing in Matthew 8–9. "Freely you have received the kingdom blessings," he says. "Freely pass them on to others."

Their activity will include miracles. Though Matthew narrates no stories in which disciples "heal the sick, raise the dead, cleanse those who have leprosy, [or] drive out demons" (verse 8), we can assume from this verse that they did such things. Should twenty-first-century disciples expect to be involved in miracles? We continue to hear abundant credible reports of healings in answer to prayer, especially in parts of the world where the gospel is penetrating for the first time—miraculous healings that astonish people and turn many to faith. Jesus anticipates great results as we pray in faith (17:20; 21:21–22). However, the complete restorative power of the kingdom—and our full authority as disciples—will come only when Jesus returns in glory (19:28; 25:34). In the meantime, we will triumph over some of the people's problems with God's help, but not over all of them. The rest of Matthew 10 speaks of many unrelieved miseries. We can count on this: whether he employs miracles as a means or not, Jesus will empower his disciples in every generation to resist darkness and to draw lost sheep to him.

### ■ Matthew 10:9–15, 40–42

⁹ "Do not get any gold or silver or copper to take with you in your belts—¹⁰ no bag for the journey or extra shirt or sandals or a staff, for the worker is worth his keep. ¹¹ Whatever town or village you enter, search there for some worthy person and stay at their house until you leave. ¹² As you enter the home, give it your greeting. ¹³ If the home is deserving, let your peace rest on it; if it is not, let your peace return to you. ¹⁴ If anyone will not welcome you or listen to your words, leave that home or town and shake the dust off your feet. ¹⁵ Truly I tell you, it will be more bearable for Sodom and Gomorrah on the day of judgment than for that town."

. . .

⁴⁰ "Anyone who welcomes you welcomes me, and anyone who welcomes me welcomes the one who sent me. ⁴¹ Whoever welcomes a prophet as a prophet will receive a prophet's reward,

and whoever welcomes a righteous person as a righteous person will receive a righteous person's reward. [42] And if anyone gives even a cup of cold water to one of these little ones who is my disciple, truly I tell you, that person will certainly not lose their reward."

Jesus sends them out green, as rookies. He does not wait until they are refined or skilled. They will learn by doing. They will have meager supplies, uncertain accommodations, and no ready cash or extra clothes. Theirs is a short-term mission featuring quick moves from one place to another. This passage does not forbid us to think ahead logistically for more settled missionary endeavors. In every mission, though, Jesus wants disciples to depend fundamentally on God himself and to accept help humbly from the people to whom he sends us.

The advertising slogan from a luxury cruise line, "Get out there!" applies here with a different meaning. Our journeys for him will not be luxurious or even comfortable, and they will not be about having fun. There will be plenty of adventure, though. God's work will require us to get out beyond our comfort zone, perhaps beyond our home country. Clearly, being the community of Jesus cannot mean clustering together as a self-serving subculture that keeps a safe distance from a contaminated, scary world. Jesus uses the shepherd-and-sheep imagery to say both "come" and "go." We come together in the presence of the Shepherd to receive security, confidence, and spiritual nourishment. Then we are fortified to go out "like sheep among wolves" (verse 16). Disciples of Jesus engage the world, facing dangers and deprivations in order to get out among the poor and diseased, the tax collectors and sinners. We will invest ourselves in receptive people who return our expressions of peace, not lingering among those who remain hostile (verses 13–14). God will honor and reward those who help Jesus' missionary disciples (verses 40–42). He tells us, "Get out there—and as you go, God will see you through."

## ▦  Matthew 10:16-31

¹⁶ "I am sending you out like sheep among wolves. Therefore be as shrewd as snakes and as innocent as doves. ¹⁷ Be on your guard; you will be handed over to the local councils and be flogged in the synagogues. ¹⁸ On my account you will be brought before governors and kings as witnesses to them and to the Gentiles. ¹⁹ But when they arrest you, do not worry about what to say or how to say it. At that time you will be given what to say, ²⁰ for it will not be you speaking, but the Spirit of your Father speaking through you.

²¹ "Brother will betray brother to death, and a father his child; children will rebel against their parents and have them put to death. ²² You will be hated by everyone because of me, but the one who stands firm to the end will be saved. ²³ When you are persecuted in one place, flee to another. Truly I tell you, you will not finish going through the towns of Israel before the Son of Man comes.

²⁴ "The student is not above the teacher, nor a servant above his master. ²⁵ It is enough for students to be like their teachers, and servants like their masters. If the head of the house has been called Beelzebul, how much more the members of his household!

²⁶ "So do not be afraid of them, for there is nothing concealed that will not be disclosed, or hidden that will not be made known. ²⁷ What I tell you in the dark, speak in the daylight; what is whispered in your ear, proclaim from the roofs. ²⁸ Do not be afraid of those who kill the body but cannot kill the soul. Rather, be afraid of the One who can destroy both soul and body in hell. ²⁹ Are not two sparrows sold for a penny? Yet not one of them will fall to the ground outside your Father's care. ³⁰ And even the very hairs of your head are all numbered. ³¹ So don't be afraid; you are worth more than many sparrows."

These verses look beyond the initial evangelistic journey of the Twelve. Though Jesus wants his followers to continue to witness among the Jewish people (verse 23), he envisions witness also to the Gentiles (verse 18). As disciples mercifully bring sheep into the Shepherd's fold, we will sometimes be mercilessly opposed. The worst may come from the people we most hoped would support us: our parents, brothers and sisters, sons and daughters.

How shall we respond to such opposition? First, "Be on your guard." We have to "be as shrewd as snakes" to evade the prowling wolves who seek to devour us. The second half of the saying (verse 16) is just as important: we have to be "as innocent as doves." We will be tempted to retaliate when people mistreat us, but our Shepherd always leads us in paths of righteousness. The authority he grants us is always moral authority. Shrewdness alone leaves us cynical, while innocence alone leaves us vulnerable. Street-smart wits combined with rock-solid integrity make us strong.

"The one who stands firm to the end will be saved," he says, which suggests that there is much to endure. Some will find the pressure too intense and will fall away (13:21; 24:10). But Jesus is eager to help his disciples stand strong. He will help us to know when the shrewdest, most faithful thing to do is simply to flee (verse 23). If we are captured and interrogated, the Spirit of God will be so intensely present that he will provide the words we need to say (verse 20). It is not our persecutors but God who has the last say about life and death (verse 28). Because *he* knows us so well and watches over us so attentively, we can move out without fear (verses 29–31) and proclaim his good news from the rooftops (verse 26–27).

Verses 24–25 are especially helpful for understanding discipleship. Students are to be *like* their teacher and servants *like* their master. In its immediate context, these verses say that disciples will be misunderstood and mistreated, as Jesus was. But they mean more broadly that we are to become like Jesus in our whole approach to life. The word for "student" is translated "disciple" everywhere else, so verse 25 means, "It is enough for disciples to be like their Teacher." Thus Dallas Willard defines discipleship as "a life of learning from Jesus Christ how to live in the Kingdom of God now, *as he himself did.*"[10]

## ■ Matthew 10:32-39

[32] "Whoever acknowledges me before others, I will also acknowledge before my Father in heaven. [33] But whoever disowns me before others, I will disown before my Father in heaven.

[34] "Do not suppose that I have come to bring peace to the earth. I did not come to bring peace, but a sword. [35] For I have come to turn

> "'a man against his father,
>      a daughter against her mother,
> a daughter-in-law against her mother-in-law—
>      [36] a man's enemies will be the members of his
> own household.'

[37] "Anyone who loves their father or mother more than me is not worthy of me; anyone who loves their son or daughter more than me is not worthy of me. [38] Whoever does not take up their cross and follow me is not worthy of me. [39] Whoever finds their life will lose it, and whoever loses their life for my sake will find it."

When Jesus talks about being flogged or being brought before governors and kings or being betrayed to death by a family member or learning not to fear those who kill the body, his words may seem foreign to our experience. For many in the world, however, such words are vividly relevant. A seminary classmate from Korea once told me that her family disowned her when she became a Christian. Another friend from India told me of a convert to Christ who had to flee from home, because family members threatened to kill him. There are thousands of stories like that. In many countries, it is a crime to invite people to know Jesus. My aunt and uncle went in their retirement years to a traditionally Muslim country where it was not yet criminal to evangelize. My uncle told me, nevertheless, that he had to be willing to risk his life for Christ, because without doubt some he would lead to Christ would be risking *their* lives. He did die there, killed by a disease he never would have gotten back home. My aunt, who continued her service in a neighboring country until recently, experienced the grilling from government officials that Jesus predicted. But in that far-away place, she enjoyed daily the presence of Jesus who had sent her. They both received rich satisfaction from leading people to Jesus, witnessing their radiant joy in the moment of baptism, and sharing praise to God with them during risky worship gatherings.

At the climax of his speech, Jesus makes some astonishing claims and breathtaking demands. Who else in the history of the world has ever spoken like this? "Do not suppose that I have come to bring peace to the earth." He intends to disrupt the whole world! "Anyone who loves their father or mother more than me . . . who loves their son or daughter more than me . . . who does not take up their cross [instrument of death] and follow me . . ."—such demands! "Not worthy of me . . . not worthy of me . . . not worthy of me!"—such audacity! "Whoever acknowledges me before others, I will also acknowledge before my Father in heaven. But whoever disowns me before others, I will disown before my Father in heaven." Such talk is the delusion or deceit of an egomaniac. *Or* it is the summons by God's glorious Son to serve the Father of all life.

Revolutionaries rouse one another to martyrdom for their righteous cause ("I only regret that I have but one life to lose . . ."). Military leaders appeal to "a sense of honor" and to the dream of being "the few, the proud"—*semper fideles* (unceasingly faithful) to country and comrades. Such fiercely zealous leaders understand the power of a worthy cause to call forth courageous, sacrificial service. Young men and women respond with all their heart (sometimes while family members plead for them to stay home), accepting—even relishing—the toughest assignments.

All the more, then, we rally to Jesus' side when he calls us to action. His is the greatest cause of all, the life-giving kingdom of God. He is the greatest leader of all, who makes our labor fruitful and our character worthy. Serving with him will involve risk and challenge, the very things that appeal to those who detest boredom. No call to adventure has ever been so ennobling, no camaraderie so honorable, no cause so worthy of sacrificial service.

*Jesus empowers and sends us into his great mission of salvation, equipping us for challenges as we gather people into his flock.*

**DAY 13**  |  # WHOEVER HAS EARS

Matthew 11

■ Matthew 11:1-19

**11** [1] After Jesus had finished instructing his twelve disciples, he went on from there to teach and preach in the towns of Galilee.
[2] When John, who was in prison, heard about the deeds of the Messiah, he sent his disciples [3] to ask him, "Are you the one who is to come, or should we expect someone else?"
[4] Jesus replied, "Go back and report to John what you hear and see: [5] The blind receive sight, the lame walk, those who have

leprosy are cleansed, the deaf hear, the dead are raised, and the good news is proclaimed to the poor. ⁶ Blessed is anyone who does not stumble on account of me."

⁷ As John's disciples were leaving, Jesus began to speak to the crowd about John: "What did you go out into the wilderness to see? A reed swayed by the wind? ⁸ If not, what did you go out to see? A man dressed in fine clothes? No, those who wear fine clothes are in kings' palaces. ⁹ Then what did you go out to see? A prophet? Yes, I tell you, and more than a prophet. ¹⁰ This is the one about whom it is written:

> "'I will send my messenger ahead of you,
>     who will prepare your way before you.'

¹¹ "Truly I tell you, among those born of women there has not risen anyone greater than John the Baptist; yet whoever is least in the kingdom of heaven is greater than he. ¹² From the days of John the Baptist until now, the kingdom of heaven has been subjected to violence, and violent people have been raiding it. ¹³ For all the Prophets and the Law prophesied until John. ¹⁴ And if you are willing to accept it, he is the Elijah who was to come. ¹⁵ Whoever has ears, let them hear.

¹⁶ "To what can I compare this generation? They are like children sitting in the marketplaces and calling out to others:

> ¹⁷ "'We played the pipe for you,
>     and you did not dance;
> we sang a dirge,
>     and you did not mourn.'

¹⁸ "For John came neither eating nor drinking, and they say, 'He has a demon.' ¹⁹ The Son of Man came eating and drinking, and they say, 'Here is a glutton and a drunkard, a friend of tax collectors and sinners.' But wisdom is proved right by her deeds."

I was a music major in college, studying four years at UCLA and three more at USC, right in the heart of Los Angeles, one of the world's great cultural centers. I knew the popular styles. My roommate was a disk jockey for UCLA's campus radio station, so I got to hear the first releases of the best rock albums. My trombone teacher was a great jazz musician who knew the top players in L.A., so I got to hear and even play with some of the best. Nevertheless, it was classical music that really moved me. Something deep within me responded to the music of Bach, Beethoven, and Mahler as I heard or played or sang it, so that I was sometimes exhilarated, sometimes moved to tears. I was struck by how few of my fellow students in the dorm were similarly moved by this music, but I felt a special bond with those who were.

In this chapter, Jesus compares his ministry to music making that is designed to stir people's souls, and complains that so many are unmoved by it. He speaks of children playing games in the marketplace, mimicking the musicians they had seen at weddings or funerals and trying to get the other children to join their fun. But the other children refuse to play along, as though they are deaf to the music. "Why doesn't our music move you?" the first group asks. "We fluted a playful tune, and you didn't dance; we sang you a sad song, and you didn't weep."

Jesus says that too many people of his generation resemble the children who neither dance nor weep to the music being played. John the Baptist has sung soberly, calling people to repent and prepare for judgment. Jesus sings joyfully, "Rejoice, the bridegroom has come!" With all this music sounding, he is appalled that so few eyes have become teary, so few toes have been set to tapping. Not everyone is tone-deaf, of course. Many have responded. The crowds are large, and Jesus sends out the Twelve expecting a plentiful harvest. Too many, though, hear the sounds but not the music. Some would be thrilled by his miracles and words, but others right beside them would be irritated or indifferent. One would rejoice, "Nothing like this has ever been seen in Israel," but another would accuse him, "It is by the prince of demons that he drives out demons" (9:32–34).

Jesus makes an appeal here that he will repeat later, "Whoever has ears, let them hear." His call to hear is urgent. "God is making his long-awaited advance, but not as you expected. Do you sense it? Is there any place in your heart that hears his music, any corner of your soul that quivers at the sound? Then dance for joy or come weeping and repenting, but for heaven's sake, move!"

The event that generates Jesus' urgent appeal is a visit by messengers of John the Baptist, who is still in prison (since 4:12). Personal isolation and odd bits of news have been wearing on John, and he is beginning to wonder if he has overestimated Jesus. Like Jesus, John had announced God's entrance, "Repent, for the kingdom of heaven has come near." Their melodies, though, were as different as a funeral dirge is from a wedding dance. John predicted that someone powerful would come with judgment and fire (3:10–12)—and Jesus' ministry seems awfully tame. In readiness, John abstained from wine, fasted often, and required discipline in his followers (9:14). Jesus, by contrast, enjoys food and drink and keeps scandalous company. Is Jesus serious enough, confrontational enough? The Baptist who had raised others' anticipation of the coming Messiah now sends messengers to Jesus with the agonized question, "Are you the one who is to come, or should we expect someone else?"

Jesus reassures John and his messengers. "Go back and report to John what you hear and see. God is moving; the music is playing—hear it yourselves." The signs foretold by the prophets are being fulfilled. "The blind receive sight, the lame walk, those who have leprosy are cleansed, the deaf hear, the dead are raised, and the good news is proclaimed to the poor" (Isaiah 35:5–6; 61:1). "Hear, see, recognize that my apparently unaggressive actions *are* God's long-awaited intervention for his people. The hard-hearted do not recognize the kingdom's arrival, but do not harden your own heart."

Jesus defends John to the crowd and then summarizes his own ministry since John's imprisonment: "From the days of John the Baptist until now, the kingdom of heaven has been forcefully advancing" (verse 12 NIV-1984). Jesus' words and works *have* been forceful—they have done a kind of violence to Satan's realm. Jesus exerts God's power perhaps less fiercely than John expected, but he is destroying the devil's cruel work and setting people free. In 12:29, Jesus will compare himself to a robber who invades the devil's house, overpowers him, and liberates people the devil has been oppressing.

God's activity through Jesus is evident, too, in the way people are activated by his presence. The last phrase in verse 12 refers to people who now pursue the kingdom life assertively: "forceful [people] lay hold of it" (NIV-1984). They refuse to be deterred by any obstacle. They walk long distances and stay for days, despite insufficient food, just to hear Jesus teach. They fight through the crowds to touch even the edge of his cloak. They tenaciously demand Jesus' attention, confident he can heal them and their loved ones. They "pluck out their eye" or "cut off their hand" in order to obey him fully. They stare down the opponent who strikes them on the cheek. They follow Jesus despite threats from their families. They risk all for him in order to gain life.[11] God's kingship emboldens his people to take vigorous action. Jesus has struck up the greatest music ever played, and those who can hear it are streaming in to join the mighty dance. They will not be denied. Jesus repeatedly encourages such people in their drive to gain the full kingdom life.

■ Matthew 11:20–30

20 Then Jesus began to denounce the towns in which most of his miracles had been performed, because they did not repent. 21 "Woe to you, Chorazin! Woe to you, Bethsaida! For if the miracles that were performed in you had been performed in Tyre and Sidon, they would have repented long ago in sackcloth and ashes. 22 But I tell you, it will be more bearable for Tyre and Sidon

on the day of judgment than for you. <sup>23</sup> And you, Capernaum, will
you be lifted to the heavens? No, you will go down to Hades. For
if the miracles that were performed in you had been performed in
Sodom, it would have remained to this day. <sup>24</sup> But I tell you that
it will be more bearable for Sodom on the day of judgment than
for you."

<sup>25</sup> At that time Jesus said, "I praise you, Father, Lord of heaven and
earth, because you have hidden these things from the wise and
learned, and revealed them to little children. <sup>26</sup> Yes, Father, for this
is what you were pleased to do.

<sup>27</sup> "All things have been committed to me by my Father. No one
knows the Son except the Father, and no one knows the Father
except the Son and those to whom the Son chooses to reveal him.
<sup>28</sup> "Come to me, all you who are weary and burdened, and I will
give you rest. <sup>29</sup> Take my yoke upon you and learn from me, for
I am gentle and humble in heart, and you will find rest for your
souls. <sup>30</sup> For my yoke is easy and my burden is light."

In the towns around the Sea of Galilee, many fail to see and
hear. Having witnessed Jesus' wonders, his countrymen—
even in Capernaum, his home (4:13)—resist God even more
obstinately than the pagan towns famously condemned in the Old
Testament.

Some today ask, "Where are the miracles now? Why doesn't
God act spectacularly to induce belief as he did in Jesus' day?"
From these verses, though, we see that no amount of visual
"proof" will win over people who are unwilling to change. With
such overpowering evidence of God in their midst, the Galilean
townspeople should fall to their knees in awe and repentance.
Instead, they reject Jesus. Here is a warning to those who are not
yet believers. Some honestly do not know enough yet to decide
about him and need more evidence of Jesus' truth and power.
God is pleased to help them patiently. But if in some corner
of their hearts they resent the prospect that Jesus might make

demands if they admit him into their lives, they are probably kidding themselves about just needing more evidence. A receptive heart comes first; otherwise, even miracles piled on top of miracles will not convince them.

Related to stubbornness of heart is mental rigidity. Even such a countercultural thinker as John the Baptist is in danger of falling away because Jesus is not exactly what he expects. In verse 25, Jesus warns that people who pride themselves in being mature thinkers are liable to miss out. He savors the irony: "I praise you, Father, Lord of heaven and earth, because you have hidden these things from the wise and learned, and revealed them to little children." That is, God often enables simple people to grasp what the sophisticated miss. The "wise and learned" in every era can become entrenched—even when they appear to be on the cutting edge. Jesus cautions that overconfident intellectuals may miss reality itself. The highly educated are not the only ones who can become overly certain, of course. Some of the most inflexible people we meet detest intellectuals and base their decisions more on resentments than insight. Jesus esteems the *children* in this verse: people young and old who know they still have much to learn.

In the very nature of Jesus' ministry, he confounds our certainties and turns our accustomed ideas upside down. We often hear it said, "Jesus was accepting and tolerant, never condemning." But here Jesus says, "Woe to you, Chorazin and Bethsaida! And you, Capernaum, will go down to Hades." In a recent poll, 70 percent of Americans said that they believed there are multiple paths to God and salvation. Jesus says, shockingly, "No one knows the Father except the Son and those to whom the Son chooses to reveal him." We hear that Christianity is oppressive because it makes demands and requires obedience. Jesus says, to the contrary, "Take my yoke upon you and learn from me . . . and you will find rest for your souls. For my yoke is easy and my burden is light." Jesus cannot be put in a box. True disciples will be mentally flexible, ready to change course as Jesus refashions our expectations.

Jesus redefines what it means to be wise and learned when he says, "Wisdom is proved right by her deeds" (verse 19). For example, Jesus is wiser than his "wise" critics when he dines with tax collectors and sinners. He is pleased to eat with outsiders the elites would never go near, because these despised ones see life and truth in him that the sophisticated cannot see. By contrast to the "wise and learned," Jesus is "humble in heart," which is the foundation for becoming truly wise. We who would follow him have good reason to be humble. When Jesus says that no one knows the Father except those to whom the Son reveals him, he declares how completely we depend on him to understand God and his ways.

Jesus identifies with those musical children in the marketplace. He delights in people who will play along with him, by contrast to those who fold their arms, too cool to play. Music making is such a helpful image, because we know music in a different way than we know facts. Jesus reveals the Father not just by teaching about him, but by touching our hearts. Similarly, music gets under our skin and connects with something inside us so that we love it and experience joy or sadness that comes straight from the music. It is not that music bypasses our mind: to the contrary, it stimulates our intellect and provokes us to learn. But it penetrates deeper. The way we know music and are moved by it is like the way we know that someone loves us—a very real kind of knowing that involves both mind and heart. With *that* kind of knowing we know Jesus, who is alive with us and loves us. Those who know him know what I am talking about. Those who are just awakening (or reawakening) to his presence have an inkling of what I am talking about. Even children can get it, but adults who discount anything but intellectual knowing cannot.

The exhortation, "Whoever has ears, let them hear," comes from the one who is able to retune our ears and reshape our hearts so that we resonate with him more and more. As we learn his word and say yes to him hour by hour, our apprenticeship as disciples becomes like a great music education. Musicians are trained not just to play their part, but to listen carefully and adjust as they play. We listen constantly to Jesus, imitating his style, ever adjusting so that we are in tune and in rhythm with him.

We learn the melodies by heart so that we can play and sing them for others. As we make music by our words and deeds, we need not be discouraged that only some respond to us. Jesus had the same experience. Some will hear our dirge and weep, or they will hear our fluting and dance. Others will remain unmoved. Those will likely find us strange or irritating. It will do no good to blast the song louder and force it into their ears. Rather, we pray that the Son, who alone can reveal the Father, will make him known to them.

The Savior says, "Come to me." That is his theme, woven into all of his music. Through the ins and outs of each day, our lives are to be a persistent coming to Jesus in intimate personal connection of heart and mind. Our coming to him will include times of solitude set aside just to listen—listening takes time. The command in verse 29, "learn of me" (that is, "be a disciple of me"), never ceases. We never graduate from Jesus' mentoring. We will always need him. As we take up the load he asks us to bear, it turns out to be much lighter than the burdens of people who cling to the illusion that they are self-sufficient. Even as he says, "Take up your cross and follow me," we hear him say without contradiction that the yoke he places on our necks is easy, and the burden he puts on our shoulders is light. Jesus brings rest for our souls, and we can trust him completely.

*Jesus confounds our expectations,*
*but we keep in step as we continually come to him*
*and retune our hearts to his music.*

# CONTROVERSIAL AUTHORITY

Matthew 12

J esus has said in previous chapters that his disciples will encounter controversy because he himself is controversial. In Matthew 12, the conflicts multiply for Jesus and create new challenges for us.

## Matthew 12:1-14

**12** [1] At that time Jesus went through the grain fields on the Sabbath. His disciples were hungry and began to pick some heads of grain and eat them. [2] When the Pharisees saw this, they said to him, "Look! Your disciples are doing what is unlawful on the Sabbath."

[3] He answered, "Haven't you read what David did when he and his companions were hungry? [4] He entered the house of God, and he and his companions ate the consecrated bread—which was not lawful for them to do, but only for the priests. [5] Or haven't you read in the Law that the priests on Sabbath duty in the temple desecrate the Sabbath and yet are innocent? [6] I tell you that something greater than the temple is here. [7] If you had known what these words mean, 'I desire mercy, not sacrifice,' you would not have condemned the innocent. [8] For the Son of Man is Lord of the Sabbath."

[9] Going on from that place, he went into their synagogue, [10] and a man with a shriveled hand was there. Looking for a reason to bring charges against Jesus, they asked him, "Is it lawful to heal on the Sabbath?"

¹¹ He said to them, "If any of you has a sheep and it falls into a pit on the Sabbath, will you not take hold of it and lift it out? ¹² How much more valuable is a person than a sheep! Therefore it is lawful to do good on the Sabbath."

¹³ Then he said to the man, "Stretch out your hand." So he stretched it out and it was completely restored, just as sound as the other. ¹⁴ But the Pharisees went out and plotted how they might kill Jesus.

The Pharisees pressed their fellow Israelites to keep the Law of Moses so that God would bless and restore the nation. Many Pharisees were convinced that Jesus undermined proper regard for God's Law, especially by his apparently cavalier attitude toward the Sabbath commandment. The Sabbath is God's gift of rest, a mercy for overworked people. But Jesus says the Pharisees are draining the mercy right out of the Sabbath. In the first story, mercy means food for hungry men. In the second, it means healing for a man's ruined hand. Jesus tells the Pharisees to learn the Scriptures they claim to defend, especially God's words in Hosea 6:6, "I desire mercy, not sacrifice."

Jesus does more, though, than plead for a deeper understanding of God's mercy. He points to his own authority, piling one astonishing assertion on another. In the previous chapter, he claimed to be in charge as God's Son, saying, "All things have been committed to me by my Father." He now adds a double claim. First, he is the "Son of Man," referring back to the prophet Daniel's vision:

There before me was one like a *son of man*, coming with the clouds of heaven. He approached the Ancient of Days [that is, God] and was led into his presence. [The son of man] was given authority, glory, and sovereign power; all nations and peoples of every language worshiped him. His dominion is an everlasting dominion that will not pass away, and his kingdom is one that will never be destroyed. (Daniel 7:13–14)

Not only is Jesus the glorious Son of Man, whom all peoples will worship and serve (25:31–32; 26:64), he is the "Lord of the Sabbath," a title any Jew would have attributed only to God. Sabbath is God's gift of rest. Now Jesus claims that he fulfills the meaning of Sabbath: "Come to *me* . . . and *I* will give you rest" (11:28). He further claims that his presence and ministry is "greater than the temple," where God dwells (12:5–6)! It is hard to exaggerate how brazen and blasphemous this series of claims must have sounded in the ears of pious Pharisees. No wonder they begin to plot and gather evidence against him. To these men who are so careful to be sure everyone does what is right, Jesus insists, "The essential thing is to be right about who I am."

## Matthew 12:15-21

<sup>15</sup> Aware of this, Jesus withdrew from that place. A large crowd followed him, and he healed all who were ill. <sup>16</sup> He warned them not to tell others about him. <sup>17</sup> This was to fulfill what was spoken through the prophet Isaiah:

<sup>18</sup> "Here is my servant whom I have chosen,
the one I love, in whom I delight;
   I will put my Spirit on him,
and he will proclaim justice to the nations.
   <sup>19</sup> He will not quarrel or cry out;
no one will hear his voice in the streets.
   <sup>20</sup> A bruised reed he will not break,
and a smoldering wick he will not snuff out,
   till he has brought justice through to victory.
<sup>21</sup> In his name the nations will put their hope."

We are surprised, after Jesus makes such bold claims about himself, that he "warned them not to tell others about him." We have seen such admonitions before (8:4; 9:30), and we will see them again (16:20; 17:9). Why does he command this? We could attribute it to his humility, to his refusal to showboat or pursue fame. But there is more to it. His warning is related to the Pharisees' plotting to kill him (verse 14). The disciples are not to tell about him for now, because doing so could cause further trouble. Jesus particularly wants to postpone having the crowds speak of him as Messiah (that is, King; see 16:20). To be called a king while living under Roman rule is politically explosive, and it will get him killed in due time. Jesus withdraws for a while. He knows when to arouse controversy and when to prevent it.

We need his restraint and wisdom, because Jesus is still controversial. We may recognize that he is God's Messiah, but then actually hinder his cause if we speak about him too soon or too uninhibitedly. (Of course, many of us are so cautious that we never speak about Jesus at all, but let's assume for a moment that our problem is being overly eager to speak.) We need to discern how much a person is ready to hear and to choose the right time and place. Sometimes we have to limit our conversation for the sake of a laudable immediate objective. For example, we may work for a secular business that we hope to influence to operate more justly. Getting "too religious" might turn off some fellow employees who would otherwise help us lobby for more ethical policies. Those same fellow employees might be more open to hearing about Jesus later, once they get to know our heart. Consider, too, Jesus' instruction not to "throw your pearls to pigs" (7:6). Some people are simply hostile and may turn on us and use our well-meaning testimony to betray us. If we pray and learn to be sensitive to the prompting of God's Spirit, we will discern when and how to speak. When we do tell people about Jesus, we want to convey respect for their convictions and experiences. It never helps to be argumentative or pushy.

Matthew says that Jesus' restraint about publicity fulfills a prophecy from Isaiah. The prophet marvels at how quiet God's chosen servant is: "He will not quarrel or cry out; no one will hear his voice in the streets." He is gentle to vulnerable people: "A bruised reed he will not break, and a smoldering wick he will not snuff out." This considerate Savior is different from the stormy prophet whom John the Baptist anticipated or the conquering rebel-king many in the crowds expect. Jesus is certainly confrontational when the occasion calls for it, but with the common people, he is "gentle and humble in heart." He is the hope of the nations. Sometimes gently and sometimes boldly, he will "bring justice through to victory." We join him in his pursuit of justice and imitate his wisdom and self-control.

## ■ Matthew 12:22-32

22 Then they brought him a demon-possessed man who was blind and mute, and Jesus healed him, so that he could both talk and see. 23 All the people were astonished and said, "Could this be the Son of David?"

24 But when the Pharisees heard this, they said, "It is only by Beelzebul, the prince of demons, that this fellow drives out demons."

25 Jesus knew their thoughts and said to them, "Every kingdom divided against itself will be ruined, and every city or household divided against itself will not stand. 26 If Satan drives out Satan, he is divided against himself. How then can his kingdom stand? 27 And if I drive out demons by Beelzebul, by whom do your people drive them out? So then, they will be your judges. 28 But if it is by the Spirit of God that I drive out demons, then the kingdom of God has come upon you.

29 "Or again, how can anyone enter a strong man's house and carry off his possessions unless he first ties up the strong man? Then he can plunder his house.

30 "Whoever is not with me is against me, and whoever does not gather with me scatters. 31 And so I tell you, every kind of sin and slander can be forgiven, but blasphemy against the Spirit will not be forgiven. 32 Anyone who speaks a word against the Son of Man will be forgiven, but anyone who speaks against the Holy Spirit will not be forgiven, either in this age or in the age to come."

Whereas Jesus kept silent publicly about his identity as Messiah, he certainly wanted his disciples to grasp who he was. Matthew keeps the question squarely before his readers, noting that after Jesus heals the blind and mute demoniac, the crowd responds in astonishment, "Could this be the Son of David?" "Son of David" is code for "Messiah," the anticipated descendant of King David whom God would send to restore Israel. The people are wondering, "Are we witnessing God's climactic intervention to rescue his people?"

"No, you fools!" say the Pharisees, "This is not God at work, but the devil—it is only by Beelzebul, the prince of demons, that this fellow drives out demons," repeating a charge they have made before (9:34; 10:25). Jesus responds that the Pharisees make no sense: the devil would not fight himself! Then in the short space of verses 28–29, he makes three of the most important assertions in the Gospel thus far: (1) The power at work in Jesus is the Spirit of God; (2) This confirms that the kingdom of God is present *now*; and (3) Jesus exerts this power in order to disable the devil and liberate all who are under his control.

Jesus portrays the greatness of his power in the short parable of the home invasion robbery, verse 29. The thief in the story represents Jesus, and the strong man whom he robs is the devil. The imagery suggests violent power, since Jesus ties up the devil and plunders his house, but Jesus' power is different. He overcomes the devil and liberates those the devil has oppressed through such gentle acts as healing the blind, mute demoniac. Ultimately, he will defeat the demonic powers by the apparent powerlessness of being nailed to a cross. Jesus' humiliation at the cross will be his greatest act of power and will define the kind of power by which his disciples will change the world. The good news is that "the kingdom of God has come" through the ministry of this man who overpowers evil without using worldly force.

His mysterious kind of power comes from God's Holy Spirit. Only people whose hearts are open can detect the Spirit's presence.

Jesus' point about the "blasphemy of the Holy Spirit" is that some hearts are so dark and hard that they are beyond rescue. Despite their outward piety, these particular Pharisees are so deeply perverse that they defame (blaspheme) the Holy Spirit who works in Jesus, calling him the devil. They will never turn and be included in Jesus' eternal benefits. It is startling to hear Jesus speak of any "unforgivable sin," but readers who worry that they may already have committed such a sin show that they have not done so by their tender-hearted concern about it. People who have committed such a sin remain disdainfully sure they have not.

### Matthew 12:33-37

33 "Make a tree good and its fruit will be good, or make a tree bad and its fruit will be bad, for a tree is recognized by its fruit. 34 You brood of vipers, how can you who are evil say anything good? For the mouth speaks what the heart is full of. 35 A good man brings good things out of the good stored up in him, and an evil man brings evil things out of the evil stored up in him. 36 But I tell you that everyone will have to give account on the day of judgment for every empty word they have spoken. 37 For by your words you will be acquitted, and by your words you will be condemned."

By his illustration of the fruit tree, Jesus asserts that the controversy about him stems from his opponents' corrupt hearts. Just as the quality of "a tree is recognized by its fruit," so people reveal the quality and content of their hearts by their words. It is a life-or-death matter whether a person's heart is tender or hardened toward God.

### Matthew 12:38-45

38 Then some of the Pharisees and teachers of the law said to him, "Teacher, we want to see a sign from you."
39 He answered, "A wicked and adulterous generation asks for a

sign! But none will be given it except the sign of the prophet Jonah. [40] For as Jonah was three days and three nights in the belly of a huge fish, so the Son of Man will be three days and three nights in the heart of the earth. [41] The men of Nineveh will stand up at the judgment with this generation and condemn it; for they repented at the preaching of Jonah, and now something greater than Jonah is here. [42] The Queen of the South will rise at the judgment with this generation and condemn it; for she came from the ends of the earth to listen to Solomon's wisdom, and now something greater than Solomon is here.

[43] "When an impure spirit comes out of a person, it goes through arid places seeking rest and does not find it. [44] Then it says, 'I will return to the house I left.' When it arrives, it finds the house unoccupied, swept clean and put in order. [45] Then it goes and takes with it seven other spirits more wicked than itself, and they go in and live there. And the final condition of that person is worse than the first. That is how it will be with this wicked generation."

The Pharisees' request for a sign is transparently insincere. What kind of sign would satisfy them? The countryside abounds with eyewitnesses to his mighty acts, so that he is well known as a miracle worker. This request is no plea for help so they can believe and become faithful followers. These are skeptics saying, "Prove it!" (A useful skill for sharing our faith is to distinguish a genuine inquirer from a cynic.) Jesus does not entirely refuse their request. He promises a momentous sign: the miracle of his own resurrection from the dead on the third day, symbolized by the prophet Jonah's renewed life after being rescued from death. But Jesus is sure that not even his resurrection, the "sign of Jonah," will be enough to convince these skeptics. Some of the pagans in the Old Testament were more spiritually discerning than Jesus' critics.[12]

He warns his generation using the strange story about the evil spirit who is cast out only to return later with more demons. The hearts of his fellow Israelites cannot safely remain unoccupied and neutral. If they receive his healings but do not then turn their hearts to the Healer, their relief will not last. Instead, worse days are in store. It will not do to receive benefits from Jesus, but then turn aside from the Savior himself. Jesus warns our generation, too. If we accept his aid in our moments of crisis but then refuse him his rightful place as Lord of our lives, we are really rejecting him. Jesus wants to do much more than fix our immediate problems. He wants to make his home in our hearts—to take charge there for our benefit.

The core idea in the controversy stories of Matthew 12 is that Jesus' presence compels decision. People whose hearts are tender toward God will perceive that something extraordinary is happening in Jesus and will pursue relationship with him. People who do not take steps to pursue him are at least temporarily choosing to keep distant. Jesus says in verse 30, "Whoever is not with me is against me, and whoever does not gather with me scatters." This stunning statement rules out neutrality. To know about Jesus but withhold full loyalty is actually to do damage, to be an obstacle to his deep-healing work in the world. Even people who contribute significantly to solving humanity's problems inevitably become obstacles to Jesus along the way when they live independently from him.

By what right does Jesus make such scandalous demands for loyalty? The Gospel repeatedly brings us back to the question of who Jesus is. If Matthew is right that Jesus made such sweeping claims about himself (see pages 307–15), and if Jesus was not just delusional—that is, if God has entered the human story in the person of Jesus as uniquely and powerfully as Matthew 11–12 indicates— it is surely the most important thing that has ever happened. If he is the Son of God who uniquely reveals his Father, the Son of Man whom God has destined for unending global dominion, and the Lord of the Sabbath who is the source of heavenly rest; if he is the one in whom God is doing something greater than in all the biblical kings or prophets or temple; if he is able to fulfill the sign of Jonah and rise victorious over death; if he is God's chosen servant, bearer of the Holy Spirit, hope of the nations—in short, if Jesus is the one through whom the reign of God has come upon us, then the scandal will not be that Jesus makes such demands but that anyone would ignore him.

### ▪ Matthew 12:46-50

46 While Jesus was still talking to the crowd, his mother and brothers stood outside, wanting to speak to him. 47 Someone told him, "Your mother and brothers are standing outside, wanting to speak to you."
48 He replied to him, "Who is my mother, and who are my brothers?" 49 Pointing to his disciples, he said, "Here are my mother and my brothers. 50 For whoever does the will of my Father in heaven is my brother and sister and mother."

The parallel to this passage in Mark 3:20–21, 31–35, accounts for Jesus' apparent disregard toward his family of origin by pointing to their attempt to suspend his ministry—to remove him from public life for his own good. But Jesus is fortified by the new parents and siblings who now surround him. Disciples (explicitly male *and* female in verse 49) are Jesus' eternal family who labor with him in the family enterprise. The Lord of the nations is assertive, but also vulnerable. He acknowledges his need for motherly love and brotherly companionship. The Savior did not live a solitary life. Disciples, likewise, need each other.

*We learn to be prudent but unashamed when showing the way to our controversial Savior, the Lord and Hope of the nations.*

# HIDDEN TREASURE

**DAY 15**

Matthew 13:1-52

We have arrived at the third "red patch" if you have one of those Bibles that shows Jesus' words in red ink—the third of Matthew's five great collections of Jesus' teachings (Matthew 5–7, 10, 13, 18, 24 25). The set of parables here in chapter 13 stands at the center. These short illustrative stories nearly all begin, "The kingdom of heaven is like . . ." Taken together, they climax Jesus' call to the people to abandon passivity and take hold of the new kingdom life—that is, to become disciples.

## ▪ Matthew 13:1-9

**13** [1] That same day Jesus went out of the house and sat by the lake. [2] Such large crowds gathered around him that he got into a boat and sat in it, while all the people stood on the shore. [3] Then he told them many things in parables, saying: "A farmer went out to sow his seed. [4] As he was scattering the seed, some fell along the path, and the birds came and ate it up. [5] Some fell on rocky places, where it did not have much soil. It sprang up quickly, because the soil was shallow. [6] But when the sun came up, the plants were scorched, and they withered because they had no root. [7] Other seed fell among thorns, which grew up and choked the plants. [8] Still other seed fell on good soil, where it produced a crop—a hundred, sixty or thirty times what was sown. [9] Whoever has ears, let them hear."

T his first parable features a contrast. The seed from the farmer's shoulder bag falls onto four kinds of soil. Because of problems in the first three (hardness, rocks, or thorny weeds), the seed produces nothing. Even seeds that initially sprout die away. Not so the seed spread upon the fourth kind, the good soil. It returns a hundred or sixty or thirty times what was planted. Palestinian farmers averaged about a tenfold yield, so a return of thirtyfold would have been quite a good crop, and sixty- or hundredfold returns would have been amazing. Jesus tells his story of the contrasting results—enormous returns or none at all—and leaves it to the crowd to figure out what he means.

## ▉ Matthew 13:10-17

¹⁰ The disciples came to him and asked, "Why do you speak to the people in parables?"

¹¹ He replied, "Because the knowledge of the secrets of the kingdom of heaven has been given to you, but not to them. ¹² Whoever has will be given more, and they will have an abundance. Whoever does not have, even what they have will be taken from them. ¹³ This is why I speak to them in parables:

> "Though seeing, they do not see;
>> though hearing, they do not hear or understand.'

¹⁴ "In them is fulfilled the prophecy of Isaiah:

> "'You will be ever hearing but never understanding;
>> you will be ever seeing but never perceiving.
> ¹⁵ For this people's heart has become calloused;
>> they hardly hear with their ears,
>> and they have closed their eyes.
> Otherwise they might see with their eyes,
>> hear with their ears,
>> understand with their hearts
> and turn, and I would heal them.'

<sup>16</sup> "But blessed are your eyes because they see, and your ears because they hear. <sup>17</sup> For truly I tell you, many prophets and righteous people longed to see what you see but did not see it, and to hear what you hear but did not hear it."

Suspecting that the crowd might be as mystified by Jesus' story as they are, his disciples ask him, "Why do you speak to the people in parables?" In answer, he lays out another contrast. "The knowledge of the secrets of the kingdom of heaven has been given to you, but not to them. You are among those who already have much and will gain more, while others who have little will lose even what they have." It resembles the contrast in the parable where seeds sprouting in good soil increase abundantly while the seeds sprouting in poor soil lose what vitality they have and die away.

Jesus clarifies that the product that people will either gain or lose is *understanding* of the kingdom's availability and power. Some will increase dramatically in understanding, while others will actually lose the insight that has begun to awaken in them. Because the kingdom is unobtrusive and mysterious, some can perceive its presence and others cannot. Many look at Jesus but do not really see what is happening; they hear his words but remain unmoved (verses 13–15). By contrast, the disciples' eyes and ears perceive that God's long-awaited action of salvation is operating right in front of them (verses 16–17).

The divide, then, is between those who perceive the kingdom's dynamic presence in the person of Jesus and those who do not. Jesus' parables themselves have this divisive effect. They leave much of the crowd in a fog, but they provoke others to ask questions and go deeper. As the curious seek him out, they grow greatly in understanding—blessed are they (verse 16). Those who listen idly, though, may never catch on. As a result, they will not turn and receive Jesus' deep healing (verse 15).

■ Matthew 13:18-23

¹⁸ "Listen then to what the parable of the sower means: ¹⁹ When anyone hears the message about the kingdom and does not understand it, the evil one comes and snatches away what was sown in their heart. This is the seed sown along the path. ²⁰ The seed falling on rocky ground refers to someone who hears the word and at once receives it with joy. ²¹ But since they have no root, they last only a short time. When trouble or persecution comes because of the word, they quickly fall away. ²² The seed falling among the thorns refers to someone who hears the word, but the worries of this life and the deceitfulness of wealth choke the word, making it unfruitful. ²³ But the seed falling on good soil refers to someone who hears the word and understands it. This is the one who produces a crop, yielding a hundred, sixty or thirty times what was sown."

Because the disciples have sought to understand more deeply, they get to hear Jesus' explanation. He tells them that the sower's seed is the message about the kingdom, and the soils represent the hearts of various people who hear the word. Three kinds of hearts prove to be unreceptive. First, some are as impenetrable as a hardened footpath, so Jesus' words never sink in at all. Second, some hearts respond initially with joy, "This is for me—I want to be part of this," but they wither like sprouts scorched by the sun. The persecution and troubles they face as they follow Jesus prove to be too much. Some of them are defeated by even minor difficulties, such as worrying that they won't fit in; or finding that going to church is hard to coordinate with their work schedule; or having old friends hint, "You used to be fun," or, "You used to be sophisticated, but now you're an embarrassment." They fall away, deciding that following Jesus is too much trouble.

Third, some initially responsive hearts are choked by "the worries of this life and the deceitfulness of wealth." Life with Jesus sounds rewarding, but thorny thoughts multiply: "I like money, but I may not make as much of it if I follow Jesus," or, "God might uproot me from my current job or home," or, "The romantic partner I long for may lose interest in me if I pursue Jesus." Choked by worldly concerns, their budding spiritual life shrivels up.

When Jesus ends the parable in verse 9 by saying, "Whoever has ears, let them hear," he is saying, "If you are able to grasp at all what I'm talking about, then jump up and pursue it. Come to me. Ask, seek, and knock for more comprehension about your God! If you put this off or get distracted, you risk losing the life-giving insight that is dawning within you now—perhaps permanently and fatally." But true disciples of Jesus are good soil. Their hearts are receptive, and they take action on what they hear. Fullness of life with Jesus awaits them—spiritual vitality and benefits far beyond what they imagine at the beginning. The seed multiplying thirty, sixty, or a hundred times reflects the extraordinary life-giving power of God's kingdom.

## Matthew 13:24-30, 36-43

24 Jesus told them another parable: "The kingdom of heaven is like a man who sowed good seed in his field. 25 But while every-one was sleeping, his enemy came and sowed weeds among the wheat, and went away. 26 When the wheat sprouted and formed heads, then the weeds also appeared.

27 "The owner's servants came to him and said, 'Sir, didn't you sow good seed in your field? Where then did the weeds come from?' 28 "'An enemy did this,' he replied.

"The servants asked him, 'Do you want us to go and pull them up?' 29 "'No,' he answered, 'because while you are pulling the weeds, you may uproot the wheat with them. 30 Let both grow together until the harvest. At that time I will tell the harvesters: First collect the weeds and tie them in bundles to be burned; then gather the wheat and bring it into my barn.'"

. . .

<sup>36</sup> Then he left the crowd and went into the house. His disciples came to him and said, "Explain to us the parable of the weeds in the field."

<sup>37</sup> He answered, "The one who sowed the good seed is the Son of Man. <sup>38</sup> The field is the world, and the good seed stands for the people of the kingdom. The weeds are the people of the evil one, <sup>39</sup> and the enemy who sows them is the devil. The harvest is the end of the age, and the harvesters are angels.

<sup>40</sup> "As the weeds are pulled up and burned in the fire, so it will be at the end of the age. <sup>41</sup> The Son of Man will send out his angels, and they will weed out of his kingdom everything that causes sin and all who do evil. <sup>42</sup> They will throw them into the blazing furnace, where there will be weeping and gnashing of teeth. <sup>43</sup> Then the righteous will shine like the sun in the kingdom of their Father. Whoever has ears, let them hear."

In every parable in this chapter, Jesus is making a point about the kingdom, the dynamic reign of God. In this one, the kingdom is compared to a bountiful crop that is emerging despite growing up in the midst of weeds. The wheat crop has to mature while intermingled with weeds, only to be distinguished at the harvest. Jesus explains that the wheat represents people of the kingdom: the people who say "yes" to Jesus' call into life with God. The weeds represent people who "belong to the evil one," who are "sources of evil"—sobering designations for people who reject Jesus. The field is the world. When we experience malice and ill treatment, one of our most pressing questions is why God does not just root out evil from the world completely and permanently. Jesus says that he *will* do that at the harvest, but not yet.

God does not want any wheat to be uprooted with the weeds; that is, he wants none of his own to be lost. The crop of faithful lives that Jesus plants must be allowed to accumulate and mature, hence his patient wait until the harvest. In the meantime, the true glory of God's people is obscured from view. The "age to come" (the kingdom) has been planted into our world. God's future world has entered into the present and exists simultaneously with it for a while, the eternal intermingling with the mortal. We who belong to that new world (the kingdom) live undetected among people who, however respectable they may appear, are captivated by this old world, walking its fatal path. When Jesus comes in glory and judgment, this world will end, and the full splendor of what God has done in us will become obvious for all to see.

Science fiction and fantasy literature are full of stories of people discovering another dimension that exists simultaneously with their world while remaining undetected by most people. In some of the stories, the other dimension turns out to be more real and solid than the world everyone knows (as in the movie *The Matrix*); also more astonishing and appealing (as in J.K. Rowling's *Harry Potter*). Typically, those who recognize and experience the new dimension are unable to convince their more down-to-earth, "mature" friends of its existence (Lucy, for example, early in C.S. Lewis's *The Lion, the Witch, and the Wardrobe*). Such stories use imagination, but Jesus proclaims reality as he tells a parable about coexisting "worlds," one dying, the other eternal. He tells of the kingdom, this newly accessible world permeated by the very personal, authoritative, living God. Then he beckons again, "Whoever has ears to hear, let them hear." He is saying, "If you can detect this hidden new world that has now penetrated into your own, come *now* and live in it. Here is real life!" (What a blunder to dismiss *this* as fantasy literature!) "Your destiny is glory—to shine like the sun in the kingdom of your Father!" The alternative is unthinkable.

## ▪ Matthew 13:31–35

[31] He told them another parable: "The kingdom of heaven is like a mustard seed, which a man took and planted in his field. [32] Though it is the smallest of all seeds, yet when it grows, it is the largest of garden plants and becomes a tree, so that the birds come and perch in its branches."

³³ He told them still another parable: "The kingdom of heaven is like yeast that a woman took and mixed into about sixty pounds of flour until it worked all through the dough."

³⁴ Jesus spoke all these things to the crowd in parables; he did not say anything to them without using a parable. ³⁵ So was fulfilled what was spoken through the prophet:

> "I will open my mouth in parables;
>> I will utter things hidden since the creation of the world."

The running theme in these parables of the kingdom is concealed wonders that are now being disclosed (verse 35)—hidden bounty and power now available to those who can perceive it. The tiny mustard seed generates a grand tree in which God's creatures find rest. Concealed in that tiny seed is surprising power for good. Who would have thought that so much could come from so little, from a source so unpromising? God's kingdom is like that. Who would anticipate that Jesus' little band of nobodies could change the world? Who would imagine that a bloodied man hanging from a cross is actually conquering death and liberating millions? The nature of God's kingship is that he exerts his great power through what appears small, weak, and impotent.

The idea of an uncontainable benevolent force is present in another image: the woman working yeast into a big ball of dough. Yeast is mysterious. It invades the dough in a hidden way and infects the whole lump so that it can be baked into fragrant, nourishing food. No part of the dough is unaffected. The image suggests that the kingdom's penetrating reach into our world is unstoppable. The "age to come" invades the present world, not just intermingling with it, but transforming it gradually and powerfully. God's healing reign is working its way into the world unceasingly through Jesus' disciples, generally undetected by those around them. Just as we are light and salt in the world, we are yeast, agents of God's penetrating, life-giving power. Jesus envisions that members of his church will fortify each other in gatherings for worship and prayer and then will go out and leaven the world. Every believer has a unique sphere of influence, whether in our families, neighborhoods, schools, workplaces, athletic teams, artistic ensembles, service organizations, political connections, or church families. God uses us—our witness and loving activity in these relationships—to penetrate into the world. Here is purpose and meaning for our lives. Here is the mandate to stir up our imaginations about what God could do through us as we pray, "Your kingdom come, your will be done on earth"—as we collaborate with him strategically on both a small and a large scale.

## Matthew 13:44-52

44 "The kingdom of heaven is like treasure hidden in a field. When a man found it, he hid it again, and then in his joy went and sold all he had and bought that field.

45 "Again, the kingdom of heaven is like a merchant looking for fine pearls. 46 When he found one of great value, he went away and sold everything he had and bought it.

47 "Once again, the kingdom of heaven is like a net that was let down into the lake and caught all kinds of fish. 48 When it was full, the fishermen pulled it up on the shore. Then they sat down and collected the good fish in baskets, but threw the bad away. 49 This is how it will be at the end of the age. The angels will come and separate the wicked from the righteous 50 and throw them into the blazing furnace, where there will be weeping and gnashing of teeth.

51 "Have you understood all these things?" Jesus asked.

"Yes," they replied.

52 He said to them, "Therefore every teacher of the law who has become a disciple in the kingdom of heaven is like the owner of a house who brings out of his storeroom new treasures as well as old."

The parallel stories of the treasure hidden in the field and the extraordinary pearl feature a person who finds something so valuable that no price is too high. In the first story, he stumbles upon the prize; in the second, he is searching for it. In both, the discoverer rejoices at having spotted such a premium object and acts decisively to obtain it. As we learn to see with kingdom eyes, we too will eagerly lay hold of the wealth that is truly wealth. Whatever seemed valuable before is dwarfed now by the immeasurable riches of life with God. Both stories tell us that the discoverer sold all he had to buy what he found. Will we hesitate about the costs that may come with this new life? No, it is like giving up a nickel to gain a priceless jewel.

Unlike these two stories that highlight the joy of gaining the kingdom, the story of the fishnet points to the wretchedness of missing out. The dragnet is already in motion gathering the fish, and the final sorting of good from bad is soon to come. In verses 49–50, Jesus leaves behind the net imagery to speak directly about judgment at the end of the age, of weeping and despair for those who reject God's great initiative to save us.

The cumulative force of the parables is tremendous. Everyone who hears them chooses how to respond. The incentives to recognize and go after the kingdom life are appealing (fruitfulness; great joy; shining like the sun), and the warnings against passively missing out are alarming (choked out life; weeping and gnashing of teeth; blazing furnace). Perceptive observers see how great the kingdom benefits are. Perceptive listeners hear how urgent it is to take hold of them. The treasure is inexpressibly valuable: dynamic life from God that is for us—and for others whom we help to find it (verse 52).

*Disciples see and hear and joyfully pursue
what many cannot detect: God's new world
is already dynamically present.*

# LITTLE FAITH– GREAT FAITH

## Matthew 13:53-14:36; 15:21-16:12

### Matthew 13:53-58

53 When Jesus had finished these parables, he moved on from there. 54 Coming to his hometown, he began teaching the people in their synagogue, and they were amazed. "Where did this man get this wisdom and these miraculous powers?" they asked. 55 "Isn't this the carpenter's son? Isn't his mother's name Mary, and aren't his brothers James, Joseph, Simon and Judas? 56 Aren't all his sisters with us? Where then did this man get all these things?" 57 And they took offense at him.

But Jesus said to them, "A prophet is not without honor except in his own town and in his own home."

58 And he did not do many miracles there because of their lack of faith.

Sometimes my students tell me that they appreciate leaving home for college, because in the new setting they are freed from the longstanding impressions of their old neighbors. Then they mature, but become frustrated when they return home and find that many perceive them only as they were before.

Jesus returns to his hometown, and his former neighbors still think of him as just the carpenter's kid whose brothers and sisters still live in town. He returns as a national figure with the language of a genius and a reputation for extraordinary feats. "They took offense at him" means they despised the way his fame had outgrown his origins and left them behind. "Don't let it all go to your head. We knew you when you couldn't hammer a nail straight." The villagers of Nazareth are unable to grant that he has become an authoritative person, let alone Israel's King and Savior.

The result is that "he did not do many miracles there because of their lack of faith." The great theme of Matthew's next three chapters is that when people begin to recognize who Jesus is, they trust him greatly and great things happen. When they do not recognize who he is, they expect little and little happens. Here is the greatest man in history standing right in the midst of his hometown folk, and they scarcely benefit because they have a pint-sized view of who he is.

Jesus' divine identity turns out to be very practical information, not just an abstract idea to agree or disagree about. In his visit of a few days, the people of Nazareth squander an opportunity, but that is a small thing compared to modern disciples' every-day-of-our-lives opportunity, which we either waste or utilize. Jesus is "with us always" as risen Lord (28:20). He wants us to expect great things of him, which we will do only as our concept of him expands.

### ■ Matthew 14:1–14

**14** $^1$ At that time Herod the tetrarch heard the reports about Jesus, $^2$ and he said to his attendants, "This is John the Baptist; he has risen from the dead! That is why miraculous powers are at work in him."

$^3$ Now Herod had arrested John and bound him and put him in prison because of Herodias, his brother Philip's wife, $^4$ for John had been saying to him: "It is not lawful for you to have her." $^5$ Herod wanted to kill John, but he was afraid of the people, because they considered John a prophet.

$^6$ On Herod's birthday the daughter of Herodias danced for the guests and pleased Herod so much $^7$ that he promised with an oath to give her whatever she asked. $^8$ Prompted by her mother, she said, "Give me here on a platter the head of John the Baptist." $^9$ The king was distressed, but because of his oaths and his dinner guests, he ordered that her request be granted [10] and had John beheaded in the prison. [11] His head was brought in on a platter and given to the girl, who carried it to her mother. [12] John's disciples came and took his body and buried it. Then they went and told Jesus.

[13] When Jesus heard what had happened, he withdrew by boat privately to a solitary place. Hearing of this, the crowds followed him on foot from the towns. [14] When Jesus landed and saw a large crowd, he had compassion on them and healed their sick.

J esus' hometown folks may be jealous, but Herod is downright paranoid. Herod had previously beheaded John; now, hearing the reports about Jesus' power, he rants, "This is John the Baptist; he has risen from the dead!" As Jesus learns of Herod's violence toward the beloved prophet and of his paranoia regarding Jesus personally, he withdraws in grief and reflection. Throughout his ministry, Jesus receives reminders that his own suffering will come soon.

## ▪ Matthew 14:15–21
[These verses are printed in the reading for Day 1.]

W e began our journey in Matthew's Gospel by considering the story of Jesus feeding the thousands with just a few loaves and fish. In the story, the disciples bring to Jesus their concern about the hungry crowd. He astonishes them by saying, "You give them something to eat." The reason he can issue such a command when they have so little is because he knows what he can do through them. As they see more clearly who he is, they have to recalibrate their ideas of what is possible. Jesus does this wonder through his disciples so they will learn to place their faith in him. The question is whether they will remember their lesson of faith the next time they face a dilemma.

■ Matthew 14:22-33

²² Immediately Jesus made the disciples get into the boat and go on ahead of him to the other side, while he dismissed the crowd. ²³ After he had dismissed them, he went up on a mountainside by himself to pray. Later that night, he was there alone, ²⁴ and the boat was already a considerable distance from land, buffeted by the waves because the wind was against it.

²⁵ Shortly before dawn Jesus went out to them, walking on the lake. ²⁶ When the disciples saw him walking on the lake, they were terrified. "It's a ghost," they said, and cried out in fear.

²⁷ But Jesus immediately said to them: "Take courage! It is I. Don't be afraid."

²⁸ "Lord, if it's you," Peter replied, "tell me to come to you on the water."

²⁹ "Come," he said.

Then Peter got down out of the boat, walked on the water and came toward Jesus. ³⁰ But when he saw the wind, he was afraid and, beginning to sink, cried out, "Lord, save me!"

³¹ Immediately Jesus reached out his hand and caught him. "You of little faith," he said, "why did you doubt?"

³² And when they climbed into the boat, the wind died down. ³³ Then those who were in the boat worshiped him, saying, "Truly you are the Son of God."

This is not the first time the disciples have been terrified on the stormy sea. Last time, Jesus was with them in the boat, yet they feared they would drown. After he calmed the sea, he chided them for their "little faith." They were amazed and whispered, "What kind of man is this? Even the winds and the waves obey him!" (8:27). Now he walks upon the waves and exhorts them, "Take courage! It is I. Don't be afraid." Pondering again what sort of man they are dealing with, the disciples worship him, "Truly you are the Son of God."

Peter admirably explores the limits, trying to apply the lesson Jesus has taught repeatedly: the power Jesus exerts is available for his disciples to exert. He says, "Tell me to come to you on the water," and Jesus says, "Come." The power that Jesus grants to disciples is never independent of him. Faith is to keep our eyes fixed on Jesus. Fear is to look away from him and stare instead at the daunting circumstances. Peter walks in faith—oh, what a moment!—and then sinks in fear. Jesus rescues him and says, "You of little faith, why did you doubt?" We may imagine that Jesus' face is not stern, but tender.

These stories of Jesus calming the wind and waves are told because they happened that way, but also because of what they symbolize: the fearsome challenges we encounter in the course of our lives. The message is to entrust each new storm to the Savior. Jesus in turn models trust toward God in his storms, particularly the accumulating threats from violent opponents (12:14; 14:10). The story of the disciples at sea begins as Jesus pulls away to a mountainside privately to pray (verse 23), seeking the solitude with God that the crowds interrupted earlier (verses 13–14). Jesus' display of glory on the sea emerges from that quiet time on the mountainside with the Father.

## ▨ Matthew 14:34–36

[34] When they had crossed over, they landed at Gennesaret. [35] And when the men of that place recognized Jesus, they sent word to all the surrounding country. People brought all their sick to him [36] and begged him to let the sick just touch the edge of his cloak, and all who touched it were healed.

These dear people "recognized Jesus," and so they come streaming to him for help. Not only do they come, but they spread the word so others can come too. This picture of people bringing their sickly friends and begging that they be allowed to touch even the edge of his cloak expresses the message beautifully: Jesus has the power we need. Even the edge of his clothing, just a small fraction of him, will be enough to overcome all the worst that we face and to make us new.

## ■ Matthew 15:21–31

21 Leaving that place, Jesus withdrew to the region of Tyre and Sidon. 22 A Canaanite woman from that vicinity came to him, crying out, "Lord, Son of David, have mercy on me! My daughter is demon-possessed and suffering terribly."

23 Jesus did not answer a word. So his disciples came to him and urged him, "Send her away, for she keeps crying out after us."

24 He answered, "I was sent only to the lost sheep of Israel."

25 The woman came and knelt before him. "Lord, help me!" she said.

26 He replied, "It is not right to take the children's bread and toss it to the dogs."

27 "Yes it is, Lord," she said. "Even the dogs eat the crumbs that fall from their master's table."

28 Then Jesus said to her, "Woman, you have great faith! Your request is granted." And her daughter was healed at that moment.

29 Jesus left there and went along the Sea of Galilee. Then he went up on a mountainside and sat down. 30 Great crowds came to him, bringing the lame, the blind, the crippled, the mute and many others, and laid them at his feet; and he healed them. 31 The people were amazed when they saw the mute speaking, the crippled made well, the lame walking and the blind seeing. And they praised the God of Israel.

No one in Matthew's Gospel is more tenacious than the Canaanite woman! She presses Jesus, not just because of her anguish about her daughter, but because she believes in him, calling him "Lord, Son of David." She is convinced that he can help as no one else can.

Amazingly, he puts her off without saying a word. She will not let up, however, and she is driving his disciples crazy. They plead with him, "Heal the woman's daughter and send her away so we can get some peace!" Jesus repeats the point he made earlier about his mission, "I was sent only to the lost sheep of Israel." This is not the time to open a new ministry front among Gentiles in the north. He is faithful to the Father's assignment to bring "bread" to God's children, the Jews. Parents do not give the food prepared for their children to their dogs.

The woman is not disheartened; rather, she thinks with him. She appeals to Jesus according to his concerns as she discovers them. "Please do feed the children—but can't the dogs lick up what falls from the table? Won't there be a few crumbs for us Gentiles?" Jesus is won over and grants her request, saying, "You have great faith!" She recognizes him as Lord and Messiah, she persists in trusting his power, and she pays close attention to what he cares about—this is great faith.

In due time, in the aftermath of his resurrection, Jesus will open the doors to all peoples, but here the Shepherd returns to a hill by the Sea of Galilee to serve his sheep, the people of Israel. Matthew reports his miracles—the mute speaking, the crippled made well, the lame walking, and the blind seeing—using the prophet's language about the coming of God's salvation (Isaiah 35:5–6).

## ▨ Matthew 15:32-39

32 Jesus called his disciples to him and said, "I have compassion for these people; they have already been with me three days and have nothing to eat. I do not want to send them away hungry, or they may collapse on the way."

33 His disciples answered, "Where could we get enough bread in this remote place to feed such a crowd?"

34 "How many loaves do you have?" Jesus asked.

"Seven," they replied, "and a few small fish."

35 He told the crowd to sit down on the ground. 36 Then he took the seven loaves and the fish, and when he had given thanks, he broke them and gave them to the disciples, and they in turn to the people. 37 They all ate and were satisfied. Afterward the disciples

picked up seven basketfuls of broken pieces that were left over. [38] The number of those who ate was four thousand men, besides women and children. [39] After Jesus had sent the crowd away, he got into the boat and went to the vicinity of Magadan.

We notice first the endurance of the crowds who come to Jesus. Can we imagine staying anywhere for anything once the food has run out? Yet these folks stay with Jesus so long that he expects they would faint if he would send them home in their hungry condition. It kindles the imagination: what was Jesus like in person that people would come so far and endure so long just to be with him?

The story's obvious focus is the similarity to the scene in Matthew 14 where Jesus fed the multitude from a small amount of food. He tests his disciples by pointing out that the people have nothing to eat. The disciples respond as if the feeding of the five thousand had never happened: "Where could we get enough bread in this remote place to feed such a crowd?" Jesus then patiently walks them through the same process by which he fed the previous crowd: the disciples bring him what little they have; he blesses it; and they distribute it as it multiplies. As before, the great supper ends with the disciples picking up much more leftover food than they had in the first place.

We first need to marvel at what Jesus has done with the assistance of his disciples. Just because he has done something before does not mean we should become jaded when he does it again, as if it is no big deal. Jesus does this awesome work that everyone, including his disciples, assumed was impossible. We wonder, though: at what point while the event is unfolding do the disciples realize that he is reenacting what they have seen before? When do they mumble to themselves, "When am I going to catch on?"

■ Matthew 16:1 – 12

16 ¹ The Pharisees and Sadducees came to Jesus and tested him by asking him to show them a sign from heaven.

² He replied, "When evening comes, you say, 'It will be fair weather, for the sky is red,' ³ and in the morning, 'Today it will be stormy, for the sky is red and overcast.' You know how to interpret the appearance of the sky, but you cannot interpret the signs of the times. ⁴ A wicked and adulterous generation looks for a sign, but none will be given it except the sign of Jonah." Jesus then left them and went away.

⁵ When they went across the lake, the disciples forgot to take bread. ⁶ "Be careful," Jesus said to them. "Be on your guard against the yeast of the Pharisees and Sadducees."

⁷ They discussed this among themselves and said, "It is because we didn't bring any bread."

⁸ Aware of their discussion, Jesus asked, "You of little faith, why are you talking among yourselves about having no bread? ⁹ Do you still not understand? Don't you remember the five loaves for the five thousand, and how many basketfuls you gathered? ¹⁰ Or the seven loaves for the four thousand, and how many basketfuls you gathered? ¹¹ How is it you don't understand that I was not talking to you about bread? But be on your guard against the yeast of the Pharisees and Sadducees." ¹² Then they understood that he was not telling them to guard against the yeast used in bread, but against the teaching of the Pharisees and Sadducees.

Here the Twelve encounter again the same problem they have faced twice before: they have insufficient food. True, this time the setting is different; now they are in a boat alone with Jesus rather than with a big crowd. Nevertheless, Jesus expects them to take what they have seen before and apply it to the new situation. They need to say, "Jesus, we are short of food again. Please help us." Instead, Jesus has to talk them through their memories of the two feedings. "How many people did we feed the first time . . . and the second? How much did we have left over the first time . . . and the second?" How embarrassing to hear, "Do you still not understand? Don't you remember?"

How is it that the crowds in these chapters know to press toward Jesus, anticipating they will see marvels if they touch even the edge of his cloak, yet his disciples who are with him all the time have such a hard time learning to trust his power? The real challenge of faith is not just to imitate the crowds or the Canaanite woman whose particular moments of faith so impress us. They each bring a single severe infirmity to Jesus that has weighed on them for some time: being lame, blind, mute, and the like. After receiving the cure for themselves or a loved one, they return home. They are perhaps less aware of their enduring day-to-day need for Jesus. By contrast, the Twelve stay with him, because he has called them to live with him all the time. Jesus is training them to recognize in each new situation that they need his help yet again.

The two pairs of stories about the disciples have something in common (two times he calms the sea; two times he feeds a crowd). In both situations, the need has arisen simply in the normal course of life. The sea is suddenly stormy. The bread supply has run low. For disciples, the transition from "little faith" to "great faith" involves remembering. Jesus' question, "Don't you remember?" says, "I have helped you before; recall this in each new situation you face."

I am writing in a week of record rainfall. In the middle of our most severe night, our sump pump could not keep up and our basement was starting to fill with water. As I was frantically moving everything off the floor and low shelves and carrying buckets of water up the stairs, it occurred to me to stop—pause for a moment—and recognize that this was today's opportunity to enjoy Jesus' presence and seek his help. It was a minor event: the kind he uses to train us for the major ones.

Faith accumulates over time. As we walk with Jesus, he reassures us along the way, showing us repeatedly that he is willing and able to do more than we thought. He keeps putting us in new situations that challenge us to remember what he has done before and trust him further. It is a long learning process, and Jesus trains us patiently. At the same time, he is eager for us to catch on. His rebuke, "you of little faith," pricks our conscience and prods us forward in our growth. Faith matters: it unleashes divine power. We need nothing less, because he is sending us to serve a hungry, hurting world.

*Jesus trains us to expect great things of him as we see more clearly who he is and remember what he has done for us before.*

# YEAST OF THE PHARISEES

**DAY 17**

## Matthew 15:1-20

Today's reading picks up a thread from the last one (16:1–12), where Jesus warned his disciples against the "yeast of the Pharisees and Sadducees." Unlike his happy parable of the woman working yeast into dough, this yeast is something detestable, a rottenness that can spread. His critics despise him as they request a sign from heaven. Actually, their request is too small, not too large. Jesus responds, "You cannot interpret the signs of the times" (16:3). They are missing the whole scope of Jesus' ministry—its beauty and grandeur, its life-changing effect on thousands. Jesus' coming is the event of the ages, not a magic show.

Jesus says, "Beware! Don't let malicious people destabilize you." Cynical people demand proof, but Jesus does not consent to prove anything. Instead, his consistent approach is to proclaim good news, treat people compassionately, and then call for response. Disciples, similarly, are not obliged to prove anything to people who despise them for trusting Jesus. No amount of evidence can persuade a hardened skeptic—not the evidence of our changed lives; not even the "sign of Jonah," Jesus' resurrection from the dead on the third day (16:4; 12:39–40).

## ■ Matthew 15:1–14

15 ¹ Then some Pharisees and teachers of the law came to Jesus from Jerusalem and asked, ² "Why do your disciples break the tradition of the elders? They don't wash their hands before they eat!"

³ Jesus replied, "And why do you break the command of God for the sake of your tradition? ⁴ For God said, 'Honor your father and mother' and 'Anyone who curses their father or mother is to be put to death.' ⁵ But you say that if anyone declares that what might have been used to help their father or mother is 'devoted to God,' ⁶ they are not to 'honor their father or mother' with it. Thus you nullify the word of God for the sake of your tradition. ⁷ You hypocrites! Isaiah was right when he prophesied about you:

⁸ "These people honor me with their lips,
   but their hearts are far from me.
⁹ They worship me in vain;
   their teachings are merely human rules.'"

¹⁰ Jesus called the crowd to him and said, "Listen and understand. ¹¹ What goes into someone's mouth does not defile them, but what comes out of their mouth, that is what defiles them."

¹² Then the disciples came to him and asked, "Do you know that the Pharisees were offended when they heard this?"

¹³ He replied, "Every plant that my heavenly Father has not planted

will be pulled up by the roots. [14] Leave them; they are blind guides. If the blind lead the blind, both will fall into a pit."

This is a sample of the Pharisees' teaching that Jesus calls "yeast." They start with a question that is really an accusation. "Why do your disciples break the tradition of the elders? They don't wash their hands before they eat!"

What was this "tradition of the elders"? It was a long list of rules that the elders among the people had formulated and collected over two or three centuries to show how to apply the Law of Moses. For example, in the Law, God commanded the people to rest on the Sabbath. The tradition of the elders applied the Sabbath law by saying not to light a fire on the Sabbath (so that people would not work by cooking) and saying not to travel farther than a set distance, called a "Sabbath day's journey" (because walking farther would be hard work). Eventually, faithfulness to the Sabbath commandment became a matter of keeping to the limits of not lighting a fire and not walking too far rather than taking a day to refresh the soul and thank God who provides everything people labor for during the rest of the week. Jesus clashed with the Pharisees when he saw that these traditional regulations took people's eyes off of the intent of the Scriptures.

In our passage in Matthew 15, we see two instances of the tradition of the elders distracting people from the intent of God's Law. The first has to do with washing hands. The Pharisees' concern was to ensure ritual purification. Moses never commanded the washing of hands before meals, and when he did command washing, he targeted a specific set of circumstances (requiring, for example, a bath after a bodily discharge, Leviticus 15:11). The tradition of the elders had expanded the regulations for purification so that anyone who failed to wash hands before eating was thought to be defiled and unholy. Jesus is just as concerned about holiness as they are, but he asserts that they misunderstand what causes defilement and what makes for holiness. "What goes into your mouth," for example, food eaten with unclean hands, "does not defile you, but what comes out of your mouth"—for example, slandering a righteous man like Jesus!—"that is what defiles you."

Jesus presses the matter further in his second example: keeping the tradition of the elders sometimes actually caused people to *disobey* God's Law. Moses commanded the people to keep their vows. Jesus, too, requires followers to keep their word (see 5:33–37). But the tradition of the elders had become rigid, requiring people to follow through, for example, on ill-considered promises to donate money. Jesus is thinking about instances where fulfilling a premature vow to make repeated religious contributions would impoverish them enough to prevent them from taking care of their parents in their old age. When the Pharisees enforced the tradition's requirement and pressed people to continue the contributions they had rashly promised, they effectively forced them to break the commandment to honor father and mother. "Thus you nullify the word of God for the sake of your tradition," says Jesus.[13] He calls them hypocrites and calls their teaching "merely human rules."

Later Jesus shocks his hearers with a follow-up comment: "Every plant that my heavenly Father has not planted will be pulled up by the roots" (verse 13). Jews thought of the Israelite people as God's planting, his precious crop (Isaiah 60:21), yet Jesus is saying that part of Israel, including this group of critical Pharisees,[14] is not God's planting but rather a kind of weed that does not belong with his crop. Such people will be rooted out at the Judgment, and will be excluded from the awaited blessings (see 13:40–43). Jesus made a similar assertion in 8:12, "[Some] subjects of the kingdom will be thrown outside, into the darkness." They will not be included in the glorious banquet at the end of the age with Abraham, Isaac, and Jacob.

These stories are not preserved to help us feel superior to the Pharisees, but to prevent their worst habits from creeping into the fellowship of Jesus. His point is for disciples not to be manipulated or intimidated by severe people who claim to be godly. Not all who spend their lives participating in the Lord's church are his "planting." Some, even among the leaders, honor God with their lips, but their hearts are far from him. Such people are "blind guides" who lead the church astray. In the end, such weeds in the church will be rooted out. Participating in Jesus' community will require us to remove the plank of hypocrisy from our eyes (7:5) and to submit our own character to God's progressive work of renewal, so that the deepest places in our hearts will honor him.

### ■ Matthew 15:15-20

[15] Peter said, "Explain the parable to us."

[16] "Are you still so dull?" Jesus asked them. [17] "Don't you see that whatever enters the mouth goes into the stomach and then out of the body? [18] But the things that come out of a person's mouth come from the heart, and these defile them. [19] For out of the heart come evil thoughts—murder, adultery, sexual immorality, theft, false testimony, slander. [20] These are what defile a person; but eating with unwashed hands does not defile them."

Jesus is concerned to do more than stamp out hypocrisy. He challenges a whole misguided approach to righteous living. The stories of Pharisees enforcing rules about hand washing and about vows to contribute money exemplify the problem. The Pharisees blindly disregard the intent of the Law of Moses. (The disciples don't understand yet, either. "Are you still so dull?" Jesus asked them. "Don't you see . . . ?") They have not grasped that purity is fundamentally a matter of character, rather than merely do this/ don't do that. We please God not by keeping rules, but by living from a heart that is rightly oriented toward him. God measures virtue not by what we put in our mouth, but by what comes out of it—words that reveal our heart. Pharisees think of themselves as guardians of the people's purity. Because Jesus contradicts their rule making—their insistence that people should please God by heeding regulations and avoiding a list of misbehaviors—they mistakenly conclude that he is indifferent about purity and righteous living.

In reality, by challenging the supremacy of rule keeping, Jesus calls his followers to a surpassing righteousness (5:20). What a conscientious disciple does from the heart may look from the outside much like what a rule-keeper does. The difference will be that the disciple is intentionally working out faithfulness toward God, while the rule-keeper is trying not to disappoint whoever cares about the rules. The disciple may walk away from the same dubious behavior or undertake the same discipline as the rule-keeper does, but the disciple will be building up self-control and gratitude to God while the rule-keeper will increasingly think of God as a nagging imposition.

How can disciples today avoid the yeast of the Pharisees? First, we need to penetrate into God's word to discern his will for us instead of overlaying it with human-made rules. In the tradition of the elders, what may originally have been suggestions for practicing God's Law had hardened into independent regulations. Recommendations for faithfulness had degenerated into rigid, detailed boundaries for every conceivable situation.

This syndrome is still present. "Don't eat meat on Fridays. Limit yourself to two drinks in an evening. Have a daily quiet time. Attend Sunday worship without fail. Give a tenth of your income. Read the lectionary readings. Don't mow the lawn or wash the car on Sundays. Stay away from R-rated movies and dance parties. Don't spank your children. Do spank your children." Any of these may be instances of wise counsel—genuinely good practices—but they can easily turn into inflexible hallmarks of "the right way" and become our focus in their own right. God wants to be our focus.

People sense instinctively that rules are for children and adulthood means freedom. Jesus treats disciples as adults who are free to work out love for God and neighbor. Loving God with all our heart, soul, and mind makes us humble and strong so that we can receive all that God has for us. Loving people far and near as much as we love ourselves enables us to live righteously toward them and to fulfill God's Law (22:37–40). To concentrate merely on keeping rules is to remain spiritually stunted and to miss the real life God desires to give us.

Second, Jesus wants us not to fall into the Pharisaical practice of fixating on a favorite set of sins to condemn. Theoretically, all of God's Law was important to the Pharisees, but certain laws, such as keeping the Sabbath and conforming to the Old Testament dietary regulations, were obvious markers of an observant Jew. The Pharisees were toughest on people who neglected these issues, while they sometimes cared little about other violations of God's Law.

Parallel today would be leaders who devote great energy to preventing sexual immorality in their church and surrounding community but neglect matters such as injustice or addiction to wealth. Leaders in other churches may highlight issues such as racial prejudice or mistreatment of women or the poor, while neglecting the community's ignorance of God and his word. Jesus is concerned about all of these harmful things, not just a few. Selective application of God's will, in whatever particular form it takes, undercuts Jesus' mission to redeem all that is evil, sick, and miserable and to replace it with God's blessing and peace. Moreover, obsessing on our own pet issues makes us look down our noses (like the Pharisees did to Jesus) toward brothers and sisters who fail to obsess in the same way. We can begin to detect our blind spots when we respectfully observe leaders from churches of a different stripe than our own.

Third, if we are going to become true disciples, we will need to eliminate any atmosphere of condemnation and inquisition from our lives and conversations. These Pharisees and teachers of the Law have come all the way from Jerusalem to Galilee to inspect whether Jesus is misbehaving ("Aha! You didn't wash your hands!"). Jesus forbids his disciples to imitate this kind of posturing and finger wagging. Does this mean that we are just to shield our eyes and permit moral failure to multiply in the fellowship of Jesus? No. It is healthy to offer merciful, humble correction as we prompt one another to be the best we can be for God. The most effective rebuke I ever received (which happened to be for being disorganized, rather than being immoral) came from a ministry colleague named Dave, who had obviously prayed and thought hard about how to help me see my problem but also how to build me up respectfully. He motivated me tremendously by his caring approach, and I changed.

Finally, these Pharisees held Jesus at arm's length personally, but Jesus calls us to draw near. We collaborate with him to bring about our growth in holiness. The power for change comes from him as we pour ourselves into the project of becoming all that God wants us to become, both as individuals and as his spiritual family.

*Disciples develop into righteous persons who please God, not by slavish rule keeping, but by cultivating a heart rightly adjusted to his heart.*

## DAY 18 | TAKE UP YOUR CROSS AND FOLLOW

Matthew 16:13-28

■ Matthew 16:13-19

¹³ When Jesus came to the region of Caesarea Philippi, he asked his disciples, "Who do people say the Son of Man is?"

¹⁴ They replied, "Some say John the Baptist; others say Elijah; and still others, Jeremiah or one of the prophets."

[15] "But what about you?" he asked. "Who do you say I am?"

[16] Simon Peter answered, "You are the Messiah, the Son of the living God."

[17] Jesus replied, "Blessed are you, Simon son of Jonah, for this was not revealed to you by flesh and blood, but by my Father in heaven. [18] And I tell you that you are Peter, and on this rock I will build my church, and the gates of Hades will not overcome it. [19] I will give you the keys of the kingdom of heaven; whatever you bind on earth will be bound in heaven, and whatever you loose on earth will be loosed in heaven."

Ever since John the Baptist was sending messengers to ask whether Jesus is "the one who is to come" (11:3), Matthew has been highlighting the question of Jesus' identity. The folks in his hometown, most of the Pharisees, and people in many of the Galilean villages, belittle or ignore him. By contrast, crowds press upon Jesus in hope, and ask one another, "Could this be the Son of David?" As for the Twelve, they sometimes show flashes of insight. After seeing him walk on the sea, they kneel before him as Son of God in a thrill of wonder and emotion (14:33). But have they come to the kind of sober conviction about him that can withstand the strain of the crises soon to come? It is time to decide, to declare where they stand.

Jesus asks the Twelve, "Who do people say the Son of Man is?"[15] They mention favorable conjectures they have overheard: Jesus is a great prophet like John the Baptist or Elijah or Jeremiah. They ignore his opponents' characterization that he is a law-breaker, blasphemer, glutton and drunkard, or agent of the devil. The Israelites' conjectures resemble the way people today might respond about who Jesus is. People generally speak respectfully: he is a great teacher, a charismatic prophet, an itinerant philosopher, a master ethicist; he is a shaman, a guru, an avatar; he is the founder of a great religion or "one solitary life" that surpassingly influenced events. Just as the ancient crowds fell short by calling Jesus merely "one of the prophets," so these modern labels fall short. They obscure who Jesus is and deter many from following him seriously.

When asked, "Who do *you* say that I am?" Peter answers boldly, "You are the Messiah, the Son of the living God." Jesus responds with an emphatic yes. He affirms that Peter's answer is truth revealed by God himself. Jesus thereby announces, "I *am* the Messiah," (that is, Christ), the ultimate King who fulfills God's promises to David and to Israel. "I *am* the Son of the living God," the unique embodiment of God's presence and salvation for the world. He joyously adds that he will build the whole renewed people of God upon the foundation of Peter's confession that Jesus is King.

Peter's declaration that Jesus is the Messiah, the Son of the living God, is the culmination of the Gospel thus far. This identification of Jesus has far-reaching implications for our lives as disciples. This is not just an appealing teacher; Jesus is God's anointed King. Therefore, it is essential to respond to his call upon our lives. Because the Father has placed all things under his command (11:27), we need to adhere to him and never stray into independence. Because he holds divine status and authority, we need to keep him at the center of our message and our activity. Because he is the powerful Son of God, we need to re-imagine the possibilities for doing good works in a hurting world. Because kingship belongs to him, we need to abandon a self-important style for leading or contributing in the church. Because the Son of God saves us, we rightly lift up our hearts in gratitude and worship. All of this and much more flows from identifying him as Messiah, Son of God.

We first met the fisherman Simon, "who is called Peter," when Jesus summoned him to be a disciple. Jesus chose the new name. *Peter* means "rock," which suggests something firm and unshakable. Now we see the significance of this name for Simon: "You are Peter, and on this rock I will build my church." The statement is full of vision and potential. Peter is not yet the steadfast "rock" Jesus has in mind, but the Lord has not finished forming him. Just as Jesus said to him, "I will *make you* into a fisher of people," he is now saying that he will make Peter into a steadfast, faithful leader. He pledges to lift up Peter's character and moral stature and to prepare him for a central role in building his church. The rest of the Gospel of Matthew will devote special attention to Peter's development, his successes and failures, as he becomes the representative disciple.

At the very moment that he is encouraging Peter as an individual, Jesus is saying in the most direct way that his mission is to build a *community* of disciples: "I will build my church." The word *church* appears only twice in Matthew.[16] Here in 16:18, it refers to the global family of Jesus' followers, and in 18:17, it refers to any local congregation of believers. Every believer belongs to the global family by participating in its local fellowship. Jesus has no conception of a Christian life lived in isolation from others who love him. He values individuals, but he fortifies us by joining us together. We need each other. We cannot live out true discipleship on our own.

"I will build my church," says Jesus. It is *his* church, the community of his committed disciples who are grounded in the confession that he is King and Son of God. He builds it—the church is always under construction, with individual members as well as the whole church growing in integrity and faith. Moreover, Jesus empowers his church (locally and globally). He gives Peter the "keys to the kingdom"; that is, the capacity to open the way for people to enter God's kingdom. Jesus has come to "bind the strong man" (Satan) and to set loose everyone he has held captive (12:29). Now Jesus astonishingly extends to his followers the same authority to bind and to set loose—authority he gives to Peter in 16:19 and to all disciples in 18:18. Disciples will exert spiritual power along with Jesus—we will bind evil and set captives loose, unlocking doors for people to enter into the kingdom life. As we forgive each other, Jesus will bring effective forgiveness from God. As we proclaim the good news, Jesus will cause the message to take root in people's hearts. As we challenge injustice, Jesus will overcome it. As we work to feed the poor and relieve the war torn, Jesus will magnify our impact. He says of his church, "The gates of Hades will not overcome it" (16:18). He pictures the church invading a fortified prison, defeating all the forces of darkness and setting prisoners free now and forever. This is a tremendous vision of the church as a vibrant, restorative, liberating force in the world.

## ▩ Matthew 16:20-23

20 Then he ordered his disciples not to tell anyone that he was the Messiah.

21 From that time on Jesus began to explain to his disciples that he must go to Jerusalem and suffer many things at the hands of the elders, the chief priests and the teachers of the law, and that he must be killed and on the third day be raised to life.

22 Peter took him aside and began to rebuke him. "Never, Lord!" he said. "This shall never happen to you!"

23 Jesus turned and said to Peter, "Get behind me, Satan! You are a stumbling block to me; you do not have in mind the concerns of God, but merely human concerns."

To announce the beginning of Jesus' public ministry of proclaiming the kingdom (4:17), Matthew used the words, "From that time on, Jesus began to . . . " Now in 16:21, he uses the identical words to announce the second and final phase of his ministry. The hinge of Matthew's Gospel is Peter's confession at Caesarea Philippi that Jesus is the Messiah, the Son of God. Jesus enthusiastically confirms Peter's declaration, but then tells the disciples not to tell anyone that he is the Messiah. Jesus will devote the second phase of their training program to reshaping their thinking about what it means that he is the Messiah and that they are the Messiah's disciples. The Twelve and Israelites in general associated the title "Messiah" with majesty, triumph, and worldly dominance, remembering Jesus' ancestor David, Israel's militant king. Jesus will indeed triumph in resurrection and full authority, but not before walking a path Peter does not expect: "From that time on Jesus began to explain to his disciples that he must go to Jerusalem and suffer many things . . . and that he must be killed." He will go as the long-awaited king into the "city of the Great King" (5:35), but instead of acclaiming him, Jerusalem will scorn him and torture him to death.

Peter pulls Jesus aside and insists that Jesus will never experience such humiliation and suffering. Peter's "Never, Lord!" likely stems less from ambition or self-protection than from his faith in God's mercy: "Surely God will spare you this. Certainly he will be zealous for his Son's success." Jesus' rebuke to Peter is breathtakingly sharp. "Get behind me, Satan!" Just minutes earlier, Jesus was praising Peter for rejecting human ideas and voicing insight he received straight from God. Now it is all backwards: "You do not have in mind the concerns of God, but merely human concerns." By correcting Peter, Jesus is warding off temptation: "You are a stumbling block to me." At the temptation in the wilderness, Satan tried to offer Jesus a route to glory that would bypass the horrors of the cross (4:8–9), and now Peter has suggested the same thing. Jesus' response both times is, "Away from me, tempter!" The cross is God's assignment. The key word in Jesus' prediction of it is *must*: the Son of Man *must* suffer; he *must* be killed. Jesus has in mind Isaiah 53 (quoted earlier in Matthew), which speaks of God's chosen servant:

> He was pierced for our transgressions;
>> he was crushed for our iniquities;
> the punishment that brought us peace was on him,
>> and by his wounds we are healed.
> We all, like sheep, have gone astray,
>> each of us has turned to our own way;
> and the LORD has laid on him
>> the iniquity of us all. (Isaiah 53:5–6)

God has revealed his plan to rescue his people through the death of his chosen servant, and the Scriptures must be fulfilled (26:54).

Jesus has a profound duty. He will die in the people's place, and their sins will be forgiven (26:28).

## ▪ Matthew 16:24-28

24 Then Jesus said to his disciples, "Whoever wants to be my disciple must deny themselves and take up their cross and follow me. 25 For whoever wants to save their life will lose it, but whoever loses their life for me will find it. 26 What good will it be for someone to gain the whole world, yet forfeit their soul? Or what can anyone give in exchange for their soul? 27 For the Son of Man is going to come in his Father's glory with his angels, and then he will reward each person according to what they have done.

28 "Truly I tell you, some who are standing here will not taste death before they see the Son of Man coming in his kingdom."

Jesus has indicated that his coming crucifixion defines his role as Messiah. Now he says it also defines discipleship. Jesus began the first phase of his ministry by calling his disciples to "follow me." He begins the second phase by telling them, "I must go to Jerusalem to be killed. Take up your cross, and follow me *there*." The idea of bearing our cross has often been diminished to mean something insipid like putting up with the inconveniences of life. No first-century reader would have understood it that way. A cross is a horrific instrument of execution. Jesus is saying, "Come die with me." There is no "prenuptial agreement" to sign before we enter into relationship with Jesus, in case things get rough along the way and we want to bow out. To follow Jesus as disciples means to commit ourselves to him irrevocably, no matter what it may cost.

It is true that one person's actual experience of taking up the cross will differ from another's. Jesus will require some disciples to endure much greater suffering than other disciples. Moreover, in the journey of following him, we may have times of comfort and security and times of maximum danger and stress, and we will not know which is coming next.

"Deny yourselves," he says. Letting go in this way requires us to trust God. Jesus says, "Whoever wants to save their life will lose it, but whoever loses their life for me will find it." That last phrase reassures us that the Shepherd has the well-being of his sheep in mind. To yield entirely to God is to find life—the real riches of life that satisfy the soul. For Jesus' sake, we release to God everything that we have customarily insisted makes life worth living—romance and sex, money and possessions, popularity and status, passions and hobbies, fun and partying, achievement and dream-fulfillment, safety and security, home and family, food and drink. To surrender these cherished benefits is what Jesus means by the phrase "whoever loses their life for me." As we do it, we discover in due time that no accumulation of benefits can hold a candle to the life we find in him. Many times, we let go of those things without actually losing them, because Jesus retains or increases them in our lives for his purposes and our benefit. But the self-denial he commands requires that when we receive gifts from God, we do so with open palms and loose fingers, never clutching on to any of them, so that God is free to place gifts in our hands and remove them as necessary to help us serve him better and love him more.

The fatal alternative is to cling tenaciously to those things. We will want to be vigilant to identify which benefits of life we have begun to hold too tightly or yearn for too intensely. Otherwise, we are not free to be fully his—and he is life! When Jesus asks, "What good will it be for someone to gain the whole world, yet forfeit their soul?" he is presenting the unlikely best-case scenario: that we would "gain the whole world" as we turn aside from him. But scarcely anyone "gains the whole world." We hear a persistent theme in the media: go after your dreams, nothing is beyond your reach, never give up, believe in yourself. Billions of dollars are spent promoting this message. To the extent that it inspires us to discipline, confidence, and commitment to excellence, the message can be positive. But typically it brings disillusionment. Those who do not achieve their dreams feel defeated and frustrated, while those who do succeed still want more. The fulfill-yourself path fails to fulfill because it puts the wrong person in the center: yourself.

Jesus' life-giving countermessage is, "Whoever loses their life for me will find it." He is saying that as we deny ourselves for *him*, we find ourselves. We live a life of growing intimacy with the maker of our hearts, and we discover ever more completely who he has designed us to be. Jesus calls Peter "Rock" to epitomize who Jesus is forming him to be. What name does Jesus have in mind for you or for me? He has a wonderful vision for each of us as we yield to him totally and remove all barriers in our will.

Earlier Jesus said, "Take my yoke upon you and learn from me . . . and you will find rest for your souls. For my yoke is easy and my burden is light" (11:28–30). Jesus now reveals that the yoke, the burden, is a cross. As disciples, we will experience suffering, sometimes sustained and excruciating suffering. Some of us will die in our prime for Jesus' sake. His promise of rest, then, can only be *complete* through the promise of 16:27, "The Son of Man is going to come in his Father's glory with his angels, and then he will reward each person according to what they have done." Jesus promises that he is with us always during all of the ups and downs in our lives as disciples (28:20). But he speaks here of his fuller, final "coming," called elsewhere "the renewal of all things." Suffering and death do not have the last word. God raised Jesus on the third day, just as Jesus predicted here at Caesarea Philippi. By doing so, he has also defeated death for disciples. Jesus says that when he comes, the Father will reward everyone "according to what they have done." The phrase refers to what people have done with the fundamental alternatives Jesus poses: did they cling to their worldly life and therefore lose out, or did they surrender their life for Jesus and thereby find true life? Disciples "find" the promised life here and now as a foretaste—and we await final glories beyond comprehension when the Son of Man comes.

*We find life itself as we let go of what we thought was life, join the King's community, and follow him to his cross.*

# COMING DOWN THE MOUNTAIN

**DAY 19**

## Matthew 17

■ Matthew 17:1-8

**17** ¹ After six days Jesus took with him Peter, James and John the brother of James, and led them up a high mountain by themselves. ² There he was transfigured before them. His face shone like the sun, and his clothes became as white as the light. ³ Just then there appeared before them Moses and Elijah, talking with Jesus.

⁴ Peter said to Jesus, "Lord, it is good for us to be here. If you wish, I will put up three shelters—one for you, one for Moses and one for Elijah."

⁵ While he was still speaking, a bright cloud covered them, and a voice from the cloud said, "This is my Son, whom I love; with him I am well pleased. Listen to him!"

⁶ When the disciples heard this, they fell facedown to the ground, terrified. ⁷ But Jesus came and touched them. "Get up," he said. "Don't be afraid." ⁸ When they looked up, they saw no one except Jesus.

A week has passed since Jesus' disciples acknowledged him at Caesarea Philippi as Messiah, King, Son of God. He had shocked them by announcing that he must suffer and be killed, but he was not denying the majesty they attributed to him. Now he displays his majesty spectacularly for three of them.

As Matthew tells it, this whole event on the mountain takes place for the disciples' benefit. Jesus leads *them* up the mountain, he is transfigured before *them*, the great Old Testament prophets appear before *them*, the radiant cloud covers *them*, and God declares to *them*, "This is my Son whom I love; with him I am well pleased." The very voice of God confirms that the man they follow is no less than God's magnificent Son. In the coming days, the fishermen will need the certainty this moment provides.

The whole experience is overpowering. They fall facedown, terrified. It is a fore-vision, a precursor of the coming splendor of which Jesus had spoken in the final verses of Matthew 16: "The Son of Man is going to come in his Father's glory." Jesus said earlier that his disciples will someday "shine like the sun in the kingdom of their Father" (13:43). Here Jesus shines for them. Moses and Elijah appear: Israel's greatest prophets of old. The Scriptures say that those great men had prepared the people for a greater one who was yet to come (Deuteronomy 18:15; Malachi 4:4–5). Now in this moment of glory, they honor Jesus—and then he stands alone, peerless.

This is not a time for Peter or the others to participate as Jesus' partners and assistants ("we will build three shrines to honor you"), but to worship in silent awe and to absorb what they are seeing and hearing. "Listen to him," says God. "Jesus is not a friend for you to correct and advise, as you seemed to think last week at Caesarea Philippi. He is your king and your master. When he says he must go to Jerusalem and suffer many things and be killed, listen to him and submit. He is fulfilling his mission and revealing the nature of yours. Nothing Jesus says about the troubles that await him will contradict what you have seen and heard on this mountain."

As the glory cloud lifts, Jesus touches the disciples and tells them to get up. His words, "Don't be afraid," point to their frightening encounter with God's power, but also to the fearsome events they will face as they go back down the mountain. They must arise and go, for their calling is to be with him down there and all the way to Jerusalem.

## ▩ Matthew 17:9-13

⁹ As they were coming down the mountain, Jesus instructed them, "Don't tell anyone what you have seen, until the Son of Man has been raised from the dead."

¹⁰ The disciples asked him, "Why then do the teachers of the law say that Elijah must come first?"

¹¹ Jesus replied, "To be sure, Elijah comes and will restore all things. ¹² But I tell you, Elijah has already come, and they did not recognize him, but have done to him everything they wished. In the same way the Son of Man is going to suffer at their hands."

¹³ Then the disciples understood that he was talking to them about John the Baptist.

As they converse while walking down the mountain, Jesus insists that the three disciples not tell anyone about what they have just witnessed until he rises from the dead. The transfiguration is not the goal; it points forward to his glorious resurrection on Easter Sunday and forward further to his followers' resurrection at the end of the age. First, though, Jesus must suffer a horrific death. They will suffer, too.

Without sentimental lingering on the mountain top, Jesus leads the disciples back to the valley where the troubles are. Even as his disciples' minds wander to questions about Elijah, whom they have seen on the mountain, Jesus stresses again that he must die. "Why do the teachers of the law say that Elijah must come first?" they ask. Jesus points to the fruitful ministry of John the Baptist, who fulfilled the prophecies about Elijah (Malachi 4:5–6). Then he adds,

"Did you notice what the authorities did to him? They failed to recognize that God had sent him, and they put him to death. The same is in store for me."

Jesus requires the fishermen—and us—to absorb and embrace both his mountaintop glory and his downward trek into a world full of death. If we forget either part of Jesus' story, we lose our way. The vision of Jesus' glory can make us more determined to remain loyal, and the remembrance of his journey toward the cross can keep us humble. Through it all, we call to mind that God himself has vindicated Jesus and honored him as his Son.

We may find it easier to savor thoughts of Jesus' glory than to come back down the mountain with him. I recall that every year when I was a youth pastor, the youth did not want their summer camp in the mountains to end. The rich experiences of God's presence and power, the joyful intimacy with new friends, and the distance from the problems of day-to-day life down in the city all made them want to stay at camp and never get back on the bus. But life with Jesus will not be a prolonged vacation of getting away from it all. If we are going to be salt and light and yeast in the world, we have to end our isolation and get back into the world.

## ■ Matthew 17:14-23

14 When they came to the crowd, a man approached Jesus and knelt before him. 15 "Lord, have mercy on my son," he said. "He has seizures and is suffering greatly. He often falls into the fire or into the water. 16 I brought him to your disciples, but they could not heal him."

17 "You unbelieving and perverse generation," Jesus replied, "how long shall I stay with you? How long shall I put up with you? Bring the boy here to me." 18 Jesus rebuked the demon, and it came out of the boy, and he was healed at that moment.

19 Then the disciples came to Jesus in private and asked, "Why couldn't we drive it out?"

20 He replied, "Because you have so little faith. Truly I tell you, if you have faith as small as a mustard seed, you can say to this mountain, 'Move from here to there,' and it will move. Nothing will be impossible for you."

22 When they came together in Galilee, he said to them, "The Son of Man is going to be delivered into the hands of men. 23 They will kill him, and on the third day he will be raised to life." And the disciples were filled with grief.

The scene at the bottom of the mountain is discouraging. The nine disciples confront a demon-possessed boy brought to them by his hopeful father. In front of a large crowd, they have tried and failed to relieve the boy's trouble. Life is messy down in the valley. The devil is active, and the problems are unmanageable.

We are startled to hear Jesus' harsh words to his disciples: "How long shall I stay with you? How long shall I put up with you?" Previously when he has called their generation unbelieving and perverse, he has seemed to exempt his circle of disciples. Not this time. The disciples have been unable to prevent the boy's seizures and suffering, but the problem is not that the demonic power is too strong. Jesus heals the boy immediately. The problem is their failure to put their faith in God, as Jesus says twice (verses 17 and 20). In that condition, they are scarcely more helpful in Jesus' work than the people who reject him outright.

When Jesus says the disciples have "so little faith," he is not saying that they ought to muster a larger volume of faith, as if faith is something to be quantified with scales or gauges. To the contrary, he tells them, "If you have faith as small as a [tiny] mustard seed . . ." no obstacle will be too great. Their problem is less a matter of miniscule faith than misdirected faith. They need to trust God more and themselves less. They ask, "Why couldn't we drive it out?" Presumably they have succeeded before in their attempts to heal. Jesus gave them authority to heal and to drive out demons, and he sent them out

to do it (10:1, 5, 8). The danger, though, in the aftermath of succeeding is to forget who the source of the success is. When God has
empowered our ministry, onlookers become impressed with us, and
we begin to be impressed with ourselves. We become self-sufficient
and start to flex our muscles. Finally, superiority toward others sets
in, and we look more and more like the arrogant people of Jesus'
generation whom he frequently criticized. It is a terrible syndrome.

Jesus turns the disciples' defeat into an important training
experience. Already embarrassed by their failed attempt to heal
the boy, they receive Jesus' public rebuke. He is beginning to
teach them humility, the theme he will press for the next four
chapters. Faith toward God and humility go hand in hand.
All of the power is his. The authority Jesus has given disciples
to work in power is entirely a gift from God, never a basis for
boasting or self-advancement. Our endeavor is not to amass some
breakthrough quantity of faith (and so become impressed with
ourselves), but to depend more and more humbly upon God.
By trusting fully in God's power rather than our own, we will do
great things. God will remove obstacles the size of mountains for
us so we can carry on his compassionate ministry.

Lest the disciples miss the connection between divine power and
humility, Jesus tells them again about his own coming humiliation and death (verses 22–23). Jesus the King will take the lowliest
road—all the way to a cross—and will thereby achieve the greatest
deliverance for a hurting world. God will validate Jesus' trust and
humility by raising him from the dead.

Matthew's seventeenth chapter highlights the downward
movement to which Jesus calls his disciples—downward from the
mountaintop, downward from pride and superiority. As we descend
from our spiritual sanctuaries into the messy world, we meet the
very situations where our faith can grow. True, we cultivate faith
by withdrawing with Jesus from time to time to the proverbial
mountaintop, whether alone for silence and prayer or with others
for refreshment in God's word. These are essential times. But we

cultivate faith even further by coming back down to where the troubles are. There we discover our dependence on God, because the problems are so monumental. And we discover the greatness of God, because he proves to be so effective. The most confounding dilemmas prepare us to see God's hand most wonderfully.

## ▪ Matthew 17:24-27

24 After Jesus and his disciples arrived in Capernaum, the collectors of the two-drachma temple tax came to Peter and asked, "Doesn't your teacher pay the temple tax?"

25 "Yes, he does," he replied.

When Peter came into the house, Jesus was the first to speak. "What do you think, Simon?" he asked. "From whom do the kings of the earth collect duty and taxes—from their own children or from others?"

26 "From others," Peter answered.

"Then the children are exempt," Jesus said to him. 27 "But so that we may not cause offense, go to the lake and throw out your line. Take the first fish you catch; open its mouth and you will find a four-drachma coin. Take it and give it to them for my tax and yours."

Politics is an especially messy part of the messy world into which Jesus leads his disciples. The Savior is on his way to Jerusalem where he will tangle with the Jews who hold political power. Their power centers on the temple, which functioned for centuries as the hub of Jewish religious life and remained independent from direct Roman control. In this story in Capernaum, Jesus meets collectors of the temple tax, which financed the Jerusalem authorities. They approach his disciples: "Your teacher pays the temple tax, doesn't he?" The question is not *whether* Jesus and his disciples will enter into the politics of the capital, but when and how.

Jesus is convinced that the temple authorities are corrupt, and the temple tax feeds their misconduct. They preside over the whole temple enterprise, a chaos of disreputable practices that Jesus will famously condemn when he enters the temple (21:12). The tax also pays the soldiers who will capture Jesus for an unjust trial. For now, Jesus postpones the conflict. As we have seen in previous situations (12:14–15; 14:12–13), Jesus does not enter into controversy impulsively or needlessly. He will speak with the boldness of a prophet when the time and setting are right, but for now, he arranges to pay the tax for Peter and himself, "so that we may not cause offense." Jesus models wisdom. He does not expect his followers to do battle immediately about every problem we confront, but rather to seek him about where to concentrate our efforts and when and how to challenge the wrongs in society. Disciples who get involved politically have as much to learn from his discretion and civility here in Capernaum as from his boldness later in Jerusalem.

The peculiar miracle with the fish who has gulped up a shiny coin represents God's provision for his servants as we do what is right. As we live prudently, God supplies what we need to do our duty, including paying our taxes. But Jesus makes an additional point. The harvested coin covers the temple tax instead of Jesus and Peter paying the tax from their own resources. Though they live under oppressive political authorities, this coin from God symbolizes that they are free in a deeper way because they belong to God. Jesus' saying about kings who do not tax their own children illustrates disciples' special standing as God's children. Jesus and his followers are the king's family, heirs to the king's fortune. As disciples, we have a heavenly heritage that surpasses nationality or country, a kingdom citizenship that merits our deepest allegiance.

Serving with Jesus in the chaotic world down below the mountain will sometimes require us to involve ourselves in politics. Some problems (injustices, for example) require that we influence the government (or the management of our workplace), and Jesus calls some of his followers to enter the fray intensively. Because we are first and foremost disciples of Jesus, we will approach politics differently than people who do not belong to him. Remembering his tremendous majesty on the mountain, we will "listen to him" humbly and obediently. We will be as shrewd as snakes while remaining as innocent as doves. We will relinquish the need to control everything ourselves. We will reconcile with others rather than retaliate, undertaking creative initiatives in order to diminish tensions.[17] We will love our enemies (personal detractors, political opponents, the nation's enemies) and remember that God loves those enemies. We will not mistake our own political convictions for God's will. Rather, we will humbly consider that our traditional opponents may be better attuned to some of God's concerns than we are. We will not confuse our ambition to make a difference with ambition for status and power. And when necessary, we will lose our (political) lives for righteousness's sake. God is our King, and only as we are true to that highest allegiance are we free to serve him well as salt and light and yeast in the world.

*On the mountaintop, Jesus shows disciples his reassuring glory and then leads them back down into the troubled world, which he must redeem and we must serve.*

# DAY 20 | GATHERED IN HIS NAME

Matthew 18

We come now to the fourth of Matthew's five collections of Jesus' teachings, the one about disciples' responsibility for one another in the family of faith. Jesus shows his determination to hold us together.

### ■ Matthew 18:1–5

**18** ¹ At that time the disciples came to Jesus and asked, "Who, then, is the greatest in the kingdom of heaven?"

² He called a little child to him and placed the child among them. ³ And he said: "Truly I tell you, unless you change and become like little children, you will never enter the kingdom of heaven. ⁴ Therefore, whoever takes the lowly position of this child is the greatest in the kingdom of heaven. ⁵ And whoever welcomes one such child in my name welcomes me."

Jesus makes humility central to his solution for every problem that arises in the next several chapters, including the problem of how to live harmoniously as his family. By asking, "Who is the greatest in the kingdom?" the disciples are really saying, "I want to be acknowledged as the greatest. How do I make sure I will come out ahead of others?" They ask self-confidently, too, as if to say, "Surely, I am already well ahead in the race." Jesus answers soberly that if they do not abandon their habit of jostling for position, they will never enter the kingdom, let alone be the greatest in it.

Jesus does not dismiss their desire for greatness; he turns greatness upside down. They have confused greatness with status. Regarding status, Jesus requires them to be pleased with the lowly position of a child. Only then can they become great, in the likeness of their "gentle and humble" King (11:29). Jesus has announced a kingdom owned by the poor in spirit, the meek, and the persecuted, the very people whom worldly power brokers disdain and ignore. His churches are made up of "little people" who receive other "little people" (whether they are young or old) and treat them as great people. By doing this, we honor Jesus: "Whoever welcomes one such child in my name welcomes me." To "change and become like little children" does not come overnight. Status is so delicious, so alluring! But God helps us make the change as we repent of our pride and begin to value others the way he values them.

## Matthew 18:6-14

6 "If anyone causes one of these little ones—those who believe in me—to stumble, it would be better for them to have a large millstone hung around their neck and to be drowned in the depths of the sea. 7 Woe to the world because of the things that cause people to stumble! Such things must come, but woe to the person through whom they come! 8 If your hand or your foot causes you to stumble, cut it off and throw it away. It is better for you to enter life maimed or crippled than to have two hands or two feet and be thrown into eternal fire. 9 And if your eye causes you to stumble, gouge it out and throw it away. It is better for you to enter life with one eye than to have two eyes and be thrown into the fire of hell.

10 "See that you do not despise one of these little ones. For I tell you that their angels in heaven always see the face of my Father in heaven.

12 "What do you think? If a man owns a hundred sheep, and one of them wanders away, will he not leave the ninety-nine on the hills and go to look for the one that wandered off? 13 And if he finds it, truly I tell you, he is happier about that one sheep than about the ninety-nine that did not wander off. 14 In the same way your Father in heaven is not willing that any of these little ones should perish."

The God who sends Jesus to gather his sheep does not want any of them to be lost. We are situated in a world that is full of evil and temptation, perils that could cause Jesus' vulnerable young followers to quit following—to "stumble" away from him and be lost. "Woe to the world because of things that cause people to stumble," Jesus says. Woe to warmongers and oppressors who fill their victims with resentment and hopelessness. Woe to authorities and anti-Christian zealots who intimidate Christian evangelists and converts. Woe to men who break the spirits of women or children by beating them or using them sexually. Woe to "friends" who lure youth into drug or alcohol addiction. Woe to purveyors of entertainment that corrupts minds and hearts. Woe to swindlers and betrayers who prey on people's trust so that they no longer trust anyone, including God. Woe to adults who plant their resentment toward God or the church into adolescents' hearts. The list goes on. Such activity ruins many new believers and deters others from ever starting with Jesus. How scary for unrepentant victimizers to meet a righteous God (verse 7)!

Jesus declares that such causes of stumbling are inevitable in our corrupt world, but they must never come from within the community of Jesus. To disciples he says, "See that you do not despise [look down on, mistreat, brush off as no great loss should they fall away] one of these little ones" (verse 10). The "little ones" are, first of all, literally children and youth, but by implication, they are the at-risk believers of all ages who are seeking to work out a stable life with God—children in faith. Jesus says, "*Their* angels in heaven always see the face of my Father in heaven." God is so concerned about each new believer's security in faith that he assigns holy messengers to their care, angels who represent each one personally to the Father. We share a solemn responsibility for these tender ones in faith to whom God is so passionately committed.

Of course, if we stray, we cannot blame it on others. In verses 8–14, we see side by side two essential aspects of staying in the sheepfold: God's pursuit of us and our determination to stay close.

Jesus commands us to be careful not to stray ("Cut off whatever causes you to stumble into sin; discipline yourself to stay faithful" [verses 8–9]), and he promises that God will actively keep us close (sending guardian angels; joyfully rescuing lost sheep [verses 10–14]). God is responsible, and we are responsible. We discipline ourselves to make wise, obedient choices, and God our Shepherd watches over us and retrieves us when necessary, unwilling to lose any. Jesus' appointment at the cross shows how seriously determined God is to rescue sinners.

### ■ Matthew 18:15-20

15 "If your brother or sister sins, go and point out their fault, just between the two of you. If they listen to you, you have won them over. 16 But if they will not listen, take one or two others along, so that 'every matter may be established by the testimony of two or three witnesses.' 17 If they still refuse to listen, tell it to the church; and if they refuse to listen even to the church, treat them as you would a pagan or a tax collector.

18 "Truly I tell you, whatever you bind on earth will be bound in heaven, and whatever you loose on earth will be loosed in heaven.

19 "Again, truly I tell you that if two of you on earth agree about anything they ask for, it will be done for them by my Father in heaven. 20 For where two or three gather in my name, there am I with them."

Not only does God keep us near while we discipline ourselves to stay, we strive to help each other stay. Even when we carefully nurture newcomers in faith, setting good examples, praying and caring for each other as family, members still may wander. Jesus instructs us step-by-step in how to intervene when necessary in order to restore brothers or sisters who have begun to fall away. Our role begins when we prayerfully recognize that a beloved member has entered into sin. Sin can jeopardize the member, the church, and others. If, as we pray, we conclude that it would be healthy to bring up the matter to the friend we are concerned about, Jesus counsels us to initiate a private encounter, one-on-one, to identify the sin and to seek a change. If we do this tenderly and respectfully, we may succeed in helping our friend work out faithfulness and peace. If the friend is unresponsive, and we sense that God would have us pursue it further, our second step is to draw in one or two other disciples who can be trusted for their wisdom and their capacity to keep matters private, people who are skilled at listening and peace-making. As a group of two or three, then, we commit the matter to prayer and count on the Lord's merciful presence in our midst as we proceed, according to his promise, "Where two or three gather in my name, there am I with them" (verses 19–20).

(Of course, these two wonderful verses encourage us about all of our praying with fellow believers, not just instances of concern about a brother or sister's lapse into sin. Whenever even a few of us meet for prayer, Jesus invites us to trust that he is personally present with us, that he is involved with us in the prayers, and that our praying together is powerfully effective with the Father.)

If the small peacemaking group does not persuade the offender, the third step would be to take the matter to the assembled church. The very prospect of this may help the sinning friend decide to change, and everyone can be spared some trauma. Jesus gives the local church solemn authority to endorse a repentant member or to exclude a defiant one from fellowship (verses 17–18). Jesus tells his disciples to treat the defiant member as they would an unre-pentant pagan or a tax collector; that is, treat the member now as a nonmember. Disciples do this in the hope that it is a temporary measure, because the ultimate goal is always to restore the person.

The steps laid out in verses 15–20 are not a set of rigid rules; the effort to rescue and restore a straying friend requires wisdom. At every point, our concern is for the deepest well-being of our friend and of the family of believers.

1. Jesus' words about helping someone in our fellowship who is falling into sin come between the chapter's opening words

about being humble and the chapter's closing parable about the forgiveness we ourselves have needed from God. If we approach a wrongdoer with an attitude of superiority, we will only make things worse. We come not as judges, but as loving brothers and sisters. For a rebuke to be effective, a track record of genuine caring needs to be in place.

2. When we hold a friend accountable, we have to be aware that we may not have all the facts and might be mistaken. It is better for us to back away than to be unfair.

3. Sometimes the offense we want to confront is something the person has done to us personally.[18] Before doing anything, we need to ask ourselves why we think the other person is the one at fault. We have to remove the plank from our own eye to see clearly (7:1–5), and we need to own up to our part in any conflict. Many offenses do not need to be confronted. It won't do to be thin-skinned or easily upset. (See Proverbs 19:11.)

4. The phrase "just between the two of you" in verse 15 indicates that Jesus wants to conserve the friend's reputation and to limit his or her humiliation. We will not gossip or tattle. It may be prudent, though, to consult a wise, discreet third party for advice about how to be most effective in speaking to the offender.

5. Jesus does not say how much time should pass before taking the second or third steps. Nor does he discourage us from trying again personally rather than jumping quickly to bring in others. All who are involved in caring about the person will bathe the situation in prayer (verses 19–20). God may then use circumstances along with the collective sensitivity of the praying group to indicate whether and when to take further steps.

6. The early church gatherings were relatively small, partly because believers could only meet in homes. In our modern churches, which typically exceed fifty members, we would likely apply verse 17 by taking the matter to the church leadership rather than involving the whole church.

7. Even in the tragic case where the church decides it must limit a person's involvement or exclude the person outright, this chapter's final parable shows that we are not to withhold our forgiveness or love. We may have to keep our distance, but even if that person truly becomes the church's enemy, Jesus' standard is always to love and continue praying (5:44). We still desire to win the brother or sister eventually. We serve the Shepherd, who rejoices at the return of his lost sheep.

## ▩ Matthew 18:21-35

21 Then Peter came to Jesus and asked, "Lord, how many times shall I forgive my brother or sister who sins against me? Up to seven times?"

22 Jesus answered, "I tell you, not seven times, but seventy-seven times.

23 "Therefore, the kingdom of heaven is like a king who wanted to settle accounts with his servants. 24 As he began the settlement, a man who owed him ten thousand bags of gold was brought to him. 25 Since he was not able to pay, the master ordered that he and his wife and his children and all that he had be sold to repay the debt.

26 "At this the servant fell on his knees before him. 'Be patient with me,' he begged, 'and I will pay back everything.' 27 The servant's master took pity on him, canceled the debt and let him go.

28 "But when that servant went out, he found one of his fellow servants who owed him a hundred silver coins. He grabbed him and began to choke him. 'Pay back what you owe me!' he demanded.

29 "His fellow servant fell to his knees and begged him, 'Be patient with me, and I will pay it back.'

30 "But he refused. Instead, he went off and had the man thrown into prison until he could pay the debt. 31 When the other servants saw what had happened, they were outraged and went and told their master everything that had happened.

32 "Then the master called the servant in. 'You wicked servant,' he said, 'I canceled all that debt of yours because you begged me to.

<sup>33</sup> Shouldn't you have had mercy on your fellow servant just as I had on you?' <sup>34</sup> In anger his master handed him over to the jailers to be tortured, until he should pay back all he owed.

<sup>35</sup> "This is how my heavenly Father will treat each of you unless you forgive your brother or sister from your heart."

P eter's question prompts a challenging answer: "Forgive your brother or sister many more times than you can count." This leads to Jesus' remarkable three-scene parable. First, we see a king who forgives his servant a tremendous debt, an impossible sum—imagine millions of dollars. He forgives all of it; nothing remains to be repaid. Second, we see the same servant refuse to forgive his poor coworker a trifling debt, a few dollars. The king's magnificent kindness might have touched his servant's heart, making him grateful and kind. Instead, the servant treats his coworker harshly and humiliates him. In the final scene, the outraged king withdraws his mercy and now applies the punishing standard that the servant had applied to his coworker, except greater, relative to the magnitude of the servant's initial debt. Like the king at the beginning, God is astonishingly merciful. Like the forgiven servant, disciples owe such mercy to others. God is appropriately outraged when we withhold forgiveness from others after he has taken so great a burden upon himself to forgive us. After Jesus' sacrifice on the cross, it is unthinkable for us to turn around and withhold forgiveness from a brother or sister. The heart adjusted to God's kingship is a forgiving heart.

Jesus insists that we forgive our brothers and sisters, but it may not always be wise to *tell* those who have hurt us that we are forgiving them. If a person asks for forgiveness, then, of course, we need to express our forgiveness. At such a moment, we say, "I forgive you," not because we feel it—we may not *feel* love toward the person at all—but because Jesus commands it as a step toward reconciliation. Speaking forgiveness to someone who has not asked to be forgiven, however, may prove to be a backhanded way of accusing the person, which only heightens the tension. When we can extend mercy and healing into the lives of those we forgive, it is good and wise to speak. At its core, the act of forgiving is between ourselves and God. Our decision to forgive opens the way for God to heal us and release us from our bitterness so that we can begin to love again. Such love holds the Lord's church together.

God's healing in our hearts resembles his healing of a physical wound, a gradual restoration in which the suffering subsides over time despite periodic jolts of pain as we are reminded of the injury. A friend of mine, a pastor, told me of his experience of being mercilessly slandered and then abandoned by members of his church. A colleague advised him to put all the people he was mad at on a list and pray forgiveness and blessing for them daily. At first, he says, he could hardly look at the list, but over time he reached a stage where he could sincerely ask God to bring blessing into their lives. It was a major experience of the Great Physician's healing.

Matthew's eighteenth chapter is profoundly important to this Gospel, whose message is that Jesus has come to gather and transform and unite God's people under his merciful authority. Jesus makes God's reign effectively present by forming a loving, humble, forgiving community of disciples. "Where two or three [or two or three hundred] come together in my name, there I am with them." Then, as we are fortified as his community, we can move out effectively as salt and light into the world.

*The Father wants none of his sheep to wander away, so Jesus unites us to help each other stay securely in the fold through prayer, accountability, and forgiveness.*

# WHAT GOD HAS JOINED TOGETHER

## DAY 21

Matthew 19:1-12; 5:31-32

■ Matthew 19:1-12

**19** [1] When Jesus had finished saying these things, he left Galilee and went into the region of Judea to the other side of the Jordan. [2] Large crowds followed him, and he healed them there.

[3] Some Pharisees came to him to test him. They asked, "Is it lawful for a man to divorce his wife for any and every reason?"

[4] "Haven't you read," he replied, "that at the beginning the Creator 'made them male and female,' [5] and said, 'For this reason a man will leave his father and mother and be united to his wife, and the two will become one flesh'? [6] So they are no longer two, but one flesh. Therefore what God has joined together, let no one separate."

[7] "Why then," they asked, "did Moses command that a man give his wife a certificate of divorce and send her away?"

[8] Jesus replied, "Moses permitted you to divorce your wives because your hearts were hard. But it was not this way from the beginning. [9] I tell you that anyone who divorces his wife, except for sexual immorality, and marries another woman commits adultery."

[10] The disciples said to him, "If this is the situation between a husband and wife, it is better not to marry."

[11] Jesus replied, "Not everyone can accept this word, but only those to whom it has been given. [12] For there are eunuchs who were born that way; and there are eunuchs who have been made eunuchs by others; and there are those who choose to live like eunuchs for the sake of the kingdom of heaven. The one who can accept this should accept it."

### ▧ Matthew 5:31–32

> [31] "It has been said, 'Anyone who divorces his wife must give her a certificate of divorce.' [32] But I tell you that anyone who divorces his wife, except for sexual immorality, makes her the victim of adultery, and anyone who marries a divorced woman commits adultery."

As Jesus continues his journey toward Jerusalem and his appointment with the cross, he faces critics who test him with the challenging subject of marriage and divorce. In Matthew 19 as well as Matthew 5, Jesus responds to a long-running debate among Jews about how to apply Moses' teaching in Deuteronomy 24:1. The verse says, "If a man marries a woman who becomes displeasing to him because he finds something indecent about her, and he writes her a certificate of divorce, gives it to her and sends her from his house . . ." The debate was over the phrase "something indecent about her." The strict interpreters, following a rabbi named Shammai, emphasized the word *indecent*, and took it to mean that only a wife's sexual immorality (adultery) would provide grounds for divorce. The permissive interpreters, following an earlier rabbi named Hillel, emphasized the word *something* and took it to mean that a man could dismiss his wife for anything he found displeasing about her, even so small a matter as overcooking dinner. The Pharisees' question reflects Hillel's permissive view, as they ask whether a man is permitted to divorce his wife "for any and every reason." In 19:9 and 5:32, Jesus stands with Shammai.

However, he revolutionizes the debate. Jesus challenges their whole way of asking the question. In 19:3, the Pharisees ask whether divorce is permitted. In essence, they are asking, "What are my rights as master of my house? For how small an offense may I withhold forgiveness from my wife and dismiss her? How great is my power as a husband? How minimal are my obligations?" Such questions emerge from a heart of stone. We may assume that a man who is inquiring in this way about dismissing his wife does not plan to remain unmarried for the rest of his life. He aims to justify getting rid of his wife in order to take another one who pleases him more. ("If I go to a new woman while married, it is adultery. If I dismiss my current wife and marry a new woman, it is not.") It is a scheme to commit adultery without being tagged as an adulterer, to skirt the Law of Moses in the guise of keeping it. It is another instance of the unspoken Pharisaical principle (which we sometimes find in our churches) that self-promoting actions of all sorts are allowable so long as we don't break any rules. Jesus exposes their game: "I tell you that anyone who divorces his wife . . . and marries another woman commits adultery" (19:9).[19]

Jesus then turns their question on its head. He says, "Don't frame the question negatively; pursue God's positive intention. Don't ask, 'What does God permit?' Ask, 'What does God prefer?' Don't ask, 'What can I get away with?' Ask, 'How shall I love the Lord my God with all my heart and soul and mind and my [wife] as myself?'"

Jesus lays out God's positive intention for marriage by quoting two key verses from Genesis. He says, "At the beginning the Creator 'made them male and female' [Genesis 1:26], and said, 'For this reason a man will leave his father and mother and be united to his wife, and the two will become one flesh' [Genesis 2:24]." Then he adds his own conclusion, "So they are no longer two, but one flesh. Therefore what God has joined together, let no one separate." A marriage is something God puts together.

Jesus quotes the three phrases from Genesis 2:24 to describe God's design for marriage. First, along with the wife (whose parting from her parents is assumed), the husband leaves father and mother to form a new primary family. This is the meaning of a wedding, the gathering of the couple's families of origin along with their friends to bless the formation of the new family. Second, the husband "is united [by God] to his wife." With God's help, the two become inseparable, committed permanently and exclusively to each other. A marriage is so much more than "a piece of paper," as many today dismissively call it. It is not a certificate in a file drawer; it is a man and woman looking each other in the eye and making profound promises to each other in the presence of God and the people they care about most. It is sacred and life changing, because God is active in it. Third, in the context of becoming each other's new family and committing their lives to each other, the partners enter into sexual intimacy. Here Jesus indicates that God positively values the sexual relationship and gives it to a husband and wife to seal and enact their binding promises of love to each other. By his three-part design, God establishes the foundation for a secure relationship and a healthy setting for children.

Since Jesus has taken this positive approach to marriage, it is good for us to consider how to maximize a marriage's chances of succeeding. By far the best way to form a marriage is for two *disciples* to come together. What better way to prepare for being permanently committed to a marital partner than to practice being permanently committed to Jesus? What better way to shape our character so that we become a humble, forgiving, and caring partner? How important it is to choose an ally in the life with God rather than someone who is lukewarm or cold to it!

Jesus' teaching about lifelong marriage has a context. In Matthew 19, it comes right after instructing disciples to forgive our brother or sister over and over. We will have many opportunities to forgive each other in marriage, and we endanger our marriages when we hold grudges and allow hurts to build up. A few verses earlier (18:1–5), Jesus told them to abandon their pursuit of status and become humble. A marriage that is a power contest will bring both partners misery. In Matthew 5, the two verses against divorce occur in the section (5:17–45) in which Jesus requires a higher righteousness. He commands us to let go of anger and be reconciled, to work out our conflicts quickly, and to be faithful to our spouse from our hearts rather than to lust after others. Later in the passage, Jesus instructs disciples to love tenaciously and creatively no matter how badly we think the other person is behaving. If Jesus requires us to love even our enemies without limit, how can we do less for our husband or wife?

Some have suspected that Jesus is requiring the impossible when he so strongly advocates lifelong marriage. The Twelve thought so: "If this is the situation between a husband and wife, it is better not to marry." Their comment reflects the reality that marriage is sometimes hard. But everything he says about faithfulness and love toward our spouse is possible because the power of God's kingdom has become available to us. Dilemmas that arise along the way are new opportunities to turn to Jesus in prayer, chances to see the matter through with his help rather than to give up. As in the whole life of discipleship, so in our marriages, we pour ourselves into making it work, intentionally yielding our wills to God in every way we can think of, and trusting his power. God is able to make us new, both as individuals and as couples, as we cooperate with him.

We need to help each other in the church. We can train members to be effective husbands and wives as part of training them to be disciples. We can equip experienced couples to guide more vulnerable couples. We can encourage our leaders not to neglect their marriages in their zeal to be involved in God's work. We can say by word and example that people are not defective if they go to a counselor about marital difficulty, any more than if they go to a doctor about a cancerous lump—and getting help sooner is better than later.

I do not write this chapter as someone who has been immune from marital difficulties. About three years into my marriage with Cindi, I actively entertained the idea that ending it would be a huge relief to both of us. A friend at church named Dave led us to a pair of counselors who met with us together every week for a couple of years and enabled us to develop new patterns. Thank God for good counselors! Several other times since, tensions and disappointments have risen to painful levels, but we have found God's help and worked through to new hope and love. We are now in our fourth decade of marriage, and we are so glad that we didn't leave each other during the troubled times. In his mercy, God has granted us a deep and rich love for each other, and we are inexpressibly grateful to him.

So Jesus wants disciples to be tenacious in marriage. Does he ever allow divorce? Both times his admonition against divorce includes the phrase "except for sexual immorality," so he does not absolutely rule out divorce. It is important to recognize in our two passages that Jesus is not answering the question whether divorce is ever permitted. He is responding to the question whether Rabbi Hillel was correct that Moses allowed men to divorce their wives for any and every reason. Jesus' answer is no—marriage is too important, too sacred, to be ended simply because one partner (or both) has become dissatisfied.

But by acknowledging Moses' permission to divorce due to a partner's sexual immorality, Jesus raises the possibility that other violations of Moses' teaching about marriage—violations such as abandonment or refusal to provide care and affection—might also provide grounds for a victimized spouse to seek release.[20] Physical and emotional abuse are appalling instances of withholding obligatory care and affection. Jesus' teaching on the value and permanence of marriage does not require people who are being abused to continue subjecting themselves to the abuse by staying with their partner.

If a disciple does enter into divorce proceedings due to such offenses, all of Jesus' requirements about persistently loving even our enemies apply to how to treat the offending spouse (5:38–48; see also 5:25). The disciple will need to forgive and to resist all temptation to retaliate, trying at every step to proceed prudently and innocently (10:16).

If a couple divorces, we in their church have to pray for discernment about how to respond. On the one hand, we do not want to promote our culture's notion of a "right to happiness" no matter what it costs in broken promises and broken family members. On the other hand, we need to serve as a community of healing for adults and children who are hurting.

In 19:10–12, Jesus throws his disciples a surprise. When they exclaim that Jesus' demanding policy on permanent marriage makes it "better not to marry," they are not seriously proposing that anyone would not marry. In the Jewish culture, all were expected to marry. But Jesus seizes the opportunity to endorse singleness. He says that marriage is not for everyone. Some may be prevented from it for physical reasons. Some may discern a call from God to remain single for his special purposes.[21] Others remain single, not knowing whether this is God's temporary or permanent plan for them.

Surely Jesus' greatest support for living single is his own life. He could have pointed to John the Baptist as well. In a society that marginalized single people and suggested that something was wrong with them, Jesus lived a joyful life with God and his fellow human beings as a single man, and he affirmed singleness as a vital possibility. His message to many disciples is, "Follow me also in this aspect of my life: my singleness."

Unfortunately, our culture too is saturated with the idea that a person who has no partner is somehow deficient. But congregations do well to embrace single members in honor of their Savior. Many of our members will never marry, and many others who do marry will live long stretches of their adult lives as single persons, either because the opportunity to marry well does not come quickly or because their marriage has ended due to a death or divorce. Jesus greatly values their lives as disciples, and he sometimes offers them rewarding avenues of service that might be impractical for believers who have family obligations. He envisions that their experience of family will come from fellow disciples, just as Jesus received disciples as his family (12:48–50).

One more issue is raised in both passages: does Jesus forbid remarriage by disciples who are single due to divorce? Clearly he allows remarriage by the person who has divorced because of a partner's adultery or abandonment. When Jesus rejects remarriage in Matthew 19 and 5, he is protesting against married men who

play the adulterous game of ending their marriage out of dissatis-
faction in order to seek another marriage.

What might he say, though, to disciples who are far down the
road since a divorce? Perhaps they divorced before becoming
a follower of Jesus, or perhaps they had begun with Christ but
disobeyed him in ways that led to their divorce. Now they have
had the necessary years to come to grips with their own responsibility for the marriage's failure and have humbled themselves and
repented honestly and deeply. Is it not possible that such disciples
might receive from God a new and right marriage? Great care must
be taken, because second marriages fail at a frightful rate. It will
be tempting for these believers to adopt the worldly stance that
they have a right to marital companionship or physical satisfaction
and lurch into something ill considered. They will need patience
in order to discern the difference between God's leading and their
own restlessness or desperation. They are wise first to come to
peace with their singleness and to be wary of any potential partner
who has not done the same. Disciples who have deeply learned
that *life is in Jesus* rather than in any particular human relationship
are in the best position to enter a marriage selflessly and to succeed
where they failed before.

*Jesus restores marriage as the secure union God designed
it to be and endorses singleness, paths Jesus makes
rich for humble disciples who pursue life in him.*

# THE LAST WILL BE FIRST

## Matthew 19:13-20:16

In each passage in the next two days' readings (19:13–21:9), Jesus addresses the problem of people loving high status. He highlights the theme by saying three times that the first will be last, and the last will be first (19:30; 20:16, 27). He has been emphasizing humility ever since Peter confessed him to be the Messiah at Caesarea Philippi. We saw this most recently as he rebuked the Pharisees for hardheartedly protecting their power advantage over their wives. Today's reading is filled with people who are concerned about their standing in comparison to others.

### Matthew 19:13-15

<sup></sup>13 Then people brought little children to Jesus for him to place his hands on them and pray for them. But the disciples rebuked them. 14 Jesus said, "Let the little children come to me, and do not hinder them, for the kingdom of heaven belongs to such as these." 15 When he had placed his hands on them, he went on from there.

Jesus has already told the disciples to curb their craving for status—to change and become like children, who are at the bottom of the ladder (18:1–5). This story similarly features children, whom their parents bring to Jesus so that he would bless them and touch them prayerfully. The Twelve interfere. They rebuke the parents, apparently to protect Jesus' dignity, deciding that Jesus is too important and distinguished to be bothered with little nobodies. This is the King! But as they scold the parents, they likely have in mind their own importance as the King's inner circle. Allowing little children to approach Jesus freely could diminish the value of their position as his elite associates.

This story of Jesus delighting in little children is one of the beautiful vignettes in the Gospel. Jesus' essential message is that the kingdom of heaven belongs to such commoners, such "little people." He never puts on airs, never condescends. The Twelve are not yet like their humble King—and if they are so overeager for status, we likely have the same problem.

## ■ Matthew 19:16-26

[16] Just then a man came up to Jesus and asked, "Teacher, what good thing must I do to get eternal life?"

[17] "Why do you ask me about what is good?" Jesus replied. "There is only One who is good. If you want to enter life, keep the commandments."

[18] "Which ones?" he inquired.

Jesus replied, "'You shall not murder, you shall not commit adultery, you shall not steal, you shall not give false testimony, [19] honor your father and mother,' and 'love your neighbor as yourself.'"

[20] "All these I have kept," the young man said. "What do I still lack?"

[21] Jesus answered, "If you want to be perfect, go, sell your possessions and give to the poor, and you will have treasure in heaven. Then come, follow me."

[22] When the young man heard this, he went away sad, because he had great wealth.

[23] Then Jesus said to his disciples, "Truly I tell you, it is hard for someone who is rich to enter the kingdom of heaven. [24] Again I tell you, it is easier for a camel to go through the eye of a needle than for someone who is rich to enter the kingdom of God."

[25] When the disciples heard this, they were greatly astonished and asked, "Who then can be saved?"

[26] Jesus looked at them and said, "With man this is impossible, but with God all things are possible."

This is the sobering story of a young man who rejects the call to discipleship. It begins with his enthusiastic question, "Teacher, what good thing must I do to get eternal life?" Matthew's take on it is that the man wants to do some praiseworthy act, something that would enhance his sense of his own emerging greatness, his worthiness of eternal life. Jesus tells him to seek not the good deed, but the good One for whom he must live entirely. He must do what he already knows to do: "Keep the commandments." When the young man claims that he has meticulously kept them all, Jesus does not question him. Instead, he offers him the very thing he asked for at the beginning: the good thing to do. "Sell your possessions and give to the poor. . . . Then come, follow me." The man is stunned. Observing him, Jesus says solemnly to his disciples, "Truly I tell you, it is hard for the rich to enter the kingdom of heaven."

Jesus is not just asking the man to walk away from his money and possessions. He is requiring him to abandon the quest implied in his initial question: the quest to be regarded as above the rest. Though the man is entirely sincere and respectful, there is a bit of the show-off in his question, a bit too much weight on the word *I*. ("The commandments are for everybody; what good thing must *I* do?") Behind his question about eternal life, we may detect another: "People can see from my riches and my zeal that God already thinks well of me. What can I do to clinch the top rank?" The disciples certainly believe that the man's wealth exhibits God's delight in him. That is why they ask, "[If a man like this is shut out,] who then can be saved?" They have been raised on such passages as Deuteronomy 28:8–14, where God promises to pour out abundant prosperity upon those who are faithful to him. One verse says, "The LORD will make you the head, not the tail. . . . You will always be at the top, never at the bottom." Here is a man destined for the top, a man of wealth, the sure sign of God's pleasure and blessing. Yet Jesus says the man's wealth and prestige hinder him. He must get rid of these things if God is to welcome him into eternal life. "Come to the bottom with me—and help some others get off the bottom by relieving their poverty—and you will have heavenly treasure." The man leaves dejectedly.

I remember a time in my musician days when I performed with a fine choir at an elegant lawn party for some of the wealthiest people in Los Angeles. As a philanthropic endeavor, they had gathered to plan a dazzling fund-raising banquet in connection with the grand opening of an exclusive apparel store. Ronald Reagan would be there, and the master of ceremonies would be Hollywood's favorite, Bob Hope. The fellow who was addressing the assembly at the lawn party kept calling the coming event "a very prestigious affair." He must have said "prestigious affair" five times. Money and prestige are thoroughly intertwined.

The danger when we read the story in Matthew is that we will see it as a warning to the folks at the lawn party. No, it is a warning to all of us—certainly to anyone who has enough disposable income to buy this book. Those of us who are part of America's middle class (even the lower middle class) are all wealthy by global standards. We are just as prone to measure ourselves by how much we have as the super-rich are. Jesus says it is the wrong treasure and the wrong measuring stick.

The story of the rich young man is a warning to all of us who possess something we cherish, anything that makes us feel like we are somebody. Perhaps it is something purchased with money, but it might be less tangible—inclusion in a social group, coveted opportunities for fun or pleasure, a boyfriend or girlfriend, high standing in an organization—anything we cling to at the cost of complete loyalty to Jesus. We have to hold loosely each blessing we have received from him so that it does not enslave us.

We are sometimes shocked and defeated by our slavery to a blessing that we cherish too much. During my musician days, my cherished item was the joy and heady esteem I received from performing in that professional choir, the one at the lawn party, which also did large-scale concerts, including performances with the Los Angeles Philharmonic Orchestra. It was a thrill to sing in those concerts. The choir's founding director was unusually good to me. At the same time, it is not unfair to say that he was sometimes manipulative. In many concerts only part of the choir was used, and he alone decided who got to sing. He dangled before us the most desirable opportunities to perform. "You scratch my back, and I'll scratch yours," he would say. We all endeavored to remain in his good graces by doing what he asked us to do. Our protection came from the musicians' union's rules. He chafed under the union's restrictions on the length and frequency of his rehearsals and on his capacity to call on us for unpaid jobs (like that lawn party). I had been getting to know the union steward, a fellow member of the bass section whom I'll call "Jim." I had begun to have serious conversations with him and to share my faith with him. One day, at the end of a dress rehearsal, the choir's director wanted to continue drilling us for a while without paying overtime. When the union steward spoke up to object, the director dared us and said, "If anyone agrees with Jim, raise your hand." We all agreed with Jim, and integrity demanded that we raise our hands to support him. No one did. What was needed was a first person to raise his hand. I could not get mine out of my lap. The moment came and went quickly, and I failed. Jim was gracious to me later when I apologized, but I will always wonder what might have happened in my effort to help him know Jesus if I had been free that day to do what was right—free from the clutches of something I loved too much.

Jesus does not tell the rich young man that his money and prestige have taken ownership over him, he merely tells him to let go of those things and shows him that he cannot. Our danger of enslavement is no less than his. To loosen our grip on distracting wealth—and to loosen its grip on us—we need God's help. Jesus' comment that "it is easier for a camel to go through the eye of a needle than for someone who is rich to enter the kingdom of God" is supposed to make us laugh (nervously). What a hilariously absurd image! Lest the disciples miss his point, he looks them straight in the eye and says, "With [human beings] this is impossible." It is impossible for the rich to enter the kingdom. We are truly helpless on our own to extricate ourselves from the clutches of our money and status. "But with God all things are possible." God is our hope, and he cares enough to rescue us. As we keep a wary eye on the blessings we cherish most, repeatedly surrendering all to him while he empowers us, we can attain the freedom to be fully his. As he helps us let go, we begin to understand that we have no basis for feeling superior over anyone.

## ▩ Matthew 19:27-29

27 Peter answered him, "We have left everything to follow you! What then will there be for us?"

28 Jesus said to them, "Truly I tell you, at the renewal of all things, when the Son of Man sits on his glorious throne, you who have followed me will also sit on twelve thrones, judging the twelve tribes of Israel. 29 And everyone who has left houses or brothers or sisters or father or mother or wife or children or fields for my sake will receive a hundred times as much and will inherit eternal life."

Surprisingly, after dramatically requiring disciples to let go of wealth and status, he promises them spectacular wealth and status. Both Peter's question and Jesus' answer refer to the new situation at the final resurrection of believers. Jesus calls it "the renewal of all things," when he, the Son of Man, will come and receive from God unchallenged kingly rule over all the world (Daniel 7:13–14; Matthew 16:27; 26:64). He declares that the disciples too will reign, enthroned in glory, exalted in status beyond their wildest dreams. When he tells the Twelve that they will judge the twelve tribes of Israel, he is not saying they will decide who is rewarded or condemned on the Judgment Day. Jesus is the sole judge of all humanity (25:31; 28:18). He means that all disciples will share Jesus' royal dignity and leadership in the new world, from which he will exclude all persecutors and enemies.[22]

Jesus speaks of his future glory and theirs so that his companions will confidently bear the costs of discipleship in the meantime. Peter says, "We have left everything," and Jesus assures them that "everyone who has left houses or brothers or sisters or father or mother or wife[23] or children or fields for my sake will receive a hundred times as much and will inherit eternal life." Such "leaving" can mean never acquiring these listed benefits in the first place. Or it can mean having them but then losing them as God sends us far afield or into the path of persecutors. Those who leave behind what is precious for Jesus' sake will be rich at the final resurrection. We will additionally enjoy some of the "riches" sooner as we receive love from the family of believers and experience the surpassingly valuable presence of Jesus himself.

## Matthew 19:30–20:16

[30] "But many who are first will be last, and many who are last will be first.

**20** [1] "For the kingdom of heaven is like a landowner who went out early in the morning to hire workers for his vineyard. [2] He agreed to pay them a denarius for the day and sent them into his vineyard.

[3] "About nine in the morning he went out and saw others standing in the marketplace doing nothing. [4] He told them, 'You also go and work in my vineyard, and I will pay you whatever is right.' [5] So they went.

"He went out again about noon and about three in the afternoon and did the same thing. [6] About five in the afternoon he went out and found still others standing around. He asked them, 'Why have you been standing here all day long doing nothing?'

[7] "'Because no one has hired us,' they answered.

"He said to them, 'You also go and work in my vineyard.'

[8] "When evening came, the owner of the vineyard said to his foreman, 'Call the workers and pay them their wages, beginning with the last ones hired and going on to the first.'

[9] "The workers who were hired about five in the afternoon came and each received a denarius. [10] So when those came who were hired first, they expected to receive more. But each one of them also received a denarius. [11] When they received it, they began to grumble against the landowner. [12] 'These who were hired last worked only one hour,' they said, 'and you have made them equal to us who have borne the burden of the work and the heat of the day.'

[13] "But he answered one of them, 'I am not being unfair to you, friend. Didn't you agree to work for a denarius? [14] Take your pay and go. I want to give the one who was hired last the same as I gave you. [15] Don't I have the right to do what I want with my own money? Or are you envious because I am generous?'

[16] "So the last will be first, and the first will be last."

This parable follows from Peter's proud comment, "We have left everything to follow you! What then will there be for us?" The rich young man turned away from Jesus, but the Twelve have followed him from the start. They are worthy of special standing, then, aren't they? Jesus' parable challenges them to let go of their sense of entitlement. In the story, those who were hired first protest, saying, "You have made [the ones hired later] equal to us who have borne the burden of the work and the heat of the day." They claim a right to advantage, because they have worked longer and harder. Many of Matthew's early readers must have had similar thoughts, because they had already experienced persecution and other hardships for their years of loyalty to Jesus. It may have seemed to them that they should have special standing above members who came to Christ later and avoided the worst hardships.

Ironically, those hired first in the parable initially believed they were the fortunate ones—to be chosen earlier rather than left out. That is the perspective the landowner wants them to retain at the end. When we are thinking clearly, we realize that we who have been with Jesus a long time have been the best off all along the way. "You too go and work in my vineyard," were Jesus' words of blessing, not burden. We got to live with Jesus that much longer, and we escaped the inner isolation and wounds of a worldly life that much sooner. Following Jesus is not soft and easy, but the appeal of living independently from him is deceptive.

The notion that those who come to Jesus later are getting a better deal motivates some of my college students to postpone following Jesus, preferring instead to have some fun first. They suspect that following him will be burdensome and will deprive them of happy experiences. Peter Pan-like, they decide, "I'm going to really live for a while before I have to get serious and take on responsibilities." That choice puts them in a rut many of them never escape, constantly pursuing fun and never feeling fulfilled. Similarly, some longtime disciples are tempted to think they missed out on something because they began early with Christ and bore "the burden of the work and the heat of the day." They may be enticed, perhaps during a "midlife crisis," to sow some wild oats belatedly. It is a trap. If and when they come to their senses, they acknowledge that Jesus' burden is light, and they have found rest for their souls in him (11:30). Better to be with Jesus all the time, no matter what the cost. What if some latecomers to faith do seem to have it better than we do? We can thank God for being generous to them! Jesus begins and ends the parable with his theme statement, "the last will be first, and the first will be last." In the end—the very end, when it counts—those who become first will be the disciples who have thought least about whether they are first.

*In a kingdom that elevates the lowly and the last, the love of money and prestige is dangerously, impossibly incompatible—but thank God for his grace!*

## DAY 23 | NOT TO BE SERVED, BUT TO SERVE

Matthew 20:17-21:9

### ■ Matthew 20:17-19

<sup></sup>17 Now Jesus was going up to Jerusalem. On the way, he took the Twelve aside and said to them, 18 "We are going up to Jerusalem, and the Son of Man will be delivered over to the chief priests and the teachers of the law. They will condemn him to death 19 and will hand him over to the Gentiles to be mocked and flogged and crucified. On the third day he will be raised to life!"

Jesus intensifies his instruction about humility as he journeys with his disciples all the way to the gates of Jerusalem. He knows the abuse that awaits him there,[24] yet he presses forward toward his appointment. The reality of Jesus' coming suffering and the consequent humbling for his followers does not register with them. After Jesus' first prediction, Peter denies that any such shameful outcome could happen. After the second, the disciples argue about which among them is the greatest. Even as he tells them now for a third time about his lowly path, the Twelve obsess about their prospects for high status.

### ■ Matthew 20:20-28

20 Then the mother of Zebedee's sons came to Jesus with her sons and, kneeling down, asked a favor of him.
21 "What is it you want?" he asked.
She said, "Grant that one of these two sons of mine may sit at your right and the other at your left in your kingdom."

²² "You don't know what you are asking," Jesus said to them. "Can you drink the cup I am going to drink?"

"We can," they answered.

²³ Jesus said to them, "You will indeed drink from my cup, but to sit at my right or left is not for me to grant. These places belong to those for whom they have been prepared by my Father."

²⁴ When the ten heard about this, they were indignant with the two brothers. ²⁵ Jesus called them together and said, "You know that the rulers of the Gentiles lord it over them, and their high officials exercise authority over them. ²⁶ Not so with you. Instead, whoever wants to become great among you must be your servant, ²⁷ and whoever wants to be first must be your slave— ²⁸ just as the Son of Man did not come to be served, but to serve, and to give his life as a ransom for many."

Though we may think that sending their mother to do their pleading is childish, we can sympathize with James and John. Hasn't Jesus sent a mixed message: lowliness and power? Jesus has recently spoken to them about sitting on thrones with him and ruling in glory (19:28)—much more appealing than hearing that the king they follow is headed for flogging and crucifixion. They listen selectively, hearing what they want to hear and ignoring the rest.

Jesus treats the mother's request as coming from the sons. Their question about the seats of greatest honor at Jesus' right and left is jarring, because it comes immediately after he predicts his coming suffering. They act as if he has not said it, and they make the most blatant grab for status we have seen thus far: "Give us the places of honor second only to your own." The other ten disciples are outraged—not because the two brothers are being callous about Jesus' coming suffering, but because James and John have outmaneuvered them in their own ambitions. Status gains come at the expense of others, so if James and John move up, the best seats become unavailable for the rest. All twelve disciples agree in missing Jesus' point.

*Is* Jesus giving a mixed message? Does all he has been saying lately about being last and becoming a servant or slave contradict all he was saying earlier about participating now in Jesus' power to bring the kingdom? Is Jesus saying that, for the time being, we should operate in terms of weakness and lowliness, but wait until his return to operate in greatness and authority?

No. Jesus is not contradicting himself. He exerts real power and calls his disciples to do the same here in this life. The key is to understand how kingdom power and authority work. It is upside-down from the world's idea of power and authority, described by Jesus: "You know that, among the Gentiles, rulers lord it over their subjects, and the great make their authority felt" (20:25 REB). Roman officials maintain high rank by keeping others down. By contrast, God's kingdom power is exerted from beneath and lifts others up.

How far beneath? From a worldly perspective, the cross is as low as a person can go. It is the ultimate experience of nonstatus. Nailing a man up on a cross of wood, stripped naked, bleeding from beatings, dying slowly in unspeakable pain—this was the Romans' way of completely humiliating a man and maximizing his despair and helplessness. It was designed to display him as thoroughly defeated—the loser at the hands of those who hold all the power.

But when Jesus hangs on a cross, he is performing the consummate act of power—he liberates humankind by means of it. It is a mistake to think of Jesus as a victim; that is, as a person overpowered by others. His death on the cross is an act of conquest. He goes to Jerusalem on purpose—to conquer darkness by suffering its worst. His mission is to bind the devil and plunder his house— an act of overpowering (12:29)—and the cross is the means by which he exerts that overwhelming power. The cross continues and culminates Jesus' whole career of powerful acts: giving sight to the blind, speech to the silent, agility to the lame, and life to the dead. The cross of Christ *does* something. It is the comprehensive messianic act of service to overcome all that is sick, dark, and sinful in our world.

To explain the meaning of his death, Jesus chooses an image out of the people's combative world. His death on the cross is a *ransom*. A ransom is a price paid to liberate someone who is held captive, whether the captive has been kidnapped or enslaved or captured as a prisoner of war. Jesus gives his life as the price to set us free, the cost to redeem us from spiritual bondage and death. Thus Jesus serves us on the cross. By dying there, he liberates us to live with God now and forever.

Salvation means rescue. We needed to be rescued not just from condemnation, but from the root cause of condemnation. Hell is made of selfishness: everyone for himself; everyone for herself. Jesus dies to rescue us from a dead-end world, and the essence of that dead-end world is the scramble to be on top. The brothers' jockeying for positions at Jesus' right and left and the other ten disciples' protests that someone might get ahead of them are the world's way all over again. It could not be more foreign to Jesus' message. So he insists, "Not so with you," and it is urgent that they see the difference. It touches on the very nature of God's kingdom. Kingdom power works from the bottom up. Pagans scramble for the top, exploiting those above them, trampling on those below, serving only themselves. Disciples have been rescued from the whole contest. They settle in further down, caring about everyone they meet and serving with life-giving power, because God is with them.

On the journey of discipleship, Jesus remains out ahead. His death is unique, just as he is unique. Only *his* life can serve as a ransom for many. Only he can bring forgiveness of sins and unlimited access to God. Still, he instructs us to take up our cross and follow him. Jesus tells the ambitious brothers, "You will indeed drink from my cup" of tribulation and apparent defeat. But it is not defeat. When we imitate Jesus, we are liberated within, and we begin to make a difference for good in our world.

Jesus' service defines the nature of our discipleship. First, his cross obligates us. Because the King has laid down his life to ransom us from futility and death, we owe him everything. Whatever Jesus asks us to do we will do with hearty gratitude, because he has done so very much for us. There can be no thought of repaying Jesus or of doing enough to make up for the cost that fell to him. His gift to us is far too great. Rather, we respond to his love by loving him in all we do.

Second, his death on our behalf motivates our discipleship. When we experience his love, we want to be with him constantly. When we see his compassion for the world, we want to love like that. When we contemplate his magnificent service at the cross, we find new energy and determination to serve one another. When we see his boldness in heading straight for Jerusalem, we find courage to stay on his path.

Third, the cross of Christ sets our purpose as his disciples. On the cross, he gives his life to free others from misery and hopelessness. As his followers, we carry on his labors to bring peace and well-being to the world. On the cross, he enters into the life experience of the sick and broken, the poor and oppressed. As his apprentices, we reenvision our own hardships as the means to know Jesus and the people he cares about. On the cross, Jesus confronts the powers of darkness in order to break their grip on human lives. As his allies, we take up his battle against evil by prayer, words, and action. Our purpose in life emerges from the offering of his life: we join him in drawing the world into the liberation and well-being he died to provide.

Finally, the cross of Christ defines our style, our way of relating to others. The one who is "God with us" takes his humble place on the cross, so we humble ourselves. The Son of God makes himself a servant, so we learn to serve. This is the new "greatness." Disciples will exert spiritual power along with Jesus precisely as we cease our infatuation with worldly power, status, and honor. It is an upside-down kind of kingdom that has come near in Christ, and so we will exert world-changing power from the bottom upward.

Jesus has stressed humility so often and in so many ways. We understand that we are to "change and become like [lowly] children." The difficulty is to do it. Humility is a quality of character, so we have to remember how our character is formed in the life of the kingdom. Our character is shaped by a collaborative effort between us and God. We diligently practice what Jesus teaches us; meanwhile God transforms our hearts by his power. It is interactive: he empowers us as we take action. We seek as first priority to live in God's righteous way, and as we do, he satisfies our hunger and thirst for righteousness by changing us, slowly but surely. Periodically he may knock us down a few notches through our circumstances, with all wisdom and gentleness, so that we become more sober about our limitations and less prone to conceit. Mostly, he assists us with habit formation—the habit of serving and honoring others without seeking praise or personal gain. Then when he entrusts to us positions of leadership and responsibility, we have some chance of serving with genuine moral authority.

Jesus corrects the disciples' selfish climbing over each other, but he does not reject their desire to be leaders. He has chosen them for the purpose of making them into leaders. His response to their request is not, "Quit aspiring to be a leader," but rather, "Do you grasp what you are signing up for? Can you drink the cup I am going to drink?" Leadership is hard. Leaders can expect to be misunderstood by their own people and attacked by outsiders. They have to stick their neck out in giving direction while building consensus among diversified members who may be neither humble nor mature. Leaders help the church venture out as a team for service in a dark world, facing obstacles out there and unresolved hurts within the congregation. Leaders will drink from Jesus' cup of tribulation and indignity. At the same time, they will have rich opportunities to lean on God and to marvel at his work. We are wise to build up our leaders' confidence and to work hard with them. We can thank God that he has given them such a calling, and we can pray that they will humbly heed his voice and experience his empowerment in all the ups and downs of their ministry.

■ Matthew 20:29–34

²⁹ As Jesus and his disciples were leaving Jericho, a large crowd followed him. ³⁰ Two blind men were sitting by the roadside, and when they heard that Jesus was going by, they shouted, "Lord, Son of David, have mercy on us!"

³¹ The crowd rebuked them and told them to be quiet, but they shouted all the louder, "Lord, Son of David, have mercy on us!"

³² Jesus stopped and called them. "What do you want me to do for you?" he asked.

³³ "Lord," they answered, "we want our sight."

³⁴ Jesus had compassion on them and touched their eyes. Immediately they received their sight and followed him.

The road to the cross is not the way of defeat, but the way of power. Jesus' healing of these blind men demonstrates that his journey toward death is no denial either of his majesty as King or of his claim to bring God's kingdom (11:2–5).

The blind men are bold, and their faith is insistent: "Lord, Son of David, have mercy on us!" The people dismiss them as their inferiors—likely, they are beggars—but Jesus honors them. The last will be first. Even while they are still blind, they can see what so many in Matthew's narrative have been unable to see: that Jesus is the messianic King, descendant of King David, the Shepherd of Israel. With their eyes fully opened, they do what all disciples must do: they follow him toward Jerusalem and the cross.

■ Matthew 21:1–9

21 ¹ As they approached Jerusalem and came to Bethphage on the Mount of Olives, Jesus sent two disciples, ² saying to them, "Go to the village ahead of you, and at once you will find a donkey tied there, with her colt by her. Untie them and bring them to me. ³ If anyone says anything to you, say that the Lord needs them, and he will send them right away."

⁴ This took place to fulfill what was spoken through the prophet:

⁵ "Say to Daughter Zion,
'See, your king comes to you,
gentle and riding on a donkey,
and on a colt, the foal of a donkey.'"

⁶ The disciples went and did as Jesus had instructed them. ⁷ They brought the donkey and the colt and placed their cloaks on them for Jesus to sit on. ⁸ A very large crowd spread their cloaks on the road, while others cut branches from the trees and spread them on the road. ⁹ The crowds that went ahead of him and those that followed shouted,

"Hosanna to the Son of David!"
"Blessed is he who comes in the name of the Lord!"
"Hosanna in the highest heaven!"

To culminate these chapters about humility, Matthew presents us with a memorable picture—foreseen by the prophet—that expresses visually everything that Jesus has been saying with words. the King enters the city on a donkey's colt. The contrast to a Roman ruler—or to King David—could not be sharper. Jesus comes as a "gentle" king (the same word is translated as "meek" in the third Beatitude, 5:5). Typical kings enter with pomp and splendor on an elegant horse, fearsome with their military escort, greeted by city officials and musicians in a spectacle of power. But the greatest King of all time and eternity enters humbly on a donkey. If we as disciples can hold that picture squarely before our mind's eye, we will grasp the nature of our calling: greatness in humility. Hosanna! Praise to the King who comes in God's name to serve! Lay down your garments, your lives for such a king.

*By going to the cross, Jesus saves us, obligates and motivates us, and sets us on the path of humble service.*

**DAY 24** | # PROPHET, KING, LORD

Matthew 21:10-22:46

## ▨ Matthew 21:10-22

¹⁰ When Jesus entered Jerusalem, the whole city was stirred and asked, "Who is this?"

¹¹ The crowds answered, "This is Jesus, the prophet from Nazareth in Galilee."

¹² Jesus entered the temple courts and drove out all who were buying and selling there. He overturned the tables of the money changers and the benches of those selling doves. ¹³ "It is written," he said to them, "'My house will be called a house of prayer,' but you are making it 'a den of robbers.'"

¹⁴ The blind and the lame came to him at the temple, and he healed them. ¹⁵ But when the chief priests and the teachers of the law saw the wonderful things he did and the children shouting in the temple courts, "Hosanna to the Son of David," they were indignant.

¹⁶ "Do you hear what these children are saying?" they asked him. "Yes," replied Jesus, "have you never read,

> "'From the lips of children and infants
>     you, Lord, have called forth your praise'?"

¹⁷ And he left them and went out of the city to Bethany, where he spent the night.

¹⁸ Early in the morning, as Jesus was on his way back to the city, he was hungry. ¹⁹ Seeing a fig tree by the road, he went up to it but found nothing on it except leaves. Then he said to it, "May you never bear fruit again!" Immediately the tree withered.

20 When the disciples saw this, they were amazed. "How did the fig tree wither so quickly?" they asked.

21 Jesus replied, "Truly I tell you, if you have faith and do not doubt, not only can you do what was done to the fig tree, but also you can say to this mountain, 'Go, throw yourself into the sea,' and it will be done. 22 If you believe, you will receive whatever you ask for in prayer."

The King has entered Jerusalem. "Who is this?" the people ask. By his words and conduct, he will reveal more than enough to make the answer clear, though he will leave it to his hearers to answer for themselves. The crowd's tentative answer is, "This is Jesus, the prophet" (verses 11 and 46). His actions in Jerusalem are indeed prophetic. He boldly challenges those in power, and he demands that the people decide about him.

Disciples, too, may be called to speak in a prophetic voice. Not all of us will take on the role of the prophet, just as not all will become leaders, but in 23:34, Jesus says he will send prophets to the people (also 10:41). He means that he will commission some of his disciples to be prophets who challenge corruption and call resistant people to God. Part of our training as apprentices, then, is to observe Jesus as he enters the city not only as king but as prophet.

It is only as we understand the Israelite style of prophecy that we can make sense of his destructive action in the temple and his cursing of the fig tree. In neither story does Jesus have a temper tantrum. These are acted symbols in the ancient prophets' dramatic style—dramatized declarations of God's judgment against official corruption. In the temple, he fiercely confronts the chief priests and their lawyers, who profit from the sale of sacrifice animals. Not only are they taking advantage of the poor (selling doves, the sacrifice offered by poor families), they have turned God's house of prayer into a chaotic place. By the spectacle of driving out animals and overturning tables, Jesus reveals God's anger, and he asserts his authority as Messiah.

The fig tree that Jesus curses and the vineyard that he describes in his parable (later in the chapter) represent Israel and its leaders. They do not bear fruit for God (Micah 7:1–3). They have rejected Jesus' momentous healings of the blind and lame (verses 14–15), signals that the messianic era has begun (Isaiah 35:5–6). The withered fig tree stands for God's coming judgment, which will turn the temple in Jerusalem to rubble.

Jesus accompanies both of these prophetic dramatizations with calls for prayer. Disciples will overcome powerful leaders' corruption not by prophetic confrontations alone, but by prayer for God to exert his power. The temple was to be a house of prayer, and Jesus' family of followers must become a household of prayer. The mountain of human resistance to God's emerging kingdom can be removed by praying in faith to God (verses 21–22). (I had a seminary professor in the 1970s who declared that God was mightier than the atheist superpower, the Soviet Union, and that we should pray for its collapse. He seemed at the time to be speaking the impossible, but he was right!) We may assume from Jesus' teaching about prayer that he himself had already been praying for months for power and wisdom to face his opponents in Jerusalem. We will imitate Jesus not by anything like hurling tables or cursing trees (a language of prophecy that was meaningful then but is foreign now), but by adopting his carefully targeted boldness against corruption and his zeal for prayer.

## ■ Matthew 21:23-32

23 Jesus entered the temple courts, and, while he was teaching, the chief priests and the elders of the people came to him. "By what authority are you doing these things?" they asked. "And who gave you this authority?"

24 Jesus replied, "I will also ask you one question. If you answer me, I will tell you by what authority I am doing these things. 25 John's baptism—where did it come from? Was it from heaven, or of human origin?"

They discussed it among themselves and said, "If we say, 'From heaven,' he will ask, 'Then why didn't you believe him?' 26 But if we say, 'Of human origin'—we are afraid of the people, for they all hold that John was a prophet."

27 So they answered Jesus, "We don't know."

Then he said, "Neither will I tell you by what authority I am doing these things.

28 "What do you think? There was a man who had two sons. He went to the first and said, 'Son, go and work today in the vineyard.' 29 'I will not,' he answered, but later he changed his mind and went. 30 Then the father went to the other son and said the same thing. He answered, 'I will, sir,' but he did not go. 31 Which of the two did what his father wanted?"

"The first," they answered.

Jesus said to them, "Truly I tell you, the tax collectors and the prostitutes are entering the kingdom of God ahead of you. 32 For John came to you to show you the way of righteousness, and you did not believe him, but the tax collectors and the prostitutes did. And even after you saw this, you did not repent and believe him."

The people of Jerusalem are divided about Jesus. Joyful crowds have laid down their garments for his procession into the city. Children continue to sing, "Hosanna to the Son of David." Jesus' arrival in Jerusalem is God's great hour, foreseen by the prophets, prepared by John the Baptist. Even tax collectors and prostitutes, people who never thought they would be included in anything having to do with God, flow to Jesus in anticipation and joy. But the chief priests and ruling elders resent him. To them, Jesus' teaching and actions are impudent, and his excitement of the crowds is dangerous, given the Romans' nervousness about a possible revolt. Indignantly, they ask the Blessed One who comes in the name of the Lord, "Who gave you this authority?"

Jesus brilliantly exposes their posturing and then indicts them in return: they are willfully blind to the arrival of God's kingdom.

Like the second son in the parable, they have said "yes" to the Father early in life and become experts in his law and chiefs among his people, but now they resist his new work. By contrast, the people whose lives had been a loud "no" to the Father are beginning to walk in "the way of righteousness." These former tax collectors and prostitutes, not the Jerusalem insiders, are doing the Father's will and are entering his kingdom. Jesus is proud to associate with them.

As we live out our allegiance to the King, we too may have to stand up to some reputable people—even the religiously reputable—who are really just refined bullies. And we will unashamedly identify ourselves with some disreputable people, because they have become Jesus' people. Both acts require courage.

### ■ Matthew 21:33–22:14

33 "Listen to another parable: There was a landowner who planted a vineyard. He put a wall around it, dug a winepress in it and built a watchtower. Then he rented the vineyard to some farmers and moved to another place. 34 When the harvest time approached, he sent his servants to the tenants to collect his fruit.

35 "The tenants seized his servants; they beat one, killed another, and stoned a third. 36 Then he sent other servants to them, more than the first time, and the tenants treated them the same way. 37 Last of all, he sent his son to them. 'They will respect my son,' he said.

38 "But when the tenants saw the son, they said to each other, 'This is the heir. Come, let's kill him and take his inheritance.' 39 So they took him and threw him out of the vineyard and killed him.

40 "Therefore, when the owner of the vineyard comes, what will he do to those tenants?"

41 "He will bring those wretches to a wretched end," they replied, "and he will rent the vineyard to other tenants, who will give him his share of the crop at harvest time."

42 Jesus said to them, "Have you never read in the Scriptures:

"'The stone the builders rejected
   has become the cornerstone;
the Lord has done this,
   and it is marvelous in our eyes'?

43 "Therefore I tell you that the kingdom of God will be taken away from you and given to a people who will produce its fruit. 44 Anyone who falls on this stone will be broken to pieces; anyone on whom it falls will be crushed."

45 When the chief priests and the Pharisees heard Jesus' parables, they knew he was talking about them. 46 They looked for a way to arrest him, but they were afraid of the crowd because the people held that he was a prophet.

22 1 Jesus spoke to them again in parables, saying: 2 "The kingdom of heaven is like a king who prepared a wedding banquet for his son. 3 He sent his servants to those who had been invited to the banquet to tell them to come, but they refused to come.

4 "Then he sent some more servants and said, 'Tell those who have been invited that I have prepared my dinner: My oxen and fattened cattle have been butchered, and everything is ready. Come to the wedding banquet.'

5 "But they paid no attention and went off—one to his field, another to his business. 6 The rest seized his servants, mistreated them and killed them. 7 The king was enraged. He sent his army and destroyed those murderers and burned their city.

8 "Then he said to his servants, 'The wedding banquet is ready, but those I invited did not deserve to come. 9 So go to the street corners and invite to the banquet anyone you find.' 10 So the servants went out into the streets and gathered all the people they could find, the bad as well as the good, and the wedding hall was filled with guests.

11 "But when the king came in to see the guests, he noticed a man there who was not wearing wedding clothes. 12 He asked, 'how did you get in here without wedding clothes, friend?' The man was speechless.

<sup>13</sup> "Then the king told the attendants, 'Tie him hand and foot, and throw him outside, into the darkness, where there will be weeping and gnashing of teeth.'

<sup>14</sup> "For many are invited, but few are chosen."

John the Baptist had called Israel to "bear fruit befitting repentance." In the parable of the vineyard, a landowner seeks fruit at harvesttime from the tenants charged with managing his land (as in Isaiah 5), but the tenants violently reject his messengers. The stakes are raised when the landowner sends his son. The tenants kill him. Many generations in Jerusalem had rejected God's prophets, the most recent being John the Baptist. Now they will kill God's Son. As a result, God will oust them and put new leaders in charge of his people, including former sinners like those whom Jesus mentioned earlier (21:32), who will become the core of his church.

The parable of the wedding banquet speaks similarly of people who are eligible for God's kindness but turn him away, of divine messengers they violently reject, and of unexpected newcomers who take their vacated places of honor. "The long-awaited hour has arrived. Come enter my joy," says God. "Celebrate my Son with me in his crowning moment!" God's heavenly banquet is yet to come, but with Jesus' arrival in Jerusalem, the kingdom has arrived already, and God's invitation to participate in his kingdom preempts all other priorities that people may have.

It will not do, however, merely to accept God's invitation to come to Jesus. Those invited are to wear the garments of the wedding feast (verses 11–14), garments provided by God, the host. The garments represent the new way of life. The tax collectors and prostitutes whom Jesus spoke of earlier as examples will no longer live in their former way. We, too, who come to the Son need to reclothe ourselves in new lives appropriate to his presence.

Jesus' point in these parables is that everything pivots on responding rightly to the Messiah's arrival. He is the son whom God sends to gather fruit, the cornerstone upon which God builds his house, the groom whom God celebrates with his wedding banquet. The difference between joy and weeping, life and destruction is to revere rather than reject the King. Disciples submit to Jesus decisively and then extend the invitation to anyone we find (verse 9).

## Matthew 22:15-40

15 Then the Pharisees went out and laid plans to trap him in his words. 16 They sent their disciples to him along with the Herodians. "Teacher," they said, "we know that you are a man of integrity and that you teach the way of God in accordance with the truth. You aren't swayed by others, because you pay no attention to who they are. 17 Tell us then, what is your opinion? Is it right to pay the imperial tax to Caesar or not?"

18 But Jesus, knowing their evil intent, said, "You hypocrites, why are you trying to trap me? 19 Show me the coin used for paying the tax." They brought him a denarius, 20 and he asked them, "Whose image is this? And whose inscription?"

21 "Caesar's," they replied.

Then he said to them, "So give back to Caesar what is Caesar's, and to God what is God's."

22 When they heard this, they were amazed. So they left him and went away.

23 That same day the Sadducees, who say there is no resurrection, came to him with a question. 24 "Teacher," they said, "Moses told us that if a man dies without having children, his brother must marry the widow and raise up offspring for him. 25 Now there were seven brothers among us. The first one married and died, and since he had no children, he left his wife to his brother. 26 The same thing happened to the second and third brother, right on down to the seventh. 27 Finally, the woman died. 28 Now then, at the resurrection, whose wife will she be of the seven, since all of them were married to her?"

29 Jesus replied, "You are in error because you do not know the Scriptures or the power of God. 30 At the resurrection people will

neither marry nor be given in marriage; they will be like the angels in heaven. [31] But about the resurrection of the dead—have you not read what God said to you, [32] 'I am the God of Abraham, the God of Isaac, and the God of Jacob'? He is not the God of the dead but of the living."

[33] When the crowds heard this, they were astonished at his teaching.

[34] Hearing that Jesus had silenced the Sadducees, the Pharisees got together. [35] One of them, an expert in the law, tested him with this question: [36] "Teacher, which is the greatest commandment in the Law?"

[37] Jesus replied: "'Love the Lord your God with all your heart and with all your soul and with all your mind.' [38] This is the first and greatest commandment. [39] And the second is like it: 'Love your neighbor as yourself.' [40] All the Law and the Prophets hang on these two commandments."

In these three stories, Jesus the prophet outwits opponents who think they are shrewd. We have seen in earlier episodes that Jesus succeeds through prayer and his dependence on God's Spirit. And now, as before, we see him repeatedly penetrate through to the core of the matter by knowing the Scriptures. We too can sharpen our minds and discern what matters most by learning the Scriptures deeply.

Responding to the politically explosive question of whether Jews should pay Roman taxes, Jesus asks whose image is on the Roman coin. Calling to mind the passage in Genesis 1 which proclaims that human beings are created in God's image, he tells them to give to Caesar what has Caesar's image on it (their coins) and give to God what has God's image on it (their lives!).

He responds to the Sadducees' trap about the resurrection of the dead by reprimanding them: "You know neither the Scriptures nor the power of God." Citing the story of Moses at the burning bush (Exodus 3), Jesus declares that God's power to give life beyond the grave is a primary indicator of who he is—"He is the God of the living." Jesus' boldness in Jerusalem stems from this. He cannot be intimidated, even by the threat of execution, because he is sure that his Almighty Father will raise him from the dead.

Finally, Jesus shows his mastery of the Scriptures by summarizing their essence. The first great command, "Love the Lord your God with all your heart and with all your soul and with all your mind," obligates us to respond to God's covenant love by loving him with our entire being. Obeying his second great command is similarly a response to his love: he loves our "neighbors" no less than he loves us, and so we learn to love them as we love ourselves. Jesus, the consummate Prophet of Israel, thus obligates us who follow him to fulfill the Law and the Prophets by the way we love. Then in prophetic style, he dramatizes and embodies love toward God and neighbor by hanging on a cross. All discipleship flows from this.[25]

## Matthew 22:41–46

[41] While the Pharisees were gathered together, Jesus asked them, [42] "What do you think about the Messiah? Whose son is he?"

"The son of David," they replied.

[43] He said to them, "How is it then that David, speaking by the Spirit, calls him 'Lord'? For he says,

[44] "'The Lord said to my Lord:
   "Sit at my right hand
until I put your enemies
      under your feet."'

[45] "If then David calls him 'Lord,' how can he be his son?" [46] No one could say a word in reply, and from that day on no one dared to ask him any more questions.

Jesus turns again to Scripture (Psalm 110) to give the people a last bold clue about the question that began today's reading, "Who is this?" Earlier in private, Peter acknowledged that Jesus is more than "one of the prophets"—he is the Messiah, the

Son of God. Now in public debate, Jesus affirms that he is more than David's royal son. More than a prophet, more than a king: he is King David's Lord, every prophet's Lord—every disciple's Lord. We yield our lives to him in reverence and awe.

*Jesus enters Jerusalem as King and Prophet, righteous, bold, and shrewd. Disciples will submit to his lordship and take up his prophetic work.*

**DAY 25**

# DO NOT DO WHAT THEY DO

Matthew 23

■ Matthew 23:1-15

**23** ¹ Then Jesus said to the crowds and to his disciples: ² "The teachers of the law and the Pharisees sit in Moses' seat. ³ So you must be careful to do everything they tell you. But do not do what they do, for they do not practice what they preach. ⁴ They tie up heavy, cumbersome loads and put them on other people's shoulders, but they themselves are not willing to lift a finger to move them. ⁵ "Everything they do is done for people to see: They make their phylacteries wide and the tassels on their garments long; ⁶ they love the place of honor at banquets and the most important seats in the synagogues; ⁷ they love to be greeted with respect in the marketplaces and to be called 'Rabbi' by others.

[8] "But you are not to be called 'Rabbi,' for you have one Teacher and you are all brothers. [9] And do not call anyone on earth 'father,' for you have one Father, and he is in heaven. [10] Nor are you to be called 'instructor,' for you have one Instructor, the Messiah. [11] The greatest among you will be your servant. [12] For those who exalt themselves will be humbled, and those who humble themselves will be exalted.

[13] "Woe to you, teachers of the law and Pharisees, you hypocrites! You shut the door of the kingdom of heaven in people's faces. You yourselves do not enter, nor will you let those enter who are trying to.

[15] "Woe to you, teachers of the law and Pharisees, you hypocrites! You travel over land and sea to win a single convert, and when you have succeeded, you make them twice as much a child of hell as you are."

Jesus continues his prophetic challenge to the authorities in Jerusalem, this time in an extended speech full of warnings about the Pharisees and teachers of the law. The Pharisees and law teachers provided the only access most people had to the Scriptures, through their public readings along with teachings about how to apply them. When Jesus says to do what they teach, he is saying to obey the Scriptural law (see 5:17–20). "But do not do what they do."

Throughout the chapter, Jesus confronts the powerful teachers directly, but he simultaneously warns his disciples not to pick up their bad habits. After criticizing the Pharisees' love of prestige, he turns to his followers: "But *you* . . . the greatest among you will be your servant." Disciples must not love too much the seats of honor, coveted invitations, or honorific titles, or they too will become oppressive and condescending. We read his sharp warnings to the ancient teachers, facing the possibility that they might apply just as well to us.

The teachers' legalism goes hand in hand with their pride. They don't just love being honored and celebrated, they believe they deserve it: their expertise about requirements for piety and their fixation on details establishes them as superior. In reality, they are turning God's life-giving instruction into burdensome rules, so that common folks despair of ever pleasing God. Meanwhile, they reinforce their prestige and power by training novices to become merciless clones of themselves. Toxic pride! No, "those who humble themselves will be exalted." How important humility must be to Jesus, since he presses the point so frequently!

## ▓ Matthew 23:16-28

[16] "Woe to you, blind guides! You say, 'If anyone swears by the temple, it means nothing; but anyone who swears by the gold of the temple is bound by that oath.' [17] You blind fools! Which is greater: the gold, or the temple that makes the gold sacred? [18] You also say, 'If anyone swears by the altar, it means nothing; but anyone who swears by the gift on the altar is bound by that oath.' [19] You blind men! Which is greater: the gift, or the altar that makes the gift sacred? [20] Therefore, anyone who swears by the altar swears by it and by everything on it. [21] And anyone who swears by the temple swears by it and by the one who dwells in it. [22] And anyone who swears by heaven swears by God's throne and by the one who sits on it.

[23] "Woe to you, teachers of the law and Pharisees, you hypocrites! You give a tenth of your spices—mint, dill and cumin. But you have neglected the more important matters of the law—justice, mercy and faithfulness. You should have practiced the latter, without neglecting the former. [24] You blind guides! You strain out a gnat but swallow a camel.

[25] "Woe to you, teachers of the law and Pharisees, you hypocrites! You clean the outside of the cup and dish, but inside they are full of greed and self-indulgence. [26] Blind Pharisee! First clean the inside of the cup and dish, and then the outside also will be clean.

[27] "Woe to you, teachers of the law and Pharisees, you hypocrites! You are like whitewashed tombs, which look beautiful on the outside but on the inside are full of the bones of the dead and

everything unclean. [28] In the same way, on the outside you appear to people as righteous but on the inside you are full of hypocrisy and wickedness."

Hypocrites are people who "do not practice what they preach." They are impressive on the outside, but rotten on the inside. They are all show. They cultivate people's esteem by disguising the truth about themselves.

Blind guides are people who preach what's not worth practicing. They have plenty to say, but they lose sight of the goal and lead others onto detours and dead ends. As examples, Jesus points to the Pharisees' fussing about how to phrase their oaths, while they remain blind to the goal of being truthful; and their giving a tithe (a tenth) of every little thing they receive, while they remain blind to the goal of becoming generous. Using the comical image of filtering a gnat out of a beverage but then swallowing a camel, he ridicules their obsessing over pet subjects while being unable to see God's biggest concerns: justice, mercy, and faithfulness.

"Do not do as they do." Jesus forbids his disciples to acquire the teachers' arrogance, hypocrisy, and spiritual blindness. As a sample of how we could apply the teachings of Matthew 23 today, I propose to consider the church's dilemma regarding homosexuality. How shall disciples speak, especially when speaking on behalf of the church? How shall disciples act in order to "practice the more important matters of the law—justice, mercy and faithfulness"— without neglecting the requirements Jesus does not emphasize (verse 23)? How might humility, integrity, and clearer spiritual perception make a difference?

In the Gospels, Jesus never directly mentions the Old Testament law that sternly forbids same-sex intercourse (Leviticus 18:22; 20:13). The matter likely never came up, because there was no debate among the Jews of his day: homosexual sex was out of bounds. That Jesus would have endorsed this prohibition is evident even from Matthew's limited material. Jesus says that he came "not to abolish the [Old Testament] Law, but to fulfill it" through his disciples' righteous living (5:17–19; 23:2–3). Jesus did assert the authority to interpret the Law anew by penetrating to its core meaning, but in doing so he did not apparently reverse its standards for sexual conduct. In his list of misbehaviors that come from within and defile a person (15:19), Jesus includes *porneia*, a general term for sexual immorality, which in Jewish law and thought would have included homosexual sex. We would very likely know about it if Jesus had permitted it among his followers, because his critics would have used the issue forcefully in their public efforts to discredit him.[26] Positively, Jesus cites the biblical law's foundation, declaring God's creation intent for gender and sexuality: "At the beginning the Creator made them male and female, and said, 'for this reason a man will . . . be united to his wife and the two will become one flesh'" (19:4–5). Sexual union is for husband and wife in marriage. Without claiming to have addressed every possible question, I will proceed from this evidence that Jesus would have prohibited same-sex intercourse. Everything we say or do in light of this prohibition must be governed not by arrogance, hypocrisy, or spiritual blindness, but by what he calls the "the more important matters of the law—justice, mercy and faithfulness."

Jesus requires humility. He forbids all disdain and superior posturing by which people gain prestige from those who share their views. We would have to admit that some who speak on the subject of homosexuality in our churches exhibit disdain, encourage others to share their disdain, and build their reputations by the vigor of their scorn (toward homosexual persons or toward people in the opposite camp in the debates). The resulting angry exchanges tear churches and denominations apart. People who are attracted to the same sex (including indisputably innocent people who are not sexually active) hear church members' contemptuous words toward one another or toward homosexuals, and they decide they want nothing to do with Jesus or his people. Churches thereby effectively "shut the door of the kingdom of heaven in people's faces."

Neither side in the heated debates is immune from Pharisee-like practices. We become hypocrites and blind guides when we lose sight of the core message of the kingdom—namely, that life is in Jesus. Instead, our culture tells us above all to search for that "soul mate," that romantic love that is "forever," and to fulfill our passion for it at all costs. This idolizing of being in love often shapes the culture within our churches, and much (heterosexual) mischief and sadness follows. Teenagers have sex because they "truly love" their partner. Young adults feel embarrassed if they do not have a boyfriend or girlfriend. Some drift into marriage with an unsuitable partner for fear that this might be their last chance for love. From marriages that do not sustain a constant glow of feeling in love, some stray into adultery or divorce in pursuit of greater romance. Many who do enjoy their marriages boast about it and feed the perception that only people who experience fulfilling romance are on the right track. When people in such a setting then scold those who are attracted to the same sex for pursuing *their* romantic interests, they become hypocrites. When they do the opposite and encourage them to pursue their romantic interests as the essential means to fulfill their personal identity, they become blind guides.

To see clearly, it helps to consider wealth as an analogy for romantic life. People would like to have money. Some Christians have it abundantly, and some do not. When acquired legitimately, it is a gift from God. Money has real advantages, and a kind of happiness may come with it. But it is not life, and it disappoints those who expect it to give them life. Many would rather pursue money than faithfulness to God, so money chokes out the word of life in their hearts (13:22; 19:24). Money is not the all-important treasure in the field or the valuable pearl Jesus spoke of in his parables (13:44–45); the thing worth having at all costs is the life of the kingdom experienced through living with and for Jesus.

Now substitute romantic love for wealth, and the same statements apply. People would like to have satisfying romantic love. Some

Christians have it abundantly, and some do not. When acquired legitimately, it is a gift from God. It has real advantages, and a kind of happiness comes with it. But it is not life, and it disappoints those who expect it to give them life. Many would rather pursue romantic love than holy faithfulness to God, so it becomes one of the cares of the world that chokes out the word of life in many hearts (13:22). Romantic love is not the treasure in the field or the valuable pearl worth attaining at all costs; the thing worth having is a close, heart-to-heart bond with the living Lord Jesus.

The new life comes as we take up the cross; that is, the painful loss of what we previously thought of as life. Not to have a romantic life or a live-in family will often be perceived and experienced as a severe loss or deprivation. The same can be said about not receiving other gifts that God gives to many of his people but not to everyone, such as consistent good health, childbearing, success in the workplace, peace rather than war, and so on. We may grieve and become angry toward God when others have those benefits and we cannot. But for people who seek their life in Christ, over time God uses those very losses or "deprivations" to bring unanticipated blessings, opportunities to serve others, and deeper intimacy with him. Jesus' promise is, "Whoever loses their life for me will find it"—their life, their true self, their wholeness (16:25).

Jesus chides the Pharisees and law teachers because they "tie up heavy, cumbersome loads and put them on other people's shoulders, but they themselves are not willing to lift a finger to move them." The pressure from advocates on one side or the other in the debates increases the already heavy loads being carried by those who find themselves conflicted about their gender or attracted to the same sex. Often they have experienced rejection, even from family members. Many face a crisis of loneliness. They may also feel guilt or sadness because their experience has thrown loved ones into turmoil. Their family members and friends may carry burdens, too—pain, guilt, bafflement, or alienation. The weight of all this can be overwhelming. How can we "lift a finger" (and our backs and shoulders) to help people bear these burdens? How can churches pursue justice and mercy?

We can communicate clearly to persons who are attracted to the same sex that God embraces them as his beloved children. They are not a disappointment to him because of feelings they have which they have not chosen to have. (Remember that feeling attraction is not the same as lusting, which Jesus does forbid.) We can become models of restraint and wisdom in our humor and our politics. We can esteem singleness in honor of the Savior who personally modeled sexually abstinent singleness as a path of joy and liberty. We can become brother or sister, father or mother to those who yearn for relationship, committed to them in love as Jesus' family. We can convey respect, as having something to learn from their story, not just something to teach. We can think creatively with new converts who have been living in committed homosexual partnerships, perhaps raising children together, about how they might appropriately keep some old promises as they work out their new obedience to Jesus. In all of this, we can lighten others' burdens only as we ourselves take up Jesus' "light burden," the obedient life.

We who follow Jesus are a community of sexual sinners (through lust or physical indulgence) who have committed ourselves to leave all of that behind and become holy. We all have sexual feelings from time to time that we would be wrong to act upon, so we have reason to be compassionate rather than superior toward others who are tempted. Together we seek healing and wholeness through God's power. We become just and merciful as we thank God who forgives us and as we treat everyone respectfully. We learn to extend to each other the same combination of merciful love and call to higher righteousness that Jesus continually extends to us.

Not all will be won over to this program of renewal. For the member who insists on continuing in sinful practices—of any kind—Jesus teaches a just and merciful procedure to invite change (18:15–17). That procedure may sometimes culminate in a parting of ways. When it does, the church can pray, trusting the Shepherd to continue pursuing his sheep (18:12–14).[27]

Consensus about this subject has been notoriously difficult to achieve. Our challenge is to pursue justice, mercy, and faithfulness to God in this and every issue we face in the churches. We will do more harm than good if we do not heed Jesus' urgent warnings against arrogance, hypocrisy, and spiritual blindness. We will find our way toward peace by humbly, habitually yielding to Jesus, who calms our belligerency and holds us close (verse 37, below).

## Matthew 23:29-39

[29] "Woe to you, teachers of the law and Pharisees, you hypocrites! You build tombs for the prophets and decorate the graves of the righteous. [30] And you say, 'If we had lived in the days of our ancestors, we would not have taken part with them in shedding the blood of the prophets.' [31] So you testify against yourselves that you are the descendants of those who murdered the prophets. [32] Go ahead, then, and complete what your ancestors started!

[33] "You snakes! You brood of vipers! How will you escape being condemned to hell? [34] Therefore I am sending you prophets and sages and teachers. Some of them you will kill and crucify; others you will flog in your synagogues and pursue from town to town. [35] And so upon you will come all the righteous blood that has been shed on earth, from the blood of righteous Abel to the blood of Zechariah son of Berekiah, whom you murdered between the temple and the altar. [36] Truly I tell you, all this will come on this generation.

[37] "Jerusalem, Jerusalem, you who kill the prophets and stone those sent to you, how often I have longed to gather your children together, as a hen gathers her chicks under her wings, and you were not willing. [38] Look, your house is left to you desolate. [39] For I tell you, you will not see me again until you say, 'Blessed is he who comes in the name of the Lord.'"

This passage concludes the section about Jesus' public ministry as God's prophet in Jerusalem (21:9–23:39). In that role, he boldly challenges his people and their leaders to depart from corruption and receive him. He is brilliant and courageous in every encounter. Even when he speaks severely, he continues to love those he criticizes: "How I have longed to gather you together, as a hen gathers her chicks under her wings." His heart breaks as he rebukes them.

Discipleship entails imitating our Teacher-Prophet, Jesus. He has said that he will send out some of his disciples as prophets (verse 34)—and any of us may be required at times to speak righteous words to the powerful. It is not sub-Christian to rebuke people appropriately. A necessary part of the kingdom work is to stand against meanness and injustice. Jesus can warn arrogant leaders forcefully and effectively because he is no hypocrite. So too with disciples; only genuinely righteous people can credibly challenge corruption.

*As disciples, we neither follow nor resemble hypocritical leaders; rather we support one another justly and mercifully as we work out our obedience to God.*

# DAY 26 | WHOEVER STANDS FIRM

## Matthew 24:1-36

In this fifth and final concentrated section of Jesus' teachings (Matthew 24–25), he fortifies his disciples to help them remain steady and faithful, ready to serve him effectively in the world. He intensifies his previous warnings about devious people and ominous circumstances that could tempt his followers to collapse.

■ Matthew 24:1-3

**24** ¹ Jesus left the temple and was walking away when his disciples came up to him to call his attention to its buildings. ² "Do you see all these things?" he asked. "Truly I tell you, not one stone here will be left on another; every one will be thrown down." ³ As Jesus was sitting on the Mount of Olives, the disciples came to him privately. "Tell us," they said, "when will this happen, and what will be the sign of your coming and of the end of the age?"

Jesus predicts the destruction of Jerusalem's great buildings, including the temple, an event that did come to pass about forty years later with the Roman military action of the year 70. The disciples ask him two questions: "When will this happen, and what will be the sign of your coming and of the end of the age?" By pairing these questions, Jesus' disciples assume that the destruction in Jerusalem and the end of the age (Jesus' coming in glory) will be the same event. We who live after the year 70 recognize them as two distinct events, but Jesus' extended answer to their questions pertains to both events equally, so that his warnings and commands apply to the earliest disciples but also to every subsequent generation. Matthew 24 concentrates on the danger of falling away due to deceivers or brutal enemies. Matthew 25 warns of the more subtle danger of missing out due to apathy or loss of focus.

## Matthew 24:4-14

⁴ Jesus answered: "Watch out that no one deceives you. ⁵ For many will come in my name, claiming, 'I am the Messiah,' and will deceive many. ⁶ You will hear of wars and rumors of wars, but see to it that you are not alarmed. Such things must happen, but the end is still to come. ⁷ Nation will rise against nation, and kingdom against kingdom. There will be famines and earthquakes in various places. ⁸ All these are the beginning of birth pains.

⁹ "Then you will be handed over to be persecuted and put to death, and you will be hated by all nations because of me. ¹⁰ At that time many will turn away from the faith and will betray and hate each other, ¹¹ and many false prophets will appear and deceive many people. ¹² Because of the increase of wickedness, the love of most will grow cold, ¹³ but the one who stands firm to the end will be saved. ¹⁴ And this gospel of the kingdom will be preached in the whole world as a testimony to all nations, and then the end will come."

Jesus does not satisfy their curiosity about when the end will come, other than to say that the disciples' assigned task must be completed first. That assignment is to preach the gospel of the kingdom in the whole world. The disciples' mission to give "testimony to all nations" carries forward the Messiah's mission to fulfill Israel's destiny. God had promised Abraham, the father of Israel, that all nations would be blessed through his offspring (Genesis 12:3). God's words of testimony about Jesus at his baptism and his transfiguration recall phrases from Psalm 2 and Isaiah 42, both of which speak of the Messiah's eventual worldwide success. Jesus' vision for his disciples is that we will join him in conveying his great global salvation, which God planned from the beginning. The whole world needs to hear our proclamation of the gospel (good news) that God's merciful reign has come (verse 14). All of our accompanying efforts to heal and feed people, to overcome evil and relieve misery, serve to verify our central message that God gives life through Jesus.

To fulfill our assignment, disciples are called to stand firm to the end despite dire circumstances. Jesus admonishes us as his apprentices never to lose focus on our task, never to give up in the face of opposition. He is greatly concerned that disciples might fall away. Some certainly will, he says (verse 10), but the mark of the saved is that they stand firm to the end. What could induce disciples to fail?

### ■ Matthew 24:15-31

15 "So when you see standing in the holy place 'the abomination that causes desolation,' spoken of through the prophet Daniel—let the reader understand— 16 then let those who are in Judea flee to the mountains. 17 Let no one on the housetop go down to take anything out of the house. 18 Let no one in the field go back to get their cloak. 19 How dreadful it will be in those days for pregnant women and nursing mothers! 20 Pray that your flight will not take place in winter or on the Sabbath. 21 For then there will be great distress, unequaled from the beginning of the world until now—and never to be equaled again.

22 "If those days had not been cut short, no one would survive, but for the sake of the elect those days will be shortened. 23 At that time if anyone says to you, 'Look, here is the Messiah!' or, 'There he is!' do not believe it. 24 For false messiahs and false prophets will appear and perform great signs and wonders to deceive, if possible, even the elect. 25 See, I have told you ahead of time.

26 "So if anyone tells you, 'There he is, out in the wilderness,' do not go out; or, 'Here he is, in the inner rooms,' do not believe it. 27 For as lightning that comes from the east is visible even in the

west, so will be the coming of the Son of Man. [28] Wherever there is a carcass, there the vultures will gather.

[29] "Immediately after the distress of those days

> "'the sun will be darkened,
>     and the moon will not give its light;
> the stars will fall from the sky,
>     and the heavenly bodies will be shaken.'

[30] "Then will appear the sign of the Son of Man in heaven. And then all the peoples of the earth will mourn when they see the Son of Man coming on the clouds of heaven, with power and great glory. [31] And he will send his angels with a loud trumpet call, and they will gather his elect from the four winds, from one end of the heavens to the other."

Jesus points to two perils that could knock out disciples who hope to stand firm: hardship and deception. Violent invasion and sustained persecution will bring "distress unequaled from the beginning," a situation in which the only course is to flee without delay. Jesus can say to stand firm (verse 13) and then to flee (verse 16) without contradicting himself. God uses the relocation of his servants for his good purposes, and on the way, faithful refugees serve other refugees. To stand firm does mean to remain loyal to Jesus, no matter what. Jesus tells his disciples to expect that our praying will affect the way events unfold (verse 20). God will limit the severity and duration of our suffering.

It is bad enough when outsiders persecute believers. It is even more ominous when believers harden their hearts toward each other. Jesus predicts that some of his followers will betray and hate each other, and their love will grow cold (verses 10–12). By this warning he urges his disciples to continue to support one other—that is, to be the church to one another—and not to let our love grow cold.

Especially in times of stress, deceivers arise—charismatic leaders who manipulate impressionable or hyper-zealous people. Jesus repeatedly warns disciples not to be fooled by awe-inspiring personalities (verses 4–5, 11, 23–26). Some charlatans even claim to be the returned Messiah or claim that the Messiah has returned in a way that only the cult's insiders have detected. They lie. Jesus insists that his own return will be such a spectacular event that no one can miss it when it happens (verses 27–31).

The danger for disciples comes from dynamic leaders who speak passionately about God and who convince their loyalists that they are joining a movement of exceptionally committed, spiritual people. Such leaders demand extraordinary contributions of time, money, and sacrifice. They portray any church or movement besides their own as inferior and encourage their followers to scorn the Christians they previously respected. They exhaust their followers' time and energy so that they lose regular contact with friends and family members who could offer perspective. These egotists speak enough truth and use Jesus' name enough and cite enough Scripture that followers let their guard down. Some heighten their appeal by performing public "signs and wonders." Jesus commands his disciples, "Watch out that no one deceives you." Sometimes the most serious Christians are the most vulnerable to being deceived, because they are attracted to such leaders' call to great commitment. Jesus has taught us to examine the character of these "prophets" ("by their fruit you will recognize them," 7:15–20) and to immerse ourselves sufficiently in Scripture to recognize when they distort its message (22:29). Jesus himself remains the center of reality, and the mark of a trustworthy leader is humble submission to him.

## Matthew 24:32-36

³² "Now learn this lesson from the fig tree: As soon as its twigs get tender and its leaves come out, you know that summer is near. ³³ Even so, when you see all these things, you know that it is near, right at the door. ³⁴ Truly I tell you, this generation will certainly not pass away until all these things have happened. ³⁵ Heaven and earth will pass away, but my words will never pass away.

³⁶ "But about that day or hour no one knows, not even the angels in heaven, nor the Son, but only the Father."

Jesus' purpose with these words is to strengthen his disciples' commitment and faithfulness to him. He limits the shock of the coming troubles by predicting them. If he had not given these warnings, his followers who get caught in the violent crossfire of world events might conclude that God's reign is not penetrating into the world after all. But the Savior himself goes to a cross, and so disciples will not be immune from violence. Jesus has a bitter cup to drink, and his disciples will drink that cup with him (20:23). Many disciples in the world's trouble spots will face intensified danger precisely because they participate in giving "testimony to all nations." "See to it that you are not alarmed," he says. "Such things must happen."

Jesus appears to be intentionally ambiguous about when the end will come. We are permitted to "know that it is near, right at the door," yet he insists that "about that day or hour no one knows." The mystery is heightened by the double horizon of his prophecy. By their double question in 24:3, the disciples weave together two events: the coming destruction of the temple and the end of time. Jesus similarly integrates the two events in his answer. His prophecies apply indistinguishably to the coming judgment upon Jerusalem in the year 70 and to the final destruction of God's enemies when Jesus will return in glory.

This phenomenon that prophecies often have more than one horizon helps us make sense of much that we find in Matthew. I think back to a visit to King's Canyon, one of California's beautiful national parks. I followed a trail up a high peak, from which I could look out and see seven distinct mountain ranges, each more distant than the one before. A photograph of that scene can capture some of its beauty, but the distance between the several ranges disappears. It flattens out and looks like a single range. Biblical prophecy is often like the photograph. It portrays short-term events and far-distant events in one picture so that the distance between them is obscured. For example, Isaiah's prophecy about a child's birth indicating "God with us" pointed in the first instance to political events surrounding King Ahaz hundreds of years before Jesus. Matthew sees a new and greater fulfillment of "God with us" in the Virgin Mary's son (1:22–23). Similarly, John the Baptist's announcement of salvation (3:2–3) fulfills Isaiah 40, whose initial horizon was Israel's return home from the Babylonian exile centuries earlier.

But John himself is perplexed by the double horizon of the Old Testament's prophecies about the Day of the Lord. He sees only a single horizon: he expects that Jesus' emergence in Galilee is God's appointed time of final judgment (3:10–12), and so he becomes disillusioned with Jesus' gentleness and sends messengers to seek assurance that Jesus really is the one who was to come (11:2–3). But Jesus sees two horizons: the kingdom is present already in Jesus' ministry (just as John announced), but God's ultimate judgment remains in the future when Jesus will return in glory.

As we read Matthew 24, we find ourselves between two horizons. Jesus' prophecy of judgment toward Jerusalem is already fulfilled in our past, but his return to judge humanity and complete his victory over evil remains in our future. His decision not to disentangle his dual prophecies of judgment as he speaks to the Twelve on the Mount of Olives provides an important benefit to disciples. It helped the first Christians to remain faithful and strong during the Roman destruction of Jerusalem, but also to continue spreading the good news when the times of distress turned out not to be the end. We too can prepare for each new crisis with the seriousness appropriate to the end of time, but whether or not our crisis turns out to be the end, we can remain focused on our assignment to transform our hurting world and make Jesus known.

Jesus' prophecy about tribulations and deceivers prior to the end helps disciples remain steadfast. We could say that his prophecy is like that view from the California mountaintop in that not just two horizons but several horizons stretch out beyond Jesus' day. In many times and places over the centuries since Jesus spoke, disciples have faced such sustained and intense tribulation that his words about coming troubles seemed to describe their very situation. Because he warned in advance about how intense the troubles could become, his followers have received strength to endure unspeakable suffering while remaining true to Jesus. Whenever persecutors and deceivers temporarily succeed, Jesus' words reassure us that God is still in control.

Jesus' "lesson from the fig tree" counsels believers to fortify one another during tribulation as if the end has come, so that we do not fall away. At the same time, by insisting that we will not know the day or the hour, he warns us not to get caught up in speculating about precisely when this may happen. Those who speculate or make pronouncements about the time of Jesus' coming distract many from the work he has given us to do and damage the credibility of the Christian movement.

Jesus' paramount proclamation in this chapter is that he, the Son of Man, will prevail in the end. His boldness is breathtaking: "Heaven and earth will pass away, but my words will never pass away." He declares that God will sound his trumpet, and people worldwide (faithful and unfaithful) will "see the Son of Man coming on the clouds of heaven, with power and great glory." Whatever tribulations we face, whether they affect multitudes or just us alone, we are right to stand firmly faithful to Jesus. And we are right to continue serving him and speaking his good news as much as we are able. As I write, I have just returned from a conversation at the hospital with a friend's mother, whose body is rapidly shutting down. Today is her dying day. She is nevertheless full of praise for Jesus, who is her hope and her certain future. Though our world as we have experienced it passes away before our eyes through suffering, disability, loss, or death, Jesus' words of promise will never pass away. He is the King of the world who will reign unopposed in the end, and we who belong to him will reign with him.

230 PARTNERING WITH THE KING

*esus fortifies us against the danger of falling away due to persecutors or deceivers so we will receive life and will persist in bearing witness about him.*

## DAY 27 | WELL DONE

Matthew 24:36-25:46

It is no surprise that persecutors or deceivers could cause believers to fall away. The hazard Jesus points to in this chapter, however, is more subtle and therefore more dangerous. Disciples may be lulled into inaction and fall away from God when daily life becomes routine and Jesus' return seems remote.

### ■ Matthew 24:36-51

36 "But about that day or hour no one knows, not even the angels in heaven, nor the Son, but only the Father. 37 As it was in the days of Noah, so it will be at the coming of the Son of Man. 38 For in the days before the flood, people were eating and drinking, marrying and giving in marriage, up to the day Noah entered the ark; 39 and they knew nothing about what would happen until the flood came and took them all away. That is how it will be at the coming of the Son of Man. 40 Two men will be in the field; one will be taken and the other left. 41 Two women will be grinding with a hand mill; one will be taken and the other left.

$^{42}$ "Therefore keep watch, because you do not know on what day your Lord will come. $^{43}$ But understand this: If the owner of the house had known at what time of night the thief was coming, he would have kept watch and would not have let his house be broken into. $^{44}$ So you also must be ready, because the Son of Man will come at an hour when you do not expect him.

$^{45}$ "Who then is the faithful and wise servant, whom the master has put in charge of the servants in his household to give them their food at the proper time? $^{46}$ It will be good for that servant whose master finds him doing so when he returns. $^{47}$ Truly I tell you, he will put him in charge of all his possessions. $^{48}$ But suppose that servant is wicked and says to himself, 'My master is staying away a long time,' $^{49}$ and he then begins to beat his fellow servants and to eat and drink with drunkards. $^{50}$ The master of that servant will come on a day when he does not expect him and at an hour he is not aware of. $^{51}$ He will cut him to pieces and assign him a place with the hypocrites, where there will be weeping and gnashing of tooth."

Here are four stories (Noah and the flood, the pairs of day laborers, the thief in the night, and the wicked servant) that illustrate a point stated four times (verses 36, 42, 44, and 50): "You must be ready, because the Son of Man will come at an hour when you do not expect him." Everyone will be accountable to Jesus, and our accountability will come at a time we do not expect. Every day we live is more important than it appears.

The people in the stories are doing the normal things of life. Noah's contemporaries are "eating and drinking, marrying and giving in marriage." The day workers are laboring in a field or grinding at a mill. The homeowner goes to bed at home night after night. The steward has daily responsibilities for an estate. None of the characters in these stories are aware that one particular day will bring a critical surprise. All are lulled into a disastrous kind of napping by the unremarkable circumstances of their lives.

In our workaday lives, we can become numb to the reality of God and of our responsibility to him. Our surroundings conspire to give us the impression that he is not around. If God comes to mind for a moment, the thought will evaporate as we get back to "real life." But it is perilous to ignore him. The last of the four stories is the most ominous, because the servant gets worse and worse. He not only loses focus on his assignment, he turns wicked and becomes a liability to his master.

The point is not that if Jesus returns when you happen to be having a bad day, you have had it. Rather, Jesus warns about a prolonged trend of life in which a person forgets God and abandons his way. Remembering God and our responsibility to him requires a constant discipline of praying and meditating on Scripture and participating in church life. By such disciplines we override the spiritually numbing effect of our surroundings.

As we bring Jesus to mind and seek for his will to be done, we will serve him well. "It will be good for that servant whose master finds him doing so when he returns. . . . He will put him in charge of all his possessions." To be entrusted with responsibility in the Lord's business is the reward. Partnership in his affairs is true life.

### ▧ Matthew 25:1–13

**25** ¹ "At that time the kingdom of heaven will be like ten virgins who took their lamps and went out to meet the bridegroom. ² Five of them were foolish and five were wise. ³ The foolish ones took their lamps but did not take any oil with them. ⁴ The wise ones, however, took oil in jars along with their lamps. ⁵ The bridegroom was a long time in coming, and they all became drowsy and fell asleep.

⁶ "At midnight the cry rang out: 'Here's the bridegroom! Come out to meet him!'

⁷ "Then all the virgins woke up and trimmed their lamps. ⁸ The foolish ones said to the wise, 'Give us some of your oil; our lamps are going out.'

⁹ "'No,' they replied, 'there may not be enough for both us and you. Instead, go to those who sell oil and buy some for yourselves.'
¹⁰ "But while they were on their way to buy the oil, the bridegroom arrived. The virgins who were ready went in with him to the wedding banquet. And the door was shut.
¹¹ "Later the others also came. 'Lord, Lord,' they said, 'open the door for us!'
¹² "But he replied, 'Truly I tell you, I don't know you.'
¹³ "Therefore keep watch, because you do not know the day or the hour."

For the third time in Matthew, Jesus compares himself to a groom at the time of a wedding (see 9:15 and 22:2). In each story, his arrival is the decisive moment for everyone around him. In this parable, the groom arrives later than his friends expect, and many of them are unprepared for the long wait. They fall asleep and their lights go out. They have anticipated joining in the groom's celebration and blessing, but instead they find themselves excluded. They knock desperately, but they hear, "I don't know you" (that is, "I don't want anything to do with you"). People who have thought they are insiders will be left horribly on the outside.

This story, like the one about the thief in the night (24:43), tells believers to "keep watch." The life of discipleship is marked by constantly expecting to see Jesus. At a down-to-earth level, we learn to detect his presence in the scenes of our day where others do not notice him. On a higher level, we joyfully anticipate his glorious return, much the same way that a soldier's children wait for Daddy to come home at last.

The wise virgins who took oil along with their lamps symbolize wise believers who think beyond the current moment. We need to consider seriously how to build our whole lives upon the rock of faithfulness to Jesus. Again, spiritual disciplines such as meditation, prayer, fasting, Bible study, worship, and service help us to maintain focus on the big picture and to sustain our devotion for the long haul. We do not undertake spiritual disciplines to prove ourselves or to earn inclusion, but to fuel our minds so that the light of Jesus shines in our hearts all the time.

## ■ Matthew 25:14-30

[14] "Again, it will be like a man going on a journey, who called his servants and entrusted his wealth to them. [15] To one he gave five bags of gold, to another two bags, and to another one bag, each according to his ability. Then he went on his journey. [16] The man who had received five bags of gold went at once and put his money to work and gained five bags more. [17] So also, the one with two bags of gold gained two more. [18] But the man who had received one bag went off, dug a hole in the ground and hid his master's money.

[19] "After a long time the master of those servants returned and settled accounts with them. [20] The man who had received five bags of gold brought the other five. 'Master,' he said, 'you entrusted me with five bags of gold. See, I have gained five more.'

[21] "His master replied, 'Well done, good and faithful servant! You have been faithful with a few things; I will put you in charge of many things. Come and share your master's happiness!'

[22] "The man with two bags of gold also came. 'Master,' he said, 'you entrusted me with two bags of gold; see, I have gained two more.'

[23] "His master replied, 'Well done, good and faithful servant! You have been faithful with a few things; I will put you in charge of many things. Come and share your master's happiness!'

[24] "Then the man who had received one bag of gold came. 'Master,' he said, 'I knew that you are a hard man, harvesting where you have not sown and gathering where you have not scattered seed. [25] So I was afraid and went out and hid your gold in the ground. See, here is what belongs to you.'

[26] "His master replied, 'You wicked, lazy servant! So you knew that I harvest where I have not sown and gather where I have not scattered seed? [27] Well then, you should have put my money on

deposit with the bankers, so that when I returned I would have received it back with interest.

<sup>28</sup> "'So take the bag of gold from him and give it to the one who has ten bags. <sup>29</sup> For whoever has will be given more, and they will have an abundance. Whoever does not have, even what they have will be taken from them. <sup>30</sup> And throw that worthless servant outside, into the darkness, where there will be weeping and gnashing of teeth.'"

Again in this parable, the question is how servants will handle their responsibility while the master is "away." All three servants are entrusted with the master's funds. He does not distribute the portions evenly, but he gives to each servant a generous portion to manage. The phrase "bag of gold" translates the word *talent*, representing the enormous sum of fifty to seventy-five pounds of gold. The word stands behind our English term *talent*, meaning "skill or gift." No one of us has been left out in God's generous distribution of gifts to use for his purposes.

The first two servants are faithful with the gold the master has entrusted to them, and they hear the words every disciple wishes to hear in the end, "Well done, good and faithful servant!" Notice again that the master's reward to his servants is to entrust to them more of the master's enterprise (verses 21 and 23; also 24:45–47). We share our master's joy as we take all that he has given us and employ it for him: our resources, our talents, our relationships, our whole lives. And our joy will soar when he comes in glory: "Come and share your master's happiness!"

By contrast, the third servant is punished for inaction. We may think of sin primarily as a matter of doing bad things, but the master is angry with his servant for doing nothing at all. The servant's heart is bitter toward his master. Inaction and loathing feed each other. The musician who practices little begins to hate practicing at all. The athlete who rarely works out hates workouts and begins to despise the coach, too. Those who serve God little begin to resent God for expecting them to serve. The very activity that could bring joy becomes something to detest. If we are feeling disgruntled toward God, often the solution is to activate our discipleship, taking up the spiritual disciplines and doing service with fellow disciples. Otherwise, we will lose all energy to serve him, our discipleship will collapse, and we will lose even the benefits we had. The characteristic of the kingdom is that people who are gaining in the life with God continue to gain more and those who are slipping away risk losing everything (verse 29; see also 13:12).

■ Matthew 25:31-46

³¹ "When the Son of Man comes in his glory, and all the angels with him, he will sit on his glorious throne. ³² All the nations will be gathered before him, and he will separate the people one from another as a shepherd separates the sheep from the goats. ³³ He will put the sheep on his right and the goats on his left.

³⁴ "Then the King will say to those on his right, 'Come, you who are blessed by my Father; take your inheritance, the kingdom prepared for you since the creation of the world. ³⁵ For I was hungry and you gave me something to eat, I was thirsty and you gave me something to drink, I was a stranger and you invited me in, ³⁶ I needed clothes and you clothed me, I was sick and you looked after me, I was in prison and you came to visit me.'

³⁷ "Then the righteous will answer him, 'Lord, when did we see you hungry and feed you, or thirsty and give you something to drink? ³⁸ When did we see you a stranger and invite you in, or needing clothes and clothe you? ³⁹ When did we see you sick or in prison and go to visit you?'

⁴⁰ "The King will reply, 'Truly I tell you, whatever you did for one of the least of these brothers and sisters of mine, you did for me.'

⁴¹ "Then he will say to those on his left, 'Depart from me, you who are cursed, into the eternal fire prepared for the devil and his angels. ⁴² For I was hungry and you gave me nothing to eat, I was thirsty and you gave me nothing to drink, ⁴³ I was a stranger and

you did not invite me in, I needed clothes and you did not clothe me, I was sick and in prison and you did not look after me.'

⁴⁴ "They also will answer, 'Lord, when did we see you hungry or thirsty or a stranger or needing clothes or sick or in prison, and did not help you?'

⁴⁵ "He will reply, 'Truly I tell you, whatever you did not do for one of the least of these, you did not do for me.'

⁴⁶ "Then they will go away to eternal punishment, but the righteous to eternal life."

Nowhere in Matthew does Jesus make a bolder claim of authority. He is the Son of Man (Daniel 7:9–10, 13–14) who will come in glory, accompanied by angels, enthroned as the Judge and Lord of humankind. He has authority both to bless lavishly and to condemn, to include people in the final joys or to exclude them. Each person will either receive an inheritance that God has prepared since creation or be expelled into a realm never intended for human beings at all, but for the devil and his demons. The distinguishing characteristic of people who are included in eternal life is their kindness toward Jesus, shown by how they have treated the lowliest human beings they encounter. The same story that proclaims Jesus' glorious majesty displays his lowly identification with people at the bottom rank. So each day of our lives, however uneventful it may seem, is more momentous than we imagine, because during that day we either respect or despise Jesus by the way we treat others. Who is the person our group tacitly agrees is fair game for ridicule? We are ridiculing Jesus. Who are the people we walk past every day whose line of work (or lack of work) puts them beneath us? It is Jesus whom we have made our inferior. Who in our city or thousands of miles away lacks the barest necessities of life? It is Jesus who feels hungry, thirsty, and cold. Disciples learn to see with new eyes, now recognizing that previously invisible people are so important that they personally represent the Son of God.

Jesus praises deeds of mercy that flow out naturally from disciples' hearts because they love him. To say that Jesus expects action and that he will reward such action at the judgment is not to say that we are saved by doing good works. Jesus delights in people who are not self-conscious or self-serving with their good works: "Lord, when did we see you hungry and feed you, or thirsty and give you something to drink?" It is not that good works achieve salvation for a person, but that merciful deeds are the mark of persons who have entered into the saved life. The acts of kindness are not something to do now in order to be OK after we die; rather, they flow routinely from people who have already transferred into the kingdom. We have been saved into a new kind of living, in which God's kindness prevails.

The parable fleshes out what it means to be ready, watchful, and prepared. It means to be actively doing the kinds of things Jesus does all the time. These verses unmistakably emphasize working to combat poverty and injustice. Earlier verses emphasized telling people the good news of God's reign through Jesus (24:14). Mercy and proclamation: the two tasks reinforce each other.

I served as pastor with a small congregation in Los Angeles that loved the good news but nevertheless had become ingrown and discouraged. Members were drifting away and the building felt emptier every week. To our surprise, a bright future opened up when we decided to quit worrying about our shrinkage and invest in caring for marginalized people outside our walls. Through sustained prayer asking for God's guidance, we were led into partnership with an inner-city church dedicated to serving the unemployed, hungry, and drug addicted. We welcomed a new congregation of poor immigrants into our facilities and our hearts. And we actively joined a network of churches that were proclaiming Jesus and doing charity among an unreached, economically depressed ethnic group halfway around the world. As a result of serving the hungry, people lacking clothes and shoes, refugees from prison, and foreigners, a church that few had wanted to join became magnetic, joyful, and fruitful.

Again, it is not that we have to prove ourselves by sufficient service. Nor is it that ministry to people within the church is devalued by contrast to ministry to those "outside." The parable's message is rather that the outflow of healthy, joyful discipleship is that we are involved for Jesus rather than being idle and callous. Our interface with the people in our world has a holy dimension. We are meeting surrogates for Jesus at every turn. The grave danger is to be lulled asleep by the ordinariness of life and miss the sacredness of the people around us and the reality of God's unseen kingdom. Blessed is the servant whom Jesus finds doing what he has commanded when he returns. Imagine hearing Jesus say in the end, "Well done, good and faithful servant! . . . Come, you who are blessed of my Father, and receive the inheritance prepared for you from the beginning of time!"

*We serve Jesus by continuing faithfully in our assigned tasks (including meeting people's most basic needs) even when he seems distant and his return seems unlikely.*

**DAY 28** | # POURED OUT FOR MANY

Matthew 26:1-29

■ Matthew 26:1-5

26 ¹ When Jesus had finished saying all these things, he said to his disciples, ² "As you know, the Passover is two days away—and the Son of Man will be handed over to be crucified." ³ Then the chief priests and the elders of the people assembled in the palace of the high priest, whose name was Caiaphas, ⁴ and they schemed to arrest Jesus secretly and kill him. ⁵ "But not during the Festival," they said, "or there may be a riot among the people."

Having concluded his exalted teaching about that Day when he will be seated on his throne in heavenly glory, Jesus brings the disciples right back down to earth. In a matter of days, he will be handed over to be crucified. He tells them so with complete certainty, and he is right to be certain: the chief priests and elders are plotting his execution. In the events that follow, he will focus on his coming death, even as his disciples fail to catch on. We have much to learn from their failures and much to gain from his saving death.

■ Matthew 26:6-29

⁶ While Jesus was in Bethany in the home of Simon the Leper, ⁷ a woman came to him with an alabaster jar of very expensive perfume, which she poured on his head as he was reclining at the table.

8 When the disciples saw this, they were indignant. "Why this waste?" they asked. 9 "This perfume could have been sold at a high price and the money given to the poor."

10 Aware of this, Jesus said to them, "Why are you bothering this woman? She has done a beautiful thing to me. 11 The poor you will always have with you, but you will not always have me. 12 When she poured this perfume on my body, she did it to prepare me for burial. 13 Truly I tell you, wherever this gospel is preached throughout the world, what she has done will also be told, in memory of her."

14 Then one of the Twelve—the one called Judas Iscariot—went to the chief priests 15 and asked, "What are you willing to give me if I deliver him over to you?" So they counted out for him thirty pieces of silver. 16 From then on Judas watched for an opportunity to hand him over.

17 On the first day of the Festival of Unleavened Bread, the disciples came to Jesus and asked, "Where do you want us to make preparations for you to eat the Passover?"

18 He replied, "Go into the city to a certain man and tell him, 'The Teacher says: My appointed time is near. I am going to celebrate the Passover with my disciples at your house.'" 19 So the disciples did as Jesus had directed them and prepared the Passover.

20 When evening came, Jesus was reclining at the table with the Twelve. 21 And while they were eating, he said, "Truly I tell you, one of you will betray me."

22 They were very sad and began to say to him one after the other, "Surely you don't mean me, Lord?"

23 Jesus replied, "The one who has dipped his hand into the bowl with me will betray me. 24 The Son of Man will go just as it is written about him. But woe to that man who betrays the Son of Man! It would be better for him if he had not been born."

25 Then Judas, the one who would betray him, said, "Surely you don't mean me, Rabbi?"

Jesus answered, "You have said so."

²⁶ While they were eating, Jesus took bread, and when he had given thanks, he broke it and gave it to his disciples, saying, "Take and eat; this is my body."

²⁷ Then he took a cup, and when he had given thanks, he gave it to them, saying, "Drink from it, all of you. ²⁸ This is my blood of the covenant, which is poured out for many for the forgiveness of sins. ²⁹ I tell you, I will not drink from this fruit of the vine from now on until that day when I drink it new with you in my Father's kingdom."

Meals are potentially festive occasions, but in both of these meals, Jesus jarringly turns the conversation to his imminent death. At the first supper he says, "You will not always have me," and, "She did it to prepare me for burial." At the second he says, "One of you will betray me," and, "This is my blood poured out." Jesus is composed and focused; the disciples remain uncomprehending. During the meals, two characters emerge into prominence: at the first supper, a devoted outsider, and at the second, a treacherous insider.

The first is a woman whose name Matthew does not preserve. Rather, he emphasizes what she does. She takes very expensive perfume, approaches Jesus directly while he is eating, and pours all of it on his head. In a world where stench abounded, to give someone a gift of fragrance was a high honor. Earlier, the Magi from the east included fragrances in their gifts to the child Jesus. Here it is clear that the woman means to honor Jesus as generously as possible. People anoint kings, so to esteem Jesus as the greatest king of all, the woman inundates him with the anointing oils. It is an act of worship, a display of unreserved devotion.

The disciples disapprove. Overfamiliar with Jesus, they become small-minded critics of someone who is awed by him. It is not the first time they have been annoyed about a woman who intrudes on their fellowship with Jesus (15:23). They do not see her as a person to respect, much less to emulate. By contrast, Jesus praises her more lavishly than anyone since he praised Peter for confessing him as Messiah. Here is the outsider whom the insiders reject but Jesus honors. She sees Jesus' greatness and pours out not just the precious oils, but herself. Her gesture could not be more fitting or her timing more appropriate.

Though the disciples demean the woman's extravagant devotion, they are right to express concern for the poor. They have learned such concern from Jesus, most memorably in his final parable about the "least of these brothers and sisters of mine." His response to his disciples, "The poor you will always have with you," is a charge to embrace the poor into their fellowship ("have them with you") and to relieve their poverty. But Jesus is the one whom the poor and all other people need, and the gospel message that he commands his disciples to proclaim throughout the world will focus on Jesus himself. This woman has correctly gauged that Jesus is the center of everything. If we can remember her adoration, her outpoured love toward Jesus, we will keep perspective on whom we are serving with our assistance to the poor ("You did it for me" [25:40]). Consider Mother Teresa's words about her daily preparations to serve the poor in Calcutta: "We try to pray through our work by doing it with Jesus, for Jesus, to Jesus."[28]

The woman at the first supper contrasts sharply with the newly prominent character at the second. She spends lavishly on Jesus, whereas Judas sells him out for a few coins. She will be celebrated around the world, but it would be better for Judas if he had never been born. In the Sermon on the Mount, speaking of treasure, Jesus had said, "If your eyes are healthy, your whole body will be full of light. But if your eyes are unhealthy . . . how great is that darkness!" (6:22–23). The woman at the supper sees Jesus to be far more valuable than all that money can buy, and she is full of light. Judas sees Jesus to be worth less than a bag of change, and how great is his darkness! Everything pivots on valuing Jesus most of all.

Jesus is shrewd as a snake (see 10:16): he knows exactly who will betray him and when and where it will happen. But he is innocent as a dove: rather than react in bitterness, he fully includes Judas in the intimacy of the meal. Reclining together at ground level around a low table, leaning on an elbow and dipping bread with the free hand into a bowl of food shared by all—this was the very picture of intimacy, a revered symbol of mutual loyalty. Jesus says that the unthinkable is happening: "The one who has dipped his hand into the bowl with me will betray me."

The other disciples are dumbstruck. They remain resistant to the whole idea that Jesus is about to die, much less that they might have any part in it. "Surely not I," they all say. They should not be so surprised at the news. In verse 2, Jesus told them, "It is two days until Passover: they are going to crucify me." Then he said that the worshiping woman at the supper "has prepared my body for burial." Then he instructed the disciples who arranged the Passover meal to tell the homeowner that "the Teacher's appointed time is near"; that is, his critical moment *has come*—it is the same expression for arrival that Jesus used about the kingdom in 4:17. Matthew uniquely records these unmistakable cues from Jesus that he will be killed soon and then shows the disciples failing to grasp that the moment has arrived. This is no traditional holiday celebration: they are in the presence of a traitor, and their leader is about to be lynched. As events unfold, it will turn out to be not only Jesus' critical moment, but theirs as well, and they will fail completely.

Surely an effective disciple will want to become as alert as possible to moments when the stakes are high. Not all moments are the same: some situations require us to stop in our tracks and focus. We are to pray constantly, but sometimes a friend is in so much danger from illness or persecution that we must pray urgently and alert others to pray with us. We face perils and temptations all around us, but sometimes we sense God tugging at us, removing our peace about what we are about to do, and we had better change plans quickly. We care about our friends all along, but sometimes we glimpse that a friend faces a life-altering decision, and we need to make ourselves available. Disciples cultivate attentiveness to Jesus. I remember the quiet testimony of an elderly woman at a church service when I was vacationing in Vermont. An old school friend's name had come to her mind repeatedly during prayer in recent days, a friend with whom she had had no contact for twenty-five years. She took the trouble to track down her friend and drive out to see her. It turns out the friend was on the verge of committing suicide, and the praying woman was able to give her hope and save her life. Can we snap out of our mindset of the routine, the everyday, the safe, in order to hear the voice of Jesus when he is speaking most urgently?

Jesus' imminent betrayal, suffering, and death are not the end, of course. Dying is essential to his mission, not coming as brakes but as a powerful thrust forward. At both suppers, Jesus points beyond his death to the ultimate triumph of his ministry. At the first supper, Jesus rejoices that his gospel will be "preached throughout the world." At the second, he promises his disciples a new kind of living with God, and he celebrates the ultimate hope of dining "new with you in my Father's kingdom."

Jesus' talk of purposeful death is hardly new. He has repeatedly predicted his suffering and death going back to the moment when Peter confessed him to be the Messiah. Jesus had said the Messiah "must" be killed (16:21). Now at the Last Supper, he explains why he must die. He associates his death with the Exodus, the greatest event of salvation in the history of God's people prior to Jesus' arrival. His death provides a new Passover (Matthew 26:2, 18, 26, 28; see Exodus 11–12), and his blood seals a new covenant, surpassing and fulfilling God's covenant with Moses and the Israelites at Mount Sinai (Matthew 26:28; see Exodus 19:1–6; 24:7–8).

In the history of God's people, the Passover had been God's defining act of liberation. It ended the power of Egypt's Pharaoh to enslave God's people. The Lord broke Pharaoh's will and his cruel dominance by bringing a plague of death into the Egyptians' homes, a plague that the Israelites escaped by placing a sacrificial lamb's blood over the entrances to their huts. Death "passed over" them, and they were freed to leave their slavery, receive God's covenant, and journey to the Promised Land.

Jesus now transforms and fulfills the Passover. His blood is the lamb's blood that saves us eternally from death, breaks the oppressor's enslaving power, and sets us on our journey with God toward our promised final home. The Lord's Supper is not the first time that Jesus describes his work as the freeing of captives. Jesus is the thief who invades the devil's house, overpowers him, and liberates those he had imprisoned (12:29). Jesus is the servant who gives his life as a ransom to set his people free (20:28). Throughout Matthew, Jesus has exerted God's kingdom power against all that is oppressive in human experience, all of the evils outside us and within us. Now, just as the sun's energy is concentrated by a magnifying glass, the full potency of the kingdom power is concentrated in Jesus' act of dying. We are not to think of the crucified Jesus as merely an inspirational man who was martyred for what he believed in. His death is his conquering act to liberate his people. By dying and being raised, Jesus establishes the final outcome of the world's story: he dooms all causes of evil and delivers his people into the eternal reign of God.

Whereas evil's defeat is sure, we still await complete liberation. It is useful to compare the cross to the impact of D-day in World War II. The Allied landing on the beaches of France in June of 1944 determined the outcome of the war in Europe. Thereafter, the Allies could not be stopped; the defeat of the Nazi oppressors had become certain. The Allies' full victory was not completed, however, until 1945, and much fighting remained between D-day and that final victory. The cross of Christ has irrevocably determined the outcome of the universal battle against evil. Now, during the period between his cross and his final triumph, we continue to fight with all the spiritual power Jesus has put at our disposal—and by the same upside-down strategy that he employed. He won through the "weakness" of dying on a cross. He continues to win through us who take up our crosses and follow—who pray and love and sacrifice and serve in all of the weak-looking ways we are learning from him.

Jesus' death not only conquers oppression and evil, it provides forgiveness and binds us securely to God. The Savior says, "This is my blood of the covenant, which is poured out for many for the forgiveness of sins." At Mount Sinai, God had entered into covenant with the Israelites, committing himself to be their God and reaffirming his choice of them to be his people. Moses led in the offering of blood sacrifices to seal that covenant (Exodus 24:6–8). When the people broke the covenant and sought forgiveness, they "poured out" blood offerings on the altar in the tabernacle (Leviticus 4:7, 18, 25, 30, 34). The prophets later spoke of God's plan to transform his people's hearts and forgive their sins by means of a new covenant (Jeremiah 31:31–34; Ezekiel 16:59–63). Now Jesus says he will "pour out" his own blood as the "blood of the covenant," fulfilling his mission to "save his people from their sins" (1:21). At immeasurable cost to himself, God removes all barriers and receives Jesus' disciples, Jew and Gentile, into an inseparable bond of being his own. How reassuring it is to savor God's secure love, promised and sealed by Jesus' death!

Jews celebrate Passover through a family meal. I learned the richness of this tradition when I was invited by some dear Jewish friends to share a Passover meal in their home. It is a time to reinforce the family heritage, to hear again the sacred stories, to rekindle hope in God's promises, and to give thanks. As the Twelve recline at the table with Jesus, they represent the family of believers whom Jesus calls and unites. Now all over the world, clusters of Jesus' disciples gather around the meal as Jesus transformed it. As we celebrate the Lord's Supper, we rediscover our identity as family to Jesus and to each other. We look back in time to his achievement of liberating us from spiritual bondage and guilt through his death. We also look forward in hope. The Lord's Supper provides a foretaste of the joy that awaits us, an anticipation of the ultimate banquet, where we will celebrate his triumphant kingship and the end of all evil. "I tell you," said Jesus, "I will not drink from this fruit of the vine from now on until that day when I drink it new with you in my

Father's kingdom." In the meantime, until he comes to drink the cup of rejoicing with us, we live in grateful fellowship, serving the Lord as members of his family, partners in his ongoing work to set people free.

*Joined sometimes by the devoted outsider, sometimes by the treacherous insider, disciples dine intimately with Jesus and receive life through his death.*

## DAY 29 | THE SHEEP WILL BE SCATTERED

Matthew 26:30–27:10

■ Matthew 26:30–35

³⁰ When they had sung a hymn, they went out to the Mount of Olives. ³¹ Then Jesus told them, "This very night you will all fall away on account of me, for it is written:

> "'I will strike the shepherd,
> and the sheep of the flock will be scattered.'

³² "But after I have risen, I will go ahead of you into Galilee." ³³ Peter replied, "Even if all fall away on account of you, I never will."

³⁴ "Truly I tell you," Jesus answered, "this very night, before the rooster crows, you will disown me three times."

³⁵ But Peter declared, "Even if I have to die with you, I will never disown you." And all the other disciples said the same.

At the supper with Jesus, the disciples asked one by one, "Surely, *I* will not betray you, will I?" No, but they will desert him. All will "fall away"—they will stumble rather than stand firm as the crisis unfolds.

Jesus had used the same expression when warning them on the Mount of Olives that they would be tempted to fall away when threatened with pain and death (24:9–10). Now he is saying that his inner circle will all succumb to that temptation before the night is over. They all protest—Peter most boldly—insisting that they will remain loyal even in the face of death. How sad it must have been for Jesus to have to contradict Peter so pointedly. "You will deny me completely,²⁹ and you will do it just hours from now."

Obviously, the *yearning* to remain faithful is not enough. All eleven commit to Jesus with heartfelt desire; yet they all fail him. It is a sober caution to every disciple since. We aspire to match their passionate loyalty to Jesus, but we take a lesson from their overconfidence: nothing is more dangerous than to be certain that we are strong.

The one person who does not fall as the crisis unfolds is Jesus. In reassuring contrast to the disciples, he models the humble, watchful, prayerful path to steadfastness. In his instruction on the Mount of Olives, he warned them but gave them hope of success: "Many will turn away . . . but the one who stands firm to the end will be saved" (24:10, 13). He is saying to us, "Be among those who stand firm. Watch me, and I will show you how."

The collapse of Jesus' entire inner circle of disciples points to our universal need for God's grace. Jesus already extends mercy and forgiveness to them, even as he predicts that they will fall away: "After I have risen, I will go ahead of you into Galilee." He is saying that despite their failure this night, he still has great plans for their ongoing service to him and to the world. Jesus humbles them through this initial failure so that they will grow steadfast after he is taken away from them. If we have already failed him and feel terrible about it, we can take comfort from Jesus' forgiving words and get back on our feet.

### ▧  Matthew 26:36-46

36 Then Jesus went with his disciples to a place called Gethsemane, and he said to them, "Sit here while I go over there and pray." 37 He took Peter and the two sons of Zebedee along with him, and he began to be sorrowful and troubled. 38 Then he said to them, "My soul is overwhelmed with sorrow to the point of death. Stay here and keep watch with me."

39 Going a little farther, he fell with his face to the ground and prayed, "My Father, if it is possible, may this cup be taken from me. Yet not as I will, but as you will."

40 Then he returned to his disciples and found them sleeping. "Couldn't you men keep watch with me for one hour?" he asked Peter. 41 "Watch and pray so that you will not fall into temptation. The spirit is willing, but the flesh is weak."

42 He went away a second time and prayed, "My Father, if it is not possible for this cup to be taken away unless I drink it, may your will be done."

43 When he came back, he again found them sleeping, because their eyes were heavy. 44 So he left them and went away once more and prayed the third time, saying the same thing.

45 Then he returned to the disciples and said to them, "Are you still sleeping and resting? Look, the hour has come, and the Son of Man is delivered into the hands of sinners. 46 Rise! Let us go! Here comes my betrayer!"

Jesus' hour of prayer (verse 40) is his time to prepare for the hour (verse 45) when his trial and tortures begin. Arriving in the Garden of Gethsemane, Jesus arrays his disciples in two groups to protect and support him in his solitary time with the Father. Jesus works through his crisis here privately so that he will be able to stand strong publicly.

The old hymn says, "Go to dark Gethsemane . . . Your Redeemer's conflict see . . . Learn of Jesus Christ to pray." What can we learn about praying as we observe him? We see his deep humanness, his candor: "I am overwhelmed with sorrow, to the point of death." This is an impressive admission to disciples who minutes earlier were outdoing each other to appear heroic. The Savior is not ashamed of his weakness or depression. We see his vulnerability and dependency—on God, but also on his friends: "Stay and watch with me." He has not only carefully preserved this time for prayer, but he has summoned his friends to pray for him. If he needs such prayer, how much more do we? It is not selfish to ask others to pray for us.

Jesus prays for himself, displaying none of the false humility that says, "I will not fuss about myself; I will think of those around me." He is restless, sometimes concentrating in prayer, sometimes walking about and noticing his disciples. In his prayer, he is realistic about the magnitude of the trial he faces: "My Father, if it is possible, may this cup be taken from me." It is hard to penetrate exactly what he is seeking, given his own firm insistence elsewhere (16:21, 23; 26:53–56) that he "must" be crucified. Does he wonder if some last-minute surprise awaits him, as had happened at the climax for Abraham when God altered his command to sacrifice Isaac (Genesis 22:10–13)? Jesus clearly would rather not go through the coming tortures. Watching him, we learn to pray what we honestly hope for, as he did. Of course, he modifies his request by saying, "Yet not as I will, but as you will." As he prays a second and third time, the idea of being spared the "cup" of suffering diminishes ("if it is *not* possible for this cup to be taken away"), while his courage to do God's will increases. As his time of praying culminates, he says, "Rise! Let us go," not meaning, "Let's escape," but, "The time has come to face my executioners, and I am ready." Having prayed it through, the matter is now settled in his mind. The cross *is* God's will, God's doing, God's great saving act, and he has received from God the needed moral strength to do what he must do. From now until his last breath, Jesus is poised and masterful. His hour in the garden culminates a whole life of praying and acting on "not my will, but yours." Jesus is our model.

Peter and his companions are not. Having been warned that they face their moment of testing, they nevertheless rest and sleep. Jesus' aching words, "Could you not watch with me one hour," express not just his desire that they would pray for him, but also that they would pray for themselves. "The spirit is willing"; that is, "you're wonderfully eager to stand tall, but you need God's help right now far more than you grasp." The disciples have squandered their opportunity to seek God's strength for their crisis, and they will collapse—Peter most bitterly.

### ■ Matthew 26:47-56

47 While he was still speaking, Judas, one of the Twelve, arrived. With him was a large crowd armed with swords and clubs, sent from the chief priests and the elders of the people. 48 Now the betrayer had arranged a signal with them: "The one I kiss is the man; arrest him." 49 Going at once to Jesus, Judas said, "Greetings, Rabbi!" and kissed him.

50 Jesus replied, "Do what you came for, friend."

Then the men stepped forward, seized Jesus and arrested him.

51 With that, one of Jesus' companions reached for his sword, drew it out and struck the servant of the high priest, cutting off his ear.

52 "Put your sword back in its place," Jesus said to him, "for all who draw the sword will die by the sword. 53 Do you think I cannot call on my Father, and he will at once put at my disposal more than twelve legions of angels? 54 But how then would the Scriptures be fulfilled that say it must happen in this way?"

55 In that hour Jesus said to the crowd, "Am I leading a rebellion, that you have come out with swords and clubs to capture me? Every day I sat in the temple courts teaching, and you did not arrest me. 56 But this has all taken place that the writings of the prophets might be fulfilled." Then all the disciples deserted him and fled.

In this tense scene, with the crowd and the disciples ready to swing swords, Jesus is the man in charge, speaking with authority and dignity. He does not recoil from the treacherous kiss, but calls Judas his friend and tells him to get on with his business. When a disciple impetuously attacks a man in the arresting party, Jesus commands him to put his sword away. What is the disciple planning to do, take on the whole mob? Jesus' quick action saves the disciple's life and averts a bloodbath. Able to call legions of angels to his defense—a divine army of terrifying power—Jesus instead yields in submission to the Scriptures and to God.

Challenging the officials who seize him for trial, he puts *them* on trial: "Am I leading a rebellion, that you have come out with swords and clubs to capture me? Every day I sat in the temple courts teaching, and you did not arrest me." They are the ones who are behaving unlawfully and risk starting a riot, not he. They stir up violence at night, whereas he has taught in their holy place in the light of day. Jesus is a formidable moral presence in the midst of thugs and fools.

What about the disciples? Imagine their shock when Jesus tells them to put their swords away. "You're not going to let us defend ourselves—or you? You're just going to submit quietly to being arrested?" They had envisioned doing heroic deeds of bravery. But their champion (not their enemy!) has taken away their weapons. Jesus' kingdom has never been about using force. Jesus did say once, "I came to bring a sword" (10:34). He did not mean, though, that disciples would take up swords, but rather that his emerging kingship would arouse opponents to raise their swords. How will faithful disciples respond in such situations? They will refuse to retaliate. They will valiantly turn the other cheek when attacked. They will relentlessly love their enemies and pray for their persecutors. Jesus aims to end the cycle of violence, the syndrome of "living by the sword and dying by it." He exerts a transforming kind of power-in-weakness that the disciples will not understand until they see him prevail over evil by dying and rising. Jesus' approach is so different from our old habits of thinking! We fail in our moments of testing when we put our confidence in imagined scenarios and worldly tactics, rather than in God and his way. Unprepared by prayer and shocked by the plot twist of Jesus' refusal to resist, the Eleven desert him and flee.

### ◼ Matthew 26:57–68

[57] Those who had arrested Jesus took him to Caiaphas the high priest, where the teachers of the law and the elders had assembled. [58] But Peter followed him at a distance, right up to the courtyard of the high priest. He entered and sat down with the guards to see the outcome.

[59] The chief priests and the whole Sanhedrin were looking for false evidence against Jesus so that they could put him to death. [60] But they did not find any, though many false witnesses came forward. Finally two came forward [61] and declared, "This fellow said, 'I am able to destroy the temple of God and rebuild it in three days.'"

[62] Then the high priest stood up and said to Jesus, "Are you not going to answer? What is this testimony that these men are bringing against you?" [63] But Jesus remained silent.

The high priest said to him, "I charge you under oath by the living God: Tell us if you are the Messiah, the Son of God."

[64] "You have said so," Jesus replied. "But I say to all of you: From now on you will see the Son of Man sitting at the right hand of the Mighty One and coming on the clouds of heaven."

[65] Then the high priest tore his clothes and said, "He has spoken blasphemy! Why do we need any more witnesses? Look, now you have heard the blasphemy. [66] What do you think?"

"He is worthy of death," they answered.

[67] Then they spit in his face and struck him with their fists. Others slapped him [68] and said, "Prophesy to us, Messiah. Who hit you?"

Jesus startles the authorities twice, first by his silence and then by his words. He is silent before their charges, refusing to dignify their false witnesses or their preposterous case by answering. One charge against him has some truth in it: Jesus had claimed, "I am able to destroy the temple of God and rebuild it in three days" (see John 2:19). He will vindicate that claim by rising bodily from his grave on the third day. The temple has been corrupted by the men who now judge him. Jesus, who is "God with us," will replace and surpass the temple as God's dwelling place among his people (12:6).

His silence frustrates them, but his words scandalize them. Asked if he claims to be the Messiah, the Son of God (as he had affirmed privately to Peter in 16:17), he says, "You have said so," which is a way of agreeing with their statement while making them responsible for its wording. (Mark's Gospel records Jesus' yes with the simple words "I am.") Far from backing away from their designation, Messiah, Son of God, Jesus reinforces it by claiming to be the divine Son of Man who will come in the clouds and judge the world when the Books are opened (Daniel 7:9–10, 13–14). Jesus is saying, "I am not only your King and God's Son, but from now on, I am your Judge. You stand in judgment over me for now, but be careful what you do, because I will have the last word." Again, Jesus reverses who is on trial.

The high priest tears his clothes in dramatic outrage and calls upon the whole council to condemn Jesus. They all concur and then abandon any further pretense of a legitimate trial, beating him, spitting on him, and mocking him. In Jesus' bold words to his accuser and in his self-control during the beating, we see the model of turning the other cheek in virtuous dignity (see 5:39).

■ Matthew 26:69–75

⁶⁹ Now Peter was sitting out in the courtyard, and a servant girl came to him. "You also were with Jesus of Galilee," she said.

⁷⁰ But he denied it before them all. "I don't know what you're talking about," he said.

⁷¹ Then he went out to the gateway, where another servant girl saw him and said to the people there, "This fellow was with Jesus of Nazareth."

⁷² He denied it again, with an oath: "I don't know the man!"

⁷³ After a little while, those standing there went up to Peter and said, "Surely you are one of them; your accent gives you away."

⁷⁴ Then he began to call down curses, and he swore to them, "I don't know the man!"

Immediately a rooster crowed. ⁷⁵ Then Peter remembered the word Jesus had spoken: "Before the rooster crows, you will disown me three times." And he went outside and wept bitterly.

P eter's meltdown is complete. As he watches the authorities' brutality toward Jesus, he forgets his bold pledge to remain faithful. Willing earlier to confront armed men, he now caves in before a slave girl—and then another. Then he adds cursing to his denial that he even knows Jesus. No rooster's call ever sounded as shattering as this one. Peter's weeping is the most honorable thing he does all night. Our best brother has fallen. We lament in humble sympathy, sobered and forewarned that we, too, are vulnerable.

## ▧ Matthew 27:1-10

**27**¹ Early in the morning, all the chief priests and the elders of the people made their plans how to have Jesus executed. ² So they bound him, led him away and handed him over to Pilate the governor.

³ When Judas, who had betrayed him, saw that Jesus was condemned, he was seized with remorse and returned the thirty pieces of silver to the chief priests and the elders. ⁴ "I have sinned," he said, "for I have betrayed innocent blood."

"What is that to us?" they replied. "That's your responsibility."

⁵ So Judas threw the money into the temple and left. Then he went away and hanged himself.

⁶ The chief priests picked up the coins and said, "It is against the law to put this into the treasury, since it is blood money." ⁷ So they decided to use the money to buy the potter's field as a burial place for foreigners. ⁸ That is why it has been called the Field of Blood to this day. ⁹ Then what was spoken by Jeremiah the prophet was fulfilled: "They took the thirty pieces of silver, the price set on him by the people of Israel, ¹⁰ and they used them to buy the potter's field, as the Lord commanded me."

Judas's story is chilling. We are disturbed to think that a member of the company of disciples could so completely fail to connect with Jesus or could turn and do such terrible, irreversible harm—to Jesus and to himself. Betrayal stories are a sad and recurring part of Christian history, so we must never be naïve. We take heart from knowing that God's plan cannot be thwarted by such a person. Indeed, God reigns so completely that he can turn Judas's act of treachery into his own righteous opportunity to redeem the world. How amazing is our God! How greatly we depend on his mercy!

*Our danger and our hope are dramatized—*
*as the disciples sleep, then collapse,*
*and as Jesus prays, then stands tall.*

**DAY
30**

# THIS IS JESUS,
# THE KING
# OF THE JEWS

Matthew 27:11-54

J esus responded with kingly dignity during his arrest and trial before the Jewish authorities, despite all the indignities thrust upon him. Now the question of his kingship dominates every scene from his Roman trial to his crucifixion.

## ◼ Matthew 27:11-26

¹¹ Meanwhile Jesus stood before the governor, and the governor asked him, "Are you the king of the Jews?"

"You have said so," Jesus replied.

¹² When he was accused by the chief priests and the elders, he gave no answer. ¹³ Then Pilate asked him, "Don't you hear the testimony they are bringing against you?" ¹⁴ But Jesus made no reply, not even to a single charge—to the great amazement of the governor.

¹⁵ Now it was the governor's custom at the Festival to release a prisoner chosen by the crowd. ¹⁶ At that time they had a well-known prisoner whose name was Jesus Barabbas. ¹⁷ So when the crowd had gathered, Pilate asked them, "Which one do you want me to release to you: Jesus Barabbas, or Jesus who is called the Messiah?" ¹⁸ For he knew it was out of self-interest that they had handed Jesus over to him.

¹⁹ While Pilate was sitting on the judge's seat, his wife sent him this message: "Don't have anything to do with that innocent man, for I have suffered a great deal today in a dream because of him."

²⁰ But the chief priests and the elders persuaded the crowd to ask for Barabbas and to have Jesus executed.

²¹ "Which of the two do you want me to release to you?" asked the governor.

"Barabbas," they answered.

²² "What shall I do, then, with Jesus who is called the Messiah?" Pilate asked.

They all answered, "Crucify him!"

²³ "Why? What crime has he committed?" asked Pilate.

But they shouted all the louder, "Crucify him!"

²⁴ When Pilate saw that he was getting nowhere, but that instead an uproar was starting, he took water and washed his hands in front of the crowd. "I am innocent of this man's blood," he said. "It is your responsibility!"

²⁵ All the people answered, "His blood is on us and on our children!"

²⁶ Then he released Barabbas to them. But he had Jesus flogged, and handed him over to be crucified.

Pilate has heard reports that among the Jewish populace, Jesus is "the one who is called the Messiah" (verses 17, 22). When he asks Jesus, "Are you the king of the Jews?" he is asking a political question: is Jesus a threat to the empire? Does he claim to be a king in challenge to Caesar's kingship and Pilate's governorship? When Jesus answers, "You have said so," he is saying, "Yes, but 'King of the Jews' is your way of putting it, and I don't mean by it what you mean by it." Political rulers will continue to govern long after Jesus triumphs on Easter Sunday. The movement he leads does not threaten the government in the way rulers are accustomed to thinking of threats. Pilate will order Jesus to be crucified alongside a pair of insurrectionists, but Jesus is not leading an insurrection. His command to his disciples to put away their swords demonstrates that. Yet his kingship will ultimately dwarf the authority of the Caesars and governors of this world. As Pilate sits in Jesus' presence, he is out of his league.

The situation quickly spins out of control for Pilate. He finds himself on trial, even as he sits as Jesus' judge. The priests' groundless accusations irritate him, and Jesus' silence[30] unnerves him. Pilate's troubled wife sends her warning not to have anything to do with this innocent man. Meanwhile, the Jewish officials stir up the throng of spectators, who scream more and more wildly, "Crucify him!" Fearing the repercussions from executing an innocent popular hero but fearing even more that the crowd in front of him might riot, Pilate finds himself squeezed in the middle and tries to make the whole thing go away. "Listen," he says, "I customarily release a prisoner at the time of your Passover Festival. Take this Jesus who is called 'Messiah.'" Scorning their chance to rescue Jesus from death, the mob roars, "No, give us Barabbas," a notorious rebel. In reply, Pilate cynically shouts again the royal title that the people ought to honor: "What shall I do with your 'Messiah'?" "Crucify him!" they shout. "Humiliate him. Crush him." Pilate caves in and condemns Jesus, imagining that he can escape liability by ostentatiously washing his hands and yelling, "It's your responsibility."

Many in the crowd would have been the same people who had already rejected Jesus in town after town (for example, 11:20–24), but some may have been part of the cheering multitude that greeted Jesus as he entered Jerusalem on Palm Sunday. How can they turn and reject him so quickly? Imagine the Jerusalem crowd's experience of seeing the famous man in whom they had put their hopes now standing there beaten and chained, paraded before them as a fraud by their leaders. Swept up by the crowd's frenzy, duped into thinking that Jesus had conned them, they turn on him with a vengeance. It is *now*, of course, that they are being conned. Still today we have to be careful not to be sucked into the emotions and prejudices of the crowd around us.

Matthew alone records the words, "His blood is on us and on our children," an oath that meant, "We are so certain this man is guilty that we have nothing to fear from a just God as we condemn him." Of course, Matthew's readers know that these people in the crowd are terribly mistaken. He includes this saying to epitomize his countrymen's widespread rejection of their Messiah, for which Jesus has predicted judgment upon Jerusalem (23:37–24:2). The verse is a last summons to Matthew's compatriots to reconsider their rejection of Jesus. Anti-Semites, however, have used the saying to justify persecuting Jews through the centuries, crazily authorizing an ancient mob to speak a curse upon all Jews in all times, as if on God's behalf. Unthinkable! Ironically, all Gentile believers worldwide owe our experience with Jesus to the courageous first witnesses in the Christian movement, who were virtually all Jewish. The famous verse is itself ironic. "His blood . . . on us" is God's way of salvation for all peoples (26:28).[31]

## ◼ Matthew 27:27-44

[27] Then the governor's soldiers took Jesus into the Praetorium and gathered the whole company of soldiers around him. [28] They stripped him and put a scarlet robe on him, [29] and then twisted together a crown of thorns and set it on his head. They put a staff in his right hand. Then they knelt in front of him and mocked him. "Hail, king of the Jews!" they said. [30] They spit on him, and took the staff and struck him on the head again and again. [31] After they had mocked him, they took off the robe and put his own clothes on him. Then they led him away to crucify him.

[32] As they were going out, they met a man from Cyrene, named Simon, and they forced him to carry the cross. [33] They came to a place called Golgotha (which means "the place of the skull"). [34] There they offered Jesus wine to drink, mixed with gall; but after tasting it, he refused to drink it. [35] When they had crucified him, they divided up his clothes by casting lots. [36] And sitting down, they kept watch over him there. [37] Above his head they placed the written charge against him: THIS IS JESUS, THE KING OF THE JEWS.

[38] Two rebels were crucified with him, one on his right and one on his left. [39] Those who passed by hurled insults at him, shaking their heads [40] and saying, "You who are going to destroy the temple and build it in three days, save yourself! Come down from the cross, if you are the Son of God!"

⁴¹ In the same way the chief priests, the teachers of the law and the elders mocked him. ⁴² "He saved others," they said, "but he can't save himself! He's the king of Israel! Let him come down now from the cross, and we will believe in him. ⁴³ He trusts in God. Let God rescue him now if he wants him, for he said, 'I am the Son of God.'" ⁴⁴ In the same way the rebels who were crucified with him also heaped insults on him.

Jesus endures brutality on a scale we can scarcely imagine. Crushing a mat of thorns onto his head and pounding on it with a rod is unspeakably sadistic. A Roman flogging would tear the flesh from his body and leave him barely alive. He is so weak afterward that he is unable to drag his crossbeam up the hill to his execution site. Crucifixion was the act of nailing a man's ankles to a post and his wrists to a crossbeam, then hanging him in midair to display his nakedness and torment as he died slowly and horribly. To see Jesus suffer this way eliminates once and for all the idea that following him will assure us a safe and pleasant life.

Matthew says little about the crucifixion itself, focusing instead on the people's contempt toward Jesus' kingship. Having crowned him with thorns, the soldiers costume him in a royal robe, put a stick in his hand for a scepter, and bow before him with the taunt, "Hail, king of the Jews!" Then as they crucify him, in derision, they hang a sign atop his bloody cross: "THIS IS JESUS, THE KING OF THE JEWS." First the passersby and then the religious leaders repeat the titles "Son of God" and "King of Israel," mocking his apparent helplessness. "He saved others, but he can't save himself." Readers of Matthew protest, "But he *is* the King of the Jews! He *is* the Son of God! He is saving others by *refusing* to save himself!"

"THIS IS JESUS, THE KING OF THE JEWS." Disciples can learn more from this picture than from any other single snapshot in the Gospel. If we can capture in our minds this picture of Jesus, wrung out, hanging on the cross with *that* sign above his head, we will begin to grasp what it means that Jesus is our Messiah

(16:16–17, 21). Here is the *obedient* King, who says, "Not my will, Father, but yours." Here is the *humble* King, who deserves honor from us because he endured such dishonor for us. Here is our *worthy* King—we owe him our all because he gave his all. Moreover, that picture of Jesus crucified beneath the word *King* portrays the nature of our discipleship—our partnership with such a king. The new "greatness" looks like *this*. *This* kind of power defeats evil. "Take up your cross and follow me. . . . Whoever would be great must become a servant . . . just as the Son of Man came not to be served but to serve and to give his life." *This* is the way to love God and transform the world. Few will understand us when we imitate him. Just as he was surrounded by uncomprehending mockers, we too will be scorned by people who are oblivious to the meaning and power of what we are doing.

## ▓ Matthew 27:45–54

45 From noon until three in the afternoon darkness came over all the land 46 About three in the afternoon Jesus cried out in a loud voice, "*Eli, Eli, lema sabachthani?*" (which means "My God, my God, why have you forsaken me?").

47 When some of those standing there heard this, they said, "He's calling Elijah."

48 Immediately one of them ran and got a sponge. He filled it with wine vinegar, put it on a staff, and offered it to Jesus to drink.

49 The rest said, "Now leave him alone. Let's see if Elijah comes to save him."

50 And when Jesus had cried out again in a loud voice, he gave up his spirit.

51 At that moment the curtain of the temple was torn in two from top to bottom. The earth shook, the rocks split 52 and the tombs broke open. The bodies of many holy people who had died were raised to life. 53 They came out of the tombs after Jesus' resurrection and went into the holy city and appeared to many people.

54 When the centurion and those with him who were guarding

Jesus saw the earthquake and all that had happened, they were terrified, and exclaimed, "Surely he was the Son of God!"

The scene is noisy, with the mockers screaming their taunts, the crucified men beside him cursing, the soldiers playing their dice game to claim his clothes, and the voyeurs hoping for a spectacle ("Did he call Elijah? Let's see if Elijah comes to save him!"). Surrounded as he is by all of these people, Jesus is alone. "My God, my God, why have you forsaken me?" As he bears the weight of humanity's sin, he endures a degree of godless isolation we will never experience. In company with the faithful over the centuries, we kneel in awe at the foot of the cross, grasping neither the depth of his emptiness nor the mystery of our forgiveness gained through his bleeding and dying. "Leave him alone," shouts the bystander, hoping for a show. He is alone all right! He is consumed in darkness so that we can live our lives and eternity in his light. All thanks and honor to Jesus.

Matthew records a cluster of wondrous signals—three hours of darkness, Jesus' loud cry of finality, a violent earthquake, the torn curtain in the temple, broken tombs, visits from deceased loved ones newly alive—signals that God is acting powerfully through Jesus' death. Evil, apparently triumphant, is conquered.

Two groups of soldiers around the cross epitomize humanity's response. The ones who throw dice to claim his clothes (verse 35) have no idea what is happening or why it matters. Donald Hagner puts it well:

> A divine drama is being enacted before the very eyes of the Roman soldiers, a drama of which they remain totally oblivious. A turning point in the ages has been reached, the accomplishment of the salvation of the world, while the soldiers like blind fools vie for the garments of the man they have crucified.[32]

By contrast, we see a centurion and his immediate circle of soldiers. How many dozens of crucifixions have they seen before? But this one is different, and they *see* it—the midday darkness, the earthquake, the demeanor of the dying man himself. "Surely he was the Son of God!" It is hard to know what their conception is of God or of Jesus as "son of God." But they reflect on what they are seeing, tremble at their role in an injustice, and stand amazed in God's presence. Jesus had such men in mind when he said, "The harvest is plentiful" (9:37)—people who show by their open hearts that they are ready to be gathered to God and become Jesus' followers if someone would invite them.

Besides the darkness, the earthquake, and Jesus' cry as he dies—so gripping to the centurion and his soldiers—Matthew gives us two brief vignettes (verses 51–53) that take place away from the scene of the cross. The first occurs in the temple in Jerusalem, which has been God's formal dwelling place with his people. The temple's curtain is torn in two from top to bottom. Matthew may mean either the huge eighty-foot-tall curtain that limited people's access to the inner sanctuary or the smaller curtain before the holy of holies that only a priest could enter annually with a blood offering. His point is to say that *God* has torn away the barrier between himself and his people—we now freely enter into God's very presence—and he has done this through Jesus' death. Jesus' sacrifice on the cross supersedes and displaces all temple sacrifices, provides the forgiveness of sins, and establishes Jesus himself as the locale of God's presence with his people.

The second vignette portrays tombs breaking open and holy people being brought to life to appear to believers in the city. These instances of the dead coming alive take place after Jesus' resurrection, but Matthew clusters them with the other wonders surrounding the crucifixion in order to show us that Jesus' dying overcomes death, our most terrible enemy. By Jesus' death on the cross and his resurrection on the third day, God opens the way for all believers to rise when Jesus returns in glory.

In the Garden of Gethsemane, Jesus had prayed intensively, "Your will be done." Now with awesome power God displays that he is working his will monumentally through Jesus' sacrifice on the cross. No more barriers, no more death—the full riches of life with God are now ours. We owe him everything. In awe and gratitude, we live to serve him.

*Though all around us mock, we kneel in awe before the King who conquers death by dying, and seeing him, we see the nature of our discipleship.*

## DAY 31 | GO AND MAKE DISCIPLES

Matthew 27:55-28:20

### ■ Matthew 27:55-61

⁵⁵ Many women were there, watching from a distance. They had followed Jesus from Galilee to care for his needs. ⁵⁶ Among them were Mary Magdalene, Mary the mother of James and Joseph, and the mother of Zebedee's sons.

⁵⁷ As evening approached, there came a rich man from Arimathea, named Joseph, who had himself become a disciple of Jesus. ⁵⁸ Going to Pilate, he asked for Jesus' body, and Pilate ordered that it be given to him. ⁵⁹ Joseph took the body, wrapped it in a clean linen cloth, ⁶⁰ and placed it in his own new tomb that he had cut out of the rock. He rolled a big stone in front of the entrance

to the tomb and went away. <sup>61</sup> Mary Magdalene and the other Mary were sitting there opposite the tomb.

In these verses, we meet some people who have the courage to be associated with Jesus when the danger is greatest. First we are told of "many women," and three in particular, who have followed Jesus and served him all the way from Galilee to his appointment at the cross. Now as he dies, two of them, both named Mary, provide him what would seem to be their last service, seeing to his burial. They will return to the tomb after the Sabbath to make sure all has been done properly and respectfully.

We also meet the rich man, Joseph of Arimathea, who has become a disciple of Jesus. That is, God has acted upon Joseph's heart, assisted by faithful people who helped him to discover Jesus, so that he has entered into the life of being Jesus' apprentice and partner. With God's help, he has overcome the impediment of his riches (19:23–26) and become Jesus' courageous loyalist. He requests Jesus' body from the same officials who had exhibited that body on a cross in order to scare away any remaining loyalists. In saying that Joseph had been (literally) "*discipled* to Jesus," Matthew uses this verbal form of "disciple" for only the second time (previously, 13:52), leading up to the third and most important time, when Jesus commissions the Eleven to *disciple* all the nations (28:19). We thank God for the faithful people who "discipled us to Jesus," and we seek opportunities to disciple others to him.

## ▪ Matthew 27:62-28:10

<sup>62</sup> The next day, the one after Preparation Day, the chief priests and the Pharisees went to Pilate. <sup>63</sup> "Sir," they said, "we remember that while he was still alive that deceiver said, 'After three days I will rise again.' <sup>64</sup> So give the order for the tomb to be made secure until the third day. Otherwise, his disciples may come and steal the body and tell the people that he has been raised from the dead. This last deception will be worse than the first."

⁶⁵ "Take a guard," Pilate answered. "Go, make the tomb as secure as you know how." ⁶⁶ So they went and made the tomb secure by putting a seal on the stone and posting the guard.

28 ¹ After the Sabbath, at dawn on the first day of the week, Mary Magdalene and the other Mary went to look at the tomb.

² There was a violent earthquake, for an angel of the Lord came down from heaven and, going to the tomb, rolled back the stone and sat on it. ³ His appearance was like lightning, and his clothes were white as snow. ⁴ The guards were so afraid of him that they shook and became like dead men.

⁵ The angel said to the women, "Do not be afraid, for I know that you are looking for Jesus, who was crucified. ⁶ He is not here; he has risen, just as he said. Come and see the place where he lay. ⁷ Then go quickly and tell his disciples: 'He has risen from the dead and is going ahead of you into Galilee. There you will see him.' Now I have told you."

⁸ So the women hurried away from the tomb, afraid yet filled with joy, and ran to tell his disciples. ⁹ Suddenly Jesus met them. "Greetings," he said. They came to him, clasped his feet and worshiped him. ¹⁰ Then Jesus said to them, "Do not be afraid. Go and tell my brothers to go to Galilee; there they will see me."

Jesus' resurrection from the dead is monumental. What other event in all of history can compare? It displays the victory of God and revolutionizes the future prospects for human existence. Matthew's portrayal of the event highlights the earth's thunderous shaking and the angel's terrifying splendor as he removes the stone to reveal that the tomb is empty. The guards who have been sent to make sure Jesus' body stays in that tomb are paralyzed with fear. The angel's first words to the women could be translated, "Don't *you* be afraid." The guards have reason to be terrified, because they are accomplices in the official effort to suppress the truth about God's great salvation. "Let these burly men shake and faint, but not you women of faith! You seek Jesus, the Crucified One. He has risen, just as he said. Look inside the tomb where you saw Joseph place him on Friday. See that he is no longer here."

In a culture that devalued women, the last have become first. These brave women who venture out unaccompanied to the criminal's tomb are not just the first to see that it is empty and to hear that Jesus has risen. God honors them with the privilege of being the first to bear human testimony about Jesus' victory over death. "Don't be afraid," says the angel. "Go and tell."

The women trust his word and move out in trembling, joyful obedience. Imagine their astonishment when Jesus himself meets them on their way! "Greetings!" What a beautiful scene, as they clasp onto his feet in worship and joy! Strikingly, Jesus repeats to them the same words the angel had spoken, "Don't be afraid; go and tell." The women have a triple confirmation of his resurrection: the angel has announced that Jesus has risen just as he said he would; they have seen the empty tomb; and they have touched the risen Jesus. Today, we base our faith and witness on that same triple confirmation: Jesus announced many times in advance that he would rise;[33] his tomb was empty on the third day; and he appeared repeatedly to his earliest disciples physically alive. To this threefold testimony about his bodily resurrection we add our own testimony about his spiritual presence in our lives. He has risen from the dead!

Jesus adds a word of grace as he repeats the angel's command to the women. The angel had said, "Tell his disciples," but Jesus says, "Tell *my brothers*." The disciples had severely disappointed themselves by abandoning Jesus on the night of his arrest. When he predicted that night that they would all fall away, he also promised them that he would go before them into Galilee after he arose. Now he fulfills his promise and reassures them that he still thinks of them as his family, his brothers. Despite their failures, they belong to him, and he will still entrust his mission to them. Neither are our failures the end of the road for us. Jesus embraces us, rebuilds us, and sends us out into his work.

### ◼ Matthew 28:11-15

11 While the women were on their way, some of the guards went into the city and reported to the chief priests everything that had happened. 12 When the chief priests had met with the elders and devised a plan, they gave the soldiers a large sum of money, 13 telling them, "You are to say, 'His disciples came during the night and stole him away while we were asleep.' 14 If this report gets to the governor, we will satisfy him and keep you out of trouble." 15 So the soldiers took the money and did as they were instructed. And this story has been widely circulated among the Jews to this very day.

The guards, too, go and tell. Presumably, they narrate to the chief priests and the elders the angelic appearance and the fact of the empty tomb. What better opportunity for these temple leaders to come to grips with the possibility that they are opposing God rather than defending his cause? But no, they immediately act to suppress this vital information and to discredit the disciples who will proclaim it. It is disturbing to think that religious people can become so certain that their view is God's view that they spurn even the most compelling evidence to the contrary and resort to deception and slander on God's behalf. We must be careful in our zeal for God never to stoop to such a thing.

Ironically, the false story that the temple leaders decide to promote asserts the very thing they had sent the guards to prevent in the first place—namely, that the disciples stole the body. They portray the guards as knowing exactly what was going on while they slept! This rumor about thieving disciples was still circulating at the time of Matthew's initial readers. By refuting the rumor, Matthew asserts firmly that the early eyewitnesses were not deceivers.[34]

## ■ Matthew 28:16-20

¹⁶ Then the eleven disciples went to Galilee, to the mountain where Jesus had told them to go. ¹⁷ When they saw him, they worshiped him; but some doubted. ¹⁸ Then Jesus came to them and said, "All authority in heaven and on earth has been given to me. ¹⁹ Therefore go and make disciples of all nations, baptizing them in the name of the Father and of the Son and of the Holy Spirit, ²⁰ and teaching them to obey everything I have commanded you. And surely I am with you always, to the very end of the age."

Encountering the risen Jesus on the mountain, the disciples are astounded and unsure how to react. "Some doubted." Their perplexity fits what they are seeing: Jesus is not a ghost, but neither is he exactly like he was before. It is a *bodily* resurrection—the tomb is empty and the women can clasp his feet—but his appearance is transformed in some sense. (Compare Luke 24:15–16, 31, 36–43; John 20:14; 21:12.) Moreover, it would be very disorienting to see him alive—the man they saw the Romans slaughter only days before. They meet him with a combination of thrill and bewilderment. (See Luke 24:41, "They still did not believe it because of joy and amazement.")

Some of the disciples spontaneously worship Jesus, and he affirms them for it, saying, "All authority in heaven and on earth has been given to me." The titles used derisively during Jesus' trials and crucifixion—King of Israel, Son of God—are now vindicated. His apparently outrageous claims—to have authority to forgive sins (9:6), to be Lord of the Sabbath (12:8), to be the peerless and final revealer of God (11:27; 24:35)—are authenticated as he stands before them victorious over death. Jesus further asserts his worthiness to be worshiped by commanding that they baptize future disciples in the name of God: Father, *Son*, and Holy Spirit. His majesty as Messiah and Son of God compels humble discipleship and provides our rationale for evangelizing the world: "All authority has been given to me; therefore go."

Now we have come full circle. Matthew began by positioning Jesus at the climax of God's long drama of saving the world through his chosen people, Israel. God had promised in the Scriptures to bless all peoples through Abraham's offspring and to gather all nations in homage to King David's descendant. Now Jesus the Messiah, the son of Abraham, the son of David, sends his followers out to bless the nations and call them to obedience. Beginning his public ministry, Jesus had called disciples, and now he sends them out to make new disciples. He had promised to make them fishers of people, and now he sends them out to fish. They are ready to proclaim their Messiah to the world. They have seen his cross, so they can finally grasp his humble, sacrificial way of power—and they have seen that his cross was not the end, so they see the greatness of that power.

Each phrase in the Great Commission (verses 19–20) is worth unpacking. Jesus' fundamental command is that his followers should *make disciples*. That's our assignment, our commission. We are to invite and equip people to become Jesus' apprentices so that they live with him and learn from him and imitate him and embrace his mission as their own. The most loving gift we can give is to disciple our friends to Jesus, because we give them life with him. Our goal is not just to bring people to a moment of initial decision, where they pray a commitment prayer or receive baptism or confirmation. Nor is it merely to assure them of life after death. We are to invite people to spend the rest of their lives with Jesus, enjoying him and collaborating with him and his followers to promote God's merciful reign on earth.

Our model for discipling people is Jesus' ministry with the Twelve. We invite and train new members to be with Jesus constantly, to obey his instructions, to mirror his actions, to depend on his power, and to conform to his character. Like Jesus, we will not only speak the good news, but we will labor to feed the hungry, heal the sick, end injustice, and meet the full array of human needs—and we will draw new disciples into those endeavors with us (9:35–38; 25:37–40).

When we *baptize* new disciples into the name of the Father, Son, and Holy Spirit, we are just beginning a long discipling process. We will not merely get them wet and say a formula of words over them; we will immerse them into God's life—into the living presence of the Father, Son, and Holy Spirit—and incorporate them into full belonging in his people, his church. They will grow to live daily with Jesus and own their identity as God's missional people only as we band together for years to nurture them—and one another—toward maturity.

Jesus commands his disciples to *go*. By contrast to his earlier command to stick to their own kind (10:5–6), he now sends them across cultural barriers to invite the Gentiles into their fellowship. By virtue of Jesus' resurrection, God has given him authority over all the earth, and so we as his disciples are to go to *"all nations"* (Greek: *ethnē*), that is, to all the world's ethnic groups, in whichever nation-states they live. Many of us have multiple nationalities living right in our hometown, and so we learn to reach beyond our customary circle of friends. Additionally, some of us will be called to travel to distant parts of the world while the rest of us support them financially and prayerfully.

Our conviction about Jesus' divine kingship and global authority does not excuse instances in Christian history when we have been arrogant or culturally insensitive or have become bedfellows with exploitative entrepreneurs and colonialists. To the contrary, such dark chapters compel us to repent and to reshape our endeavor sensitively. In a pluralistic world, how can disciples carry out the Great Commission in an ethical way? We will start by adopting Jesus' humility and gentleness. We are not superior—how can we repent of our sins at the foot of the cross and then think we are superior to anyone? Rather, we have received God's mercy gratefully, and we want to share it. We will authentically respect the people to whom God sends us, acknowledging that we have much to receive and learn from them. We will work side by side with our hosts to overcome violence and social ills. We will not impose our culture, but instead will help our newfound friends to find indigenous expressions of devotion to Christ. Most important, with God's help, we will be consistently righteous in character, conformed to our Savior.

As we go out, we pray that all people will come to recognize who Jesus is and yield allegiance to him as their King and Savior. By his ministry of healing and righteousness, by his authoritative revelation of God's love, by his saving death and once-for-all resurrection, he is unique in all of history. All authority in heaven and on earth belongs to him. The Gospel's scandalous message that Jesus must become the focus and source of life is nevertheless the loving message. We are inviting people to be immersed in his limitless love, and there is no greater gift.

We see throughout the world today that many people who are exposed to Jesus perceive a surpassing greatness in him, so that, despite their previous religious convictions, they joyfully become his followers, often in the face of danger. These new followers of Jesus, largely converting from other religions, number many millions every year,[35] far more than ever before in history.

Jesus' last instruction for discipling new followers is to *teach them to obey* everything he has commanded us. There is no discipleship apart from obedience to Jesus. This was his final point in the Sermon on the Mount (7:21–27), and it is his final point now on this mountain (28:16, 20). His majestic authority and sacrificial love compel us to cooperate with him wholeheartedly. We invite others to join us in the obedient life, and we form our churches into training and support communities for working out that obedience. What has Jesus commanded us? To seek first God's kingdom and his righteousness, to love God and our neighbor, to pray for our enemies and forgive those who hurt us, to end our lust and our love of money and status, to pursue justice, mercy, and faithfulness, and in every situation to come to him who can move mountains and calm storms and reshape our hearts. Obediently, then, we will hear his words and do them—and teach one another to do them—until that Day when he says to us, "Well done, good and faithful servants! Come and share your master's happiness!"

Jesus commanded those first women, "Don't be afraid; go and tell." Likewise, he sends us out to spread his good news. If we do feel afraid, we find relief through his final promise, "I am with you always." We never go out alone, but always with him. As with every aspect of our service as disciples, *Jesus* will meet our friends' needs—including their deep need to know the Father—but he will do so through us and with us. Despite our weaknesses and flaws, Jesus the King has called us to be his partners, serving at his side. We bring our best efforts to "go and tell" about life with him—about his easy yoke and light burden and rest for our souls—and he blesses our words and stirs our friends' hearts. We can venture across the room or across the world to draw people to Jesus, confident that he is with us always, preparing the way.

*Don't be afraid; go and tell the good news of the risen King, who summons all people into joyous, obedient discipleship.*

# STUDY AND DISCUSSION GUIDE

These questions are a resource for individual reflection or group discussion. In the group setting, I encourage leaders, after an opening prayer, to begin with their own ice-breaker questions or activities and to invite members to comment on parts of the reading that most caught their attention. Discussion of the questions below will then flow more easily and can lead to prayer for one another.

## DAY 1 YOU GIVE THEM SOMETHING TO EAT
(Matthew 14:13-21)

1. When have you observed a situation in which people's needs seemed vastly greater than the resources available to meet them? What does this chapter offer toward solving problems of that nature? What is Jesus' role and what is ours?

2. Jesus commands his disciples, "You give them something to eat." Make a list of the kinds of needs and hurts (including physical hunger) that Jesus cares about and could potentially remedy through collaborating with his modern-day disciples. To which need(s) in the world is your heart most drawn?

3. What are the symptoms of a passive kind of Christianity by contrast to active discipleship? What does solo religion look like by contrast to "together" discipleship? What factors in our culture and in our churches promote passivity and lack of connection among believers?

4. What in this chapter encourages you to think and/or act differently than before? Describe individuals or groups you have observed who seem to be living out aspects of an "intimate, active, cooperative, world-changing" collaboration with Jesus. In what ways would you like your collaboration with Jesus to expand?

## **DAY 2**  A PLACE IN GOD'S STORY
(Matthew 1 - 2)

1.   What aspects of Israel's family story is Jesus said to fulfill (pages 13–14, 18–19)? How does God's activity shown in Israel's family story contribute to your understanding of who Jesus is and what he came to do?

2.   What changes in your living and planning result from no longer asking whether God fits into your story but asking instead where you fit in his? How might it affect the way you think about career, family, church, mobility, money, goals, prayer, or other aspects of life?

3.   What does it mean to belong to the family of Jesus? Who belongs to his family whom you would not normally think of as being part of your spiritual family and heritage (prior generations, other ethnic or socio-economic groups, different denominations or traditions)? What are potential benefits from valuing those connections?

4.   What impresses you about the Magi from the East? about Jesus' earthly father, Joseph? What aspects of their response to Jesus would you like to emulate? When have you had to change course in order to cooperate with what God is doing? What were the results? What potential disruptions to your life do you face now?

## **DAY 3**  MORAL PREPARATION
(Matthew 3)

1.   What insights do you gain about what John the Baptist was like? How do various people in the passage respond to him? Which of his statements most catches your attention, and why?

2.   What have you been able to pick up so far about the meaning of John's announcement that "the kingdom of heaven has come near" (3:2)? Distinguish "kingdom of heaven" from the idea of "where we go when we die" (p. 22). What is the kingdom's "now" aspect as John announces it? In what ways is it good news? To what kinds of people (in Matthew's narrative and today) might it seem to be unwelcome news?

3.  What sorts of things put you on the defensive? For what questionable behavior do you still mentally rehearse self-justification? What concerns or fears restrain you from full honesty with God? When have you experienced relief by letting go of some bad attitude or behavior you were previously defending? What can help clear the way for God in your heart?

4.  What do the details of Matthew's narrative of Jesus' baptism reveal about Jesus? about his relationship with God the Father? about his identification with us who wish to work out life with God? Why does it matter that Jesus was baptized among the people? Does the narrative of Jesus' baptism make him seem more approachable or less so? Why?

## DAY 4 TEMPTED
(Matthew 4:1-11)

1.  To which of the three lines of temptation that Jesus faced—plenty (pursuit of material abundance), protection (yearning for safety and security), or power (love of being influential and esteemed) do you think you are most vulnerable? Which yearning has the greatest capacity to draw you into living independently from God or treating him like an intruder? Give examples.

2.  What does it look like to "put the Lord your God to the test" (that is, to create your own difficulties by impulsiveness, pride, or disobedience and then hope God will bail you out)? What instances of it have you seen in others' lives and in yours? What precautions can you take to put God more fully in charge of your future?

3.  When have you been tempted to take moral shortcuts ("compromise ethically, shade the truth, elbow aside someone unimportant") for the sake of praiseworthy objectives? When have you gained in status or clout at someone else's expense—or when has someone else gained at your expense? How did you feel afterward?

4.  How does it help to know that Jesus was tempted just as you are? What spiritual disciplines helped Jesus to triumph over temptation? Which disciplines have you found most helpful? Which could you expand as part of your equipment for remaining loyal to God?

### **DAY 5** THE CALL TO DISCIPLESHIP
(Matthew 4:12-22)

1. How does Jesus' call of the fishermen resemble God's call of Abraham and Moses (p. 38)? Now that they are followers of Jesus, how is the agenda for the disciples' lives different than it was before?

2. How is Jesus' call to "follow me" as disciples different from asking students merely to learn a set of principles or skills (p. 39)? What about Jesus makes him worthy of being followed? What questions about their future remain unresolved as the fishermen get up "immediately" to follow him? What unknowns trouble you as you work out devotion to Jesus?

3. What practical differences will the call of the fishermen make in their future living? How might a modern disciple's "calling" affect or involve "career"? All disciples, not just people with ministry careers, are called by Jesus. How might this idea affect your approach to your next five or ten years?

4. What aspects of God's will are the same for all disciples, and what aspects are specific to individuals? Retrace the process and resources for determining what God wants you personally to do (p. 40). What new actions or relationships might help you discern his will for you more clearly?

### **DAY 6** JOY INSTEAD OF MOURNING
(Matthew 4:23-25; 8:1-34)

1. Trace the displays of Jesus' authority in this chapter: authority over what and whom and for what purposes? How does Jesus' authority relate to the idea of "the good news of the kingdom"? Even though our society often devalues authority, how might Jesus' surpassing authority be good news in your life?

2. What does your family expect of you now and in the future? In what ways have you neglected the kind of concern for your family that Jesus would endorse? How might choosing loyalty to Jesus' call and guidance cause stress in your family relationships? Who among your friends have been misunderstood by their families because

they have chosen to follow Jesus seriously? How can you encourage or support them?

3. Who are some of the outsiders in this chapter whom Jesus relieves and gives new belonging as insiders? In what settings have you felt like an outsider? How does Jesus' embrace of you affect your self-concept? Whom do you think of as an outsider to your circle that you might now treat differently in light of Jesus' actions of inclusion? What are the risks and benefits of caring about people on the margins the way Jesus does?

4. The townspeople in the last story ask Jesus to leave. Why might some people today prefer for Jesus to leave them alone—to leave things the way they are? What fears or concerns might be at the root of such a rejection of Jesus' help? In what ways has Jesus disrupted your life and plans? For what inconveniences have you learned to thank him?

## DAY 7 DEEP HEALING
(Matthew 9:1-35)

1. In what ways does "sin hurt the sinner" (p. 52)? What are the potential costs to you when you indulge in what you know to be sin? How does knowing that Jesus is willing and able to forgive your sins help you to turn away from habitual sin? What benefits come from being part of a community of people who know they need the Physician's help?

2. When has a person's poor reputation blinded you to what God might be able to do in that person's life? When has your own pattern of misbehavior led you to think you might be a hopeless case? What in your life seemed impossible or beyond repair but can be reimagined now in light of Jesus' powerful presence?

3. When have you seen members' "feet-set-in-concrete certainty" about the way things ought to be done cause inertia or division in the community of Jesus? What examples can you think of where followers of Jesus have valued the wisdom of Christian tradition and experience but have also been able to think and listen anew? What spiritual practices can aid in discerning what Jesus wants done?

4.   What insight does Matthew 8–9 provide about the kingdom of heaven (pp. 59–60)? What is Jesus' mission? What role do you as a disciple play in it? What has already begun, and what do we still await? What ideas here are new or invigorating to you?

## DAY 8   GOOD NEWS OF THE KINGDOM
(Matthew 5:1 - 16)

1.   What are some marks of being "out" rather than "in" as society sees it? Who in the course of your normal day is essentially invisible to you or thought of as an unimportant person? Who are the poor in spirit, the meek, the victims of injustice, and when do you cross paths with them?

2.   What is the difference between interpreting the Beatitudes as announcements of the presence and benefits of God's kingdom as opposed to statements of what we ought to do? Try to put into other words some of the kingdom benefits noted in the Beatitudes?

3.   Define and describe discipleship in light of Matthew so far, including 5:13–16. What would be examples of small ways in which disciples could be salt and light? What would be examples of large-scale ways?

4.   In light of Jesus' summons to be salt and light in the world, discuss and pray over the questions in the last paragraph on page 67.

## DAY 9   NEW RIGHTEOUSNESS
(Matthew 5:17 - 48)

1.   When have you experienced hurt and anger that was easier to nurse and savor than let go of? What can be gained from yielding your anger to God, and what are the potential costs of continuing to nurse it?

2.   Discuss the strategy for putting a stop to lusting (pp. 72–73). What initiatives can you take to minimize falling into situations where lust becomes more likely? If married, what can you do to deepen your faithfulness to your spouse? How can you build up the mental discipline of treating everyone as sacred and valuable to Jesus?

3. List some of the transforming initiatives Jesus offers to help us end the cycle of getting even (5:39–42)? What steps toward reconciliation can you make in a tense relationship you face now? In what ways can you "do more [mercy] than others" and "love preposterously"?

4 What is your role and what is God's in the formation of your character (p. 69)? By what specific acts of obedience to Jesus' teaching in this chapter will you strengthen your character and "build your house on a rock" (7:24)?

## DAY 10 KINGDOM PRAYING
(Matthew 6:7-15, 25-34; 7:7-12; review of 8-9)

1. In whose lives would you like to see God's will done? Do not think just of friends, but also of opponents; not just of individuals, but also of family, church, town, and world.

2. What kinds of dilemmas are you most inclined to worry over rather than entrust consciously to Jesus? For what needs that the world "runs after" can you more fully trust your heavenly Father? What experiences of answered prayer have increased your faith? What aspects of Jesus' teaching here broaden your sense of God's generosity?

3. Are there some instances when you have treated God as a vending machine and then become frustrated with him? About what matters would you like to ask, seek, and knock in a sustained way? Whom can you invite to join you in praying about these matters?

4. Jesus says we are to seek first God's kingdom and his righteousness (6:33). What might you be prone to pursue "first" instead? What are the benefits for yourself, your group, your congregation, others you care about, as you own more fully the priorities of 6:33? What difference might it make in the way you pray and what you pray about?

## **DAY 11** BEWARE
(Matthew 6:1-6, 16-24; 7:1-6, 13-29)

1.  Jesus cautions us against showing off spiritually (e.g., with our giving, praying, or fasting), yet he wants us to let our light shine before others. In what ways are you tempted to show off? What is the proper goal when others are watching (5:16)? What are healthy ways to receive a compliment? Give examples of others you have seen shining without being self-promoters.

2.  How would you describe the "treasure that is most worth having"? How much money is enough? What might be some guidelines for determining whether you possess your money or it possesses you? What would be markers that you are serving God and not money? What steps could you take to "pursue the wealth that is truly wealth"?

3.  What are examples from the chapter of being "naïve" (pp. 92–94)? Are you someone who is more likely to trust people or to be suspicious? What precautions could prevent you from being conned or manipulated or betrayed?

4.  What is the proper application of Jesus' command, "Do not judge?" What is the difference between communicating condemnation versus communicating legitimate concern? How might you discern when it is best to express concern about someone's sinful or harmful pattern of living and when to keep quiet?

## **DAY 12** GATHERING PEOPLE TO JESUS
(Matthew 9:35-10:42)

1.  In your experience, has your church focused more on freeing people from hunger, disease, and injustice or on proclaiming the good news of eternal life with God (or neither)? How does Jesus' ministry in Matthew display a uniting of those two emphases? How might carrying out both emphases help to fulfill the church's mission to gather people to live with him and for him?

2.  What is your part in the Lord's sending work at this point in your life or potentially in the future? What could be the role of prayer

in Christian evangelism and service? Prayer about what? (Include 9:38.) How much training do people need to get started in outreach? What resources does Jesus give to disciples to overcome fear (10:26–31, 40–42)?

3. Jesus says that the student (disciple) is to be like the teacher (10:25). What aspects of Jesus' way of living that you have observed so far in Matthew would you like to imitate more fully?

4. What in our culture and people's experience contribute to the idea that Christian living would likely be boring? Whom do you know who might be more attracted to Jesus because Jesus sends his followers to face risks and challenges? As his partner, what aspects of Jesus' ongoing kingdom work do you find most compelling or exciting?

## DAY 13 WHOEVER HAS EARS
(Matthew 11)

1. Jesus speaks of "forceful people who lay hold of [the kingdom]." Have you known people who strike you as particularly tenacious in pursuing the kingdom life and blessings? What are the indicators of their eagerness? What is the difference between seeking first God's kingdom and his righteousness on the one hand and drivenness or fanaticism on the other?

2. The chapter speaks of people who wish to see tangible evidence of Jesus' truth and power before believing (pp. 109–10). How might you respond to someone who wants proof? Can you identify with the comment that Jesus' appeal is like music that "gets under our skin and connects with something inside us so that we love it and experience joy or sadness that comes straight from the music"? What was God's process in helping you to trust Jesus?

3. Many of Jesus' original hearers and observers did not believe, partly because he was not what they expected. What has surprised you thus far about Jesus during your journey of getting to know him? In what ways does Jesus confound our culture's expectations? In Jesus' view, what does it take to be wise?

4.  What does Jesus mean when he says that his yoke is easy and his burden is light (11:30)? What do you suppose the burden is, and why can it be characterized as light? Lighter than what? What will it mean for you at this time in your life to come to him persistently and learn of him more deeply? Can you think of times when his rest has been particularly real and reassuring to you?

## DAY 14  CONTROVERSIAL AUTHORITY
(Matthew 12)

1.  What is your approach to the Lord's Day? In what ways is it different from other days? How have you experienced Sabbath as a mercy, or how could it become a mercy to you in the busyness of life? What might help to retain its purpose to bring rest and renewal in the Lord? What, on the other hand, can make it into something burdensome?

2.  Would you classify yourself as eager or reticent to speak to those outside of the church about Jesus? What experiences have you had where speaking up was effective and helpful? What is the role of listening when you converse (or decide whether to converse) about Jesus? How can you speak winningly without softening Jesus' "scandalous demands for loyalty"? What would you like people to know about Jesus? Why?

3.  Matthew, quoting Isaiah, points to Jesus as the One who will "bring justice through to victory." In what ways can you partner with Jesus in his pursuit of justice? What injustices are you aware of that you would like to see put right? What is the difference between justice and vengeance? How is Jesus' kind of power different from worldly aggressiveness?

4.  What will it mean to "gather with Jesus" rather than to "scatter"? When have you undertaken a noble endeavor but messed things up through willfulness and inattention to Jesus? How might you contribute to reconciliation and mutual support within Jesus' gathered "family"?

## **DAY 15** HIDDEN TREASURE
(Matthew 13:1–52)

1. What is Jesus' purpose in teaching by means of parables (p. 125)? What will people gain or lose depending on their response (13:12)? What are appropriate steps for people who "have ears to hear" (p. 127)? What kinds of "troubles" or "worries of this life" can deter initially responsive people from following through on the new life with Jesus (13:21–22)? For whom are you praying, and to what distractions are they vulnerable?

2. How does perceiving the presence of the kingdom resemble the experience of characters in science fiction or fantasy literature who discover a new "dimension" or "parallel world"? What are the wonders concealed in a mustard seed, and how are an obscure group of disciples or a Galilean's death on a cross similar to the mustard seed?

3. How is God's action through Jesus and his disciples (including you) similar to yeast being worked into dough? What is your part in that leavening action now and potentially in the years to come? What could your church's part be?

4. How is the kingdom life like the treasure or the pearl (13:44–45)? What benefits—what kinds of bounty and power—does Jesus offer us through living with him and for him prior to his return? How does his offer expand what you can offer to others beyond forgiveness of sins and a secure afterlife? What do you want those you love to see and hear when they consider Jesus?

## **DAY 16** LITTLE FAITH–GREAT FAITH
(Matthew 13:53–14:36; 15:21–16:12)

1. What experience do you have of people who knew you in an earlier part of your life still thinking of you now as you were then? About whom might you need to update your impressions now that they have matured more? In what ways have your impressions of Jesus changed (enlarged?) over the years—and as you've been reading

Matthew? In what ways does understanding Jesus and what he cares about help you as you pray?

2.  What experiences in your life resemble the storms at sea in Matthew's narrative? Have you tended to focus on the circumstances fearfully or to focus on Jesus trustingly—or first one then the other? Give examples.

3.  Jesus is ready for the storm partly because he has sought solitude with God and found it despite postponements. Describe benefits you have experienced from times of solitude and retreat, especially times focused on Jesus. Do you have particular times or places where you like to withdraw with God?

4.  Part of growing in faith is remembering when God has helped us impressively in the past. What stories of Jesus' responsiveness to people's faith inspire you (stories in Matthew or of people you know)? What events of God's help to you do you like to remember particularly? When has he acted in ways that you did not expect or think possible? Why does growing in faith matter?

## **DAY 17** YEAST OF THE PHARISEES
(Matthew 15:1-20)

1.  Have you ever experienced "an atmosphere of inquisition" or spiritual intimidation from people who perceive themselves to be godly? How did you react? Toward whom are you tempted to wag the finger in a superior way? What are healthier ways to help one another work out deeper righteousness?

2.  Give positive examples of human-made rules and guidelines you have found useful and protective over the years. When have you seen guidelines turn into inflexible markers of the "right way" (p. 148)? Think of examples when a rule-keeper's actions might look to an observer like a disciple's actions? What would be the differences in those two people's motivation and growth toward spiritual maturity?

3.  In your crowd, what behaviors or attitudes are most readily judged and condemned? Why those, do you suppose? What moral concerns of Jesus tend to be neglected among your associates? What

role does your politics play in your "favorite sins to condemn" (and vice versa)?

4. Twice Jesus cautions us about the way we speak: [a] "These people honor me with their lips, but their hearts are far from me" (15:8); and [b] "For out of the heart come evil thoughts . . . false testimony, slander. These are what defile a person" (15:19–20). What changes would you like to cultivate in your heart and your words?

## DAY 18 TAKE UP YOUR CROSS AND FOLLOW
(Matthew 16:13-28)

1. What impressions of Jesus do you encounter in the secular world? What would you like people to understand about Jesus? Why? What are the implications of Jesus' being Messiah and Son of God for how you live at home, at work, in social settings, and in your participation in the church (p. 152)?

2. In his answer to Peter, what are the elements of Jesus' vision for his church: its mission, power, durability, unity (pp. 153–54)? As bearers of the "keys of the kingdom," how can churches unlock the doors to life with God and to loose their neighbors from captivity and the power of darkness? When have you seen a church act with compassionate power?

3. Evaluate the cultural theme of pursuing our dreams. How has following Jesus altered what you pursue? What aspects of your old life has Jesus required you to yield? What did that look like, and how did it go? Which of his gifts are you learning to receive and enjoy "with open palms and loose fingers" (p. 157)?

4. What are characteristics of the true life which Jesus offers? Which are you experiencing now? Which would you like to experience more fully or consistently? Can you identify with the statement that "as we deny ourselves for him, we find ourselves"? Jesus called Peter "Rock." What name might fit what he is forming you (or others in the group) to be as you mature?

## **DAY 19** COMING DOWN THE MOUNTAIN
(Matthew 17)

1.  Jesus takes three disciples up the mountain to show them his glory and then leads them back down into the messy world below. What is expressed about him by each event? How might both his glory and his coming down shape your thinking and actions as you face difficulties and dangers?

2.  What was the disciples' error regarding the boy they could not heal? Describe the kind of faith that leads to an outflow of power from God? How are humility and prayer related? Have you ever fallen into confidence in your track record of success instead of confidence in God? What were the results?

3.  Looking back over Matthew 11–17, when has Jesus been restrained and when has he been assertive in dealing with influential people? To which extreme are you most tempted: chronic avoidance of conflict or aggressiveness and disdain? From Day 19's last full paragraph, evaluate the list of ways Christians involved in politics could approach their participation differently from people who are not motivated by loyalty to Jesus. Consider specific ways to apply each item.

4.  What aspects of the world in your immediate experience are "messy"? What "messy" aspects of human life are you generally shielded from observing? Prior to Jesus' return in glory, what problems stir you to want to make a difference with Jesus' help? (See the following chart.) Brainstorm about what you or your group or your church might do?

A Partial List of the World's Evils and Miseries for
Disciples to Challenge as Partners with the King

Abandonment
Abortion
Adultery
Alcoholism

Anarchy/Chaos
Arrogance/Scorn
Blindness
Boredom/Dreariness
Broken families
Burden of guilt
Cheating/Corruption
Child labor
Covetousness/Jealousy
Cruelty
Deafness
Death
Despair/Hopelessness
Destruction
Disability/Handicaps
Disease/Epidemics
Divorce
Drought/Famine
Domestic abuse
Drug addiction
Eating disorders
Ecological damage
Estrangement from God
Exploiting the poor
Fear
Feuding/Being enemies
Fraud/Manipulation
Gambling addiction
Gluttony
Greed/Avarice
Grief/Depression
Harassment
Hatred/Hate crimes
Homelessness
Hunger
Ignorance of God's love
Illiteracy

Injustice
Intimidation
Juvenile delinquency
Kidnapping
Lack of clothing
Loneliness
Lostness/Being adrift
Lying/Dishonesty
Malice/Resentments
Mental illness/Senility
Molestation
Murder
Neglect
Natural disasters
Occult practices
Oppression
Orphanhood
Paralysis
Pollution
Pornography
Poverty
Prejudice
Profanity/Lewdness
Prostitution/Pimping
Racism/Anti-Semitism
Rape
Rejection/Exclusion
Religious repression
Sexual immorality
Sex trafficking
Sin
Slander/Gossip
Slavery
Suicide
Terrorism
Theft

Torture
Unemployment
Unwanted pregnancy
Urban blight
Violence/Persecution
War
Wrongful imprisonment

## **Day 20**
# GATHERED IN HIS NAME
(Matthew 18)

1.   What is your part, God's part, and the Christian community's part in your staying with the Shepherd and not straying? What disciplines do you use to strengthen your faithfulness to Jesus? By what strategies might believers build one another up and help prevent anyone from straying in the first place?

2.   Have you observed successful cases of a loving friend or church group helping a person get back on track once they have strayed? What contributed to their success? What struck you from the chapter's instructions and numbered suggestions as especially important or helpful? What is the ultimate goal? What all is at stake when seeking to restore a person?

3.   What are the benefits of praying together? What could you do to enhance your opportunities for this kind of praying? How can people who are shy about it be encouraged and protected and drawn into the praying?

4.   What is Jesus' rationale for stressing that disciples should forgive others? What are the benefits for you in forgiving? for the person forgiven? for the church? What did you find helpful in the suggestions and examples about how to go about forgiving? Whom do you need to forgive? What kind of help do you need from Jesus and fellow disciples in order to do it?

**Day 21**
# WHAT GOD HAS JOINED TOGETHER
(Matthew 19:1 - 12; 5:31 - 32)

1. Lay out the elements of marriage drawn from Jesus' quotation of Genesis 2:24 (pp. 179–80). In what ways does this contrast to secular views of marriage? How does God's design for marriage as the formation of a new family, permanent and exclusive commitment, and physical union in loving intimacy contribute to the experience of security by the husband and wife? How will that security affect their children?

2. The chapter points to the context of Jesus' remarks about marriage in Matthew 19 and in Matthew 5 (p. 180). How do those surrounding instructions contribute to his guidance about how to maximize a marriage's success and well-being? Consider them one by one. Why is it important that a disciple marry another disciple rather than someone who is lukewarm or cold to life with God?

3. How does Jesus' evaluation of singleness differ from his culture's view and from ours? How can you support single people in your family and in your congregation? How can you and your church affirm singleness as a way of life? What are potential benefits for a disciple and for Jesus' mission while the disciple is single?

4. Summarize and evaluate the chapter's conclusions and counsel about divorce. How can you or your church aid marriages in trouble to prevent divorce? What does a divorced person need to take into consideration when thinking about the possibility of remarriage? How might the Gospel's emphasis that "life is found in Jesus" figure in a divorcee's healing and decision making?

**Day 22**
# THE LAST WILL BE FIRST
(Matthew 19:13 - 20:16)

1. Thinking of the twelve disciples' attitude toward the children, whom do you think of (or ignore) as the unimportant people in your world by contrast to yourself? Is there someone, whom others

may have disregarded, who you have discovered is more impressive or more Christ-like than you are in some way? What are indicators that you might be over-eager for status? Status in whose eyes?

2. What is scary about the story of the rich young man? What is encouraging in it? What is possible and what is not, according to Jesus? What status-enhancing blessings have you received and to which are you most attached? Can you think of situations in which your attachment to one of them has compromised (or might compromise) your integrity or faithfulness to God?

3. Are you a veteran of years with Jesus or a relative newcomer? As a disciple, have you ever had occasion to envy or resent non-disciples or latecomers to Jesus who lived apart from him for years? What accounts for your envy or resentment? What are the advantages of following Jesus early in life and consistently?

4. How have you imagined the new world which Jesus describes as the "renewal of all things"? What new insights come from his words in 19:28–30? What will life be like? How might the anticipation affect the way you think and live now?

## Day 23
# NOT TO BE SERVED, BUT TO SERVE
(Matthew 20:17-21:9)

1. Take a look at endnote 24 (p. 320). Have you ever heard Jews blamed as a people for Jesus' execution? What is the fallacy in that claim? What is the potential damage? How might you respond to someone who makes such a comment? What are appropriate steps for disciples toward diminishing and overcoming anti-Semitism?

2. What was crucifixion, invented by the Romans, designed to do? What does Jesus' death on the cross (along with his resurrection) accomplish in God's purposes (pp. 196-97)? How is Jesus' death more than a man being victimized by governmental oppression?

3. Jesus' cross obligates us: in what ways can your life be a thank you to Jesus for his costly love? Jesus' cross motivates us: in what settings might Jesus' great sacrifice challenge you to greater love, service, or courage? In what ways will his cross determine your purpose (your

mission in life; what you pursue)? How will your style of living and relating to others and to God be defined by Jesus' cross?

4.   What are the challenges facing a disciple who aspires to lead in God's church and mission? What would "humble" look like in an effective leader in the church? What would be the distinctives of a disciple who leads effectively in the secular world? How does the picture of the Messiah on a donkey help you to think about leadership? How can your congregation support its key leaders?

## Day 24
## PROPHET, KING, LORD
(Matthew 21:10-22:46)

1.   What are the characteristics of a prophet, and in what ways does Jesus act as a prophet in these stories? When have you had to stand up to reputable or powerful people? How did it go? How can you maximize your effectiveness in such a situation? When have you needed courage to identify publicly or socially with a disreputable or unpopular person?

2.   Identify some obstacles (mountains) to God's will being done in the world or in a friend's life that you would like to pray to have removed. What obstacles does your church face? What mountains are being faced at this time by missionaries you care about?

3.   Jesus has arrived as king in Jerusalem to establish God's reign, heightening the imperative of obeying him. What do his parables and answers to his critics indicate we should do? How does the cross display Jesus' obedience to the Great Commandment (love God with your whole being) and its corollary (love others as yourself)? In what ways might you renew your obedience to these commandments this week?

4.   Ponder Jesus' actions, his assertions, his tone of voice, his responses to tricky questions. What impresses you about Jesus? What do you find troubling? How would you describe his personality and style? Why can't he be intimidated? What would you like to imitate?

**Day 25**
# DO NOT DO WHAT THEY DO
(Matthew 23)

1. What examples of hypocrisy and being blind guides does Jesus give in Matthew 23? Postponing for a moment discussion of homosexuality, which of Jesus' examples appear relevant to your church or social setting. When have you seen Christians' hypocrisy or angry discourse become barriers to people considering the kingdom life? Conversely, when have you seen people (hypocritically?) accuse Christians of being hypocrites as an excuse for ignoring Jesus?

2. Jesus climaxes his teaching by saying to the people of Jerusalem, "How often I have longed to gather your children together, as a hen gathers her chicks under her wings." What does that statement mean? How might that desire of Jesus affect the way you handle controversy and tension among believers? How can you protect coming to Jesus as the priority of your congregational life and of your own life?

3. Where have you seen the "idolizing of being in love" in our culture or heard it in your church members' conversation? What is the potential harm? What are its symptoms, and what can you and your circle do to avoid falling into it? How does it affect conversation and attitudes regarding singles? regarding people who are attracted to the same sex?

4. What ideas in this chapter were most helpful regarding the issue of homosexuality? Which comments raised further questions? How can you promote mercy, justice, faithfulness, and the lifting of burdens? How can members "extend to each other the combination of merciful love and call to higher righteousness that Jesus continually extends to us"? Which half of that combination does your circle most easily neglect?

**Day 26**
# WHOEVER STANDS FIRM
(Matthew 24:1–36)

1.  What has been your part up to now in Jesus' mandate that the gospel must be proclaimed to all the nations? How might you become informed about how to pray for those who testify for Jesus in trouble spots? What does Jesus' phrase "stand firm" mean so that it does not contradict his command to "flee" in some circumstances? What refugee populations or people under severe tribulation are you aware of? What role might you have in caring for them or aiding them?

2.  What are the characteristics of cult-like leaders? What kinds of claims and demands do they make which cause their followers to trust them excessively and distrust more familiar Christian leaders? How can you distinguish trustworthy leaders from leaders who become deceivers and controllers? How might you help members who are vulnerable to the "wolves in sheep's clothing"?

3.  What are the consequences of speculating about precisely when Jesus will return? How can the double horizon (already/not-yet) of Jesus' predictions about tribulation and about his return guide and fortify you as crises arise (pp. 227–29)? How can disciples avoid unsteadiness or collapse during crisis on the one hand and distraction from Jesus' ongoing assignments on the other? What are our ongoing assignments?

4.  What promises does Jesus make regarding large-scale tribulation? (Consider especially verses 13, 22, 31, 35). How might these help you face more personal tribulations in life, including physical decline and death? What tribulations are you or your loved ones facing at this time? How might Jesus' words here and elsewhere in Matthew help you in hard times (for example, 6:26–27; 7:24–25; 8:28; 11:28–30; 17:20; 25:23; 26:28)?

## Day 27
# WELL DONE
(Matthew 24:36-25:46)

1.  Do you ever experience a numbness to God's presence due to ordinariness and routine as described here? Have you experienced being startled in the midst of it by glimpses of his activity or goodness or displeasure? In what ways does Jesus come to disciples unexpectedly? How can you "keep watch" in the midst of your routines and busyness?

2.  Describe your experience with spiritual disciplines, perhaps including Scripture study or memorization, meditation, prayer, fasting, solitude, simplicity (that is, thrift, limiting luxuries), service, confession, worship, or seeking guidance. What has proved enriching? What would you like to try in the days ahead? How can you protect them as spiritual nourishment as opposed to burdensome duty, self-vindication, or showing off?

3.  The parable of the bags of gold speaks negatively of the person who does nothing with the gift entrusted to him. When is inactivity sinful? In what ways can inactivity contribute to stubbornness or resentment? When is inactivity a gift from God and a protection against burnout?

4.  Would you describe your church as tilting more toward proclamation or ministries of mercy? How might you pursue greater balance and integration? How can you more fully integrate caring for the poor, the prisoner, the foreigner into your routine way of living—the outflow of your love for Jesus? Talk about times when partnering with Jesus in his work of mercy and proclamation has brought you satisfaction and a foretaste of glory.

**Day 28**
## POURED OUT FOR MANY
(Matthew 26:1-29)

1. What is admirable about the woman's devotion in the first narrative of Jesus at supper? What do the disciples find off-putting about
   her? What is your attitude about individuals who go overboard,
   perhaps disruptively, in worshipping Jesus? What about her action
   here would you like to imitate?

2. Once again the subject of the poor comes up (see also 6:2–4; 19:21;
   25:34–40). What is your approach to the phenomenon of poverty
   (far away and nearby) and toward poor people themselves? What
   are the challenges? Do you have occasion to know some of the poor
   personally? How can you diminish your isolation from the poor
   and understand them and their situation better?

3. The chapter speaks of moments to stop in our tracks and focus.
   How would you describe your response to critically important
   moments? Are you slow or quick to catch on? Have you had success
   or difficulty transitioning from the routine to the urgent? Have you
   experienced having the Lord bring a matter to your mind repeatedly, either through a friend or in prayer? What turned out to be at
   stake?

4. What new information does the Lord's Supper narrative provide
   regarding the meaning and necessity of Jesus' death? What does it
   achieve? What do celebrations of the supper look back to, and what
   do they look forward to? About what do you wish to give thanks?
   How does celebrating the Lord's Supper fortify you for what is
   coming, short-term and long-term?

**Day 29**
## THE SHEEP WILL BE SCATTERED
(Matthew 26:30-27:10)

1. What do you admire about the disciples in this chapter? What
   about them would you like not to imitate? How does Jesus'
   promise in advance to meet them in Galilee after his death and

resurrection, despite their failures, help you as you undertake challenges for him?

2. What do you observe as Jesus prays in Gethsemane? What from his example is helpful to you as you pray or as you face a crisis? Jesus asked his friends to watch with him and pray for him. When has the prayer of friends helped you in the face of a crisis or a momentous decision? When have you been too shy about asking friends to pray seriously for you?

3. List instances of Jesus' poise, self-control, and authority in the aftermath of his praying at Gethsemane. What do you learn about who Jesus is and what he is like from the narratives of his arrest and late-night trial? Characterize his response to being willfully misunderstood and unjustly punished. In what ways is he a model for you in these episodes? What amazes you about him?

4. The book speaks of the disciples depending unwisely upon imagined heroic scenarios and worldly tactics. When have events unfolded unexpectedly for you in a way that either revealed your cowardice or waywardness or compelled you to turn to God? How can you prepare best for future crises?

## Day 30
# THIS IS JESUS, THE KING OF THE JEWS
(Matthew 27:11-54)

1. What situations have you observed or been part of where a group's prejudices carried the day or their emotions swept others up in misguided outrage? How might you go about keeping your head in such situations? In the trial before Pilate, did Pilate have "no choice" but to condemn Jesus? Have you ever faced an unwelcome choice between costly integrity and going with the flow? How did it go?

2. Which people from the scene at the cross intrigue you or make you sad? Imagine Jesus' experience from the story's details. What do you learn about him as he undergoes crucifixion? What do you learn about God from the events of this chapter, including the signs and wonders in the narrative as Jesus dies?

3. The centurion and his men seem, at first glance, unlikely to be impressed by Jesus. When have you been surprised by someone's unexpected openness to seeing Jesus' greatness and their own sin and need? Whom among your acquaintances might you be unfairly pigeon-holing as seeming unlikely to respond to Jesus?

4. What emotions and responses arise in you as you consider Jesus on the cross? How does the picture of the weak and humbled "King of the Jews" redefine your thinking about power and greatness? What responses arise in your heart as you ponder Jesus on the cross? What might you do differently in light of it? What would you like to say to him?

## Day 31
# GO AND MAKE DISCIPLES
(Matthew 27:55-28:20)

1. What do you observe about the women in the story? Contrast the women and the soldiers. What would it be like to be in their position? What do you admire about the women—and about Joseph of Arimathea? Matthew speaks of Joseph having been "discipled to Jesus." Who discipled (or is now discipling) you to Jesus? What have they done that helped you most?

2. What elements of encouragement do you see in the words of the angel and of Jesus to the women? Why might it have helped for the women to hear twice the command to go and tell the other disciples? Why is it significant that Jesus calls the eleven men to whom he sends the women "brothers"? When has Jesus encouraged you in the aftermath of your having let him down?

3. What do you imagine about Jesus' appearance and the disciples' reaction in the scene on the mountain in Galilee? What explanations in the reading helped you most regarding the phrases in his Great Commission? When you "go and tell," what aspects of the story and message of Jesus do you want to include? What errors of attitude and action do you want to avoid as you invite people to be disciples?

4.  What are the key elements of God's grand story from beginning to end, and what part does this scene on the mountain play in it? What have you learned about your role (and your church's role) in that grand story? What themes from the Gospel of Matthew as a whole have been most helpful and memorable to you? What has challenged or equipped or inspired you toward a fruitful partnership with the King?

# ACKNOWLEDGMENTS

I express here my humble thanks to the people who have helped me think about Matthew and write this book. Some of them have written great books: the community of biblical scholars who have taught me so much through their commentaries and theological works, and the pastoral writers, especially John Stott in my early years and Dallas Willard more recently, who have modeled how to apply the Bible to current living. Others have taught Bible and theology with me at the University of Sioux Falls and in the local church, outstanding colleagues whose input has sharpened my interpretation and improved my expression of it: Kimlyn J. Bender, Brian Han Gregg, Christina S. Hitchcock, and John D. Lierman. Family members have provided essential editorial input, especially my mother, Kay Hiigel, and my wonderfully supportive wife, Cindi, but also at crucial points my nephew, Stephen Campbell, and my sister, Barbara Campbell. Stacey Trobman has blessed me by examining the manuscript with her Jewish eyes. Jon Sweeney of Paraclete Press has improved the book immeasurably by his gracious, wise counsel and editing, and Sarah McBride is a meticulous and congenial copy editor. I am deeply grateful to the many who have prayed for me. Finally, I say thanks to my students, scores of whom have read drafts of the book, sometimes offering suggestions that I have incorporated, but mostly sharing their lives with me as they respond to Jesus. To see their growth in discipleship is my best reward.

# APPENDIX
## IS MATTHEW TRUE?

I n this book, we read Matthew according to the kind of document it is, a proclamation of good news that God has done great things through Jesus and a guidebook for participating in what God is still doing. We do not hold the Gospel at arm's length for analysis. Rather, we try to enter into the reality that it portrays and to respond personally to its summons to follow Jesus. This approach to reading the Gospel raises the unavoidable question, "Is it true?"

The question arises on two levels. First, did it all really happen? Did Jesus really say startling things like, "Anyone who loves their father or mother more than me is not worthy of me," and, "Heaven and earth will pass away, but my words will never pass away" (10:37; 24:35)? Is it true that Jesus healed hundreds of sick people (4:23–24), fed thousands with a few loaves (14:19–21; 15:36–38), and taught that his own coming death and resurrection were necessary in God's saving work (16:21–23; 26:26–29)? These are questions of historicity.

A second level is to ask whether this Gospel is true in its claims concerning God, the world, and God's activity in the world. The author of Matthew thinks according to a worldview that emerges from his community's understanding of the Hebrew Scriptures (the Bible's Old Testament) and from Jesus' teaching. To ask "Is it true?" regarding Matthew's worldview is to pose questions such as: Are human beings the creation of a loving God who gets involved in their lives and answers their prayers? Is God a kingly authority who is active to see that his beneficial will is done in the world?

Are there really darker spiritual powers—the devil or demons? Is Jesus the spearhead of a new and final reality, which this Gospel calls the kingdom of heaven? "This is my blood of the covenant, which is poured out for many for the forgiveness of sins," says Jesus in Matthew 26. The question of historicity is whether Jesus actually said such a thing. The question of worldview is whether Jesus' death really is the basis for human beings to have a barrier-free relationship with the living, faithful, personal God.

For some readers, these questions of historicity and worldview raise little concern. Either they find Matthew's presentation of Jesus so compelling that their intuition tells them to trust it, or they say, "Of course it's true," because Matthew is part of the Bible. For others, though, the question "Is it true?" requires more scrutiny, and for them, Matthew's status as Scripture is not an adequate starting point. They will want to evaluate first whether Matthew, simply as a surviving ancient document, might provide reliable information. Their process would be to read enough about Jesus as a historical figure—what he said and did—to be able to reach at least a tentative verdict about Jesus' fundamental question for his disciples: "Who do you say I am?" (16:15). The further such inquirers progress with that question, the more ready they will be to heed his call on their lives.

Considering the question of historicity, I suggest that the Gospel of Matthew provides us with enough dependable information to arrive at the necessary verdict about who Jesus is and what he cares about so that we can begin responding to him. Some commentators argue, to the contrary, that the real historical Jesus was likely quite different from Jesus as he is described in the Gospel of Matthew, partly because the document's purpose was propagandistic and theological, not historical. The Gospel of Matthew *does* have a theological agenda; that is, its primary message is not history for information's sake, but an announcement about life with God. But Matthew's very announcement is that God has done something in historical Palestine by means of a real person, Jesus, who was interacting by word and deed with real residents of the region. In that sense, the writer makes the validity of his announcement depend on the reality of the events he is describing.

What can we know about how the Gospel of Matthew came into existence? Despite dissenters here and there, scholars both liberal and conservative have generally been able to agree on this much: this first of the four Gospels in our New Testament was not the first to be written. Rather, the author of Matthew made use of already circulating sources, including the Gospel of Mark and likely another source, which scholars call Q, detectable in the material Matthew and Luke have in common. These sources emerged in a region where eyewitnesses lived and in a social environment in which their accounts of Jesus' actions and teaching were being actively discussed.

Our Gospel of Matthew likely came about by a process much like that described at the beginning of Luke: "Many have undertaken to draw up an account of the things that have been fulfilled among us [that is, the Gospel writer has in hand previously written accounts like Mark], just as they were handed down to us by those who from the first were eyewitnesses [that is, written sources were supplemented by eyewitness accounts available to the Gospel writer]. . . . [Having] carefully investigated everything from the beginning, I too decided to write an orderly account" (Luke 1:1–3). The writer of Matthew would similarly have organized information about Jesus from available writings and eyewitness testimonies into a narrative that stressed themes he thought were important.

Whenever the Gospel of Matthew was written, whether it was during the years leading up to the catastrophic Roman attack on Jerusalem in the year 70 or in the decade or two afterward, the writer was using older materials, including Mark, which were written closer in time to the events they describe. Scholars commonly date Mark in the late 60s or 70–71, though a date at least a decade earlier is possible. Mark, in turn, likely drew from even earlier written sources and personally knew eyewitnesses, likely including Peter.[36] If Mark treated his sources as respectfully as Matthew treated Mark—the variations in the telling of the story between Mark and Matthew are truly minor—then Mark preserves information collected close in time to the events themselves. The passages usually attributed to Q (mostly sayings of Jesus that are parallel in Matthew and Luke but are not present in Mark[37]) preserve a view of Jesus' identity and significance that fits so well with Mark that both Matthew and Luke intersperse material from these sources freely in their Gospels. In summary, the author of our Gospel of Matthew probably had eyewitnesses available to him, and he also extensively used at least two independent sources, Q and Mark, dating from the 60s or earlier and reflecting still earlier testimony.

Here is the point. The likely date of Jesus' death is the year 30 (perhaps 33). This leaves little time for a radical *revision* of the story of Jesus' life and teaching to replace the truth and become the "correct," authoritative Christian proclamation that we find in Mark and Matthew. Scholars who propose that Mark and Matthew contain this sort of massive revision of the true historical reality commonly assert not just that the early Christians got confused or misreported some details or somewhat embellished Jesus' words and deeds, but that they *invented* large numbers of sayings and actions to attribute to him. They created sayings about the kingdom of God, about judgment, about Jesus' saving death, and about his self-identification as Messiah, along with many miracles culminating in his resurrection from the dead. These mischievous early Christian revisionists succeeded in establishing their new orthodoxy about Jesus in the very region where multitudes of eyewitnesses to the real events were still living.

This strained hypothesis that the early Christians projected their own ideas and wishes back onto the deceased Jesus owes less to actual evidence in its favor than to a modern "maturity" about the impossibility of the supernatural in human affairs (as if to say, "Grow up! People don't rise from the dead.") and to a kind of respect for the "real" Jesus who is relevant because he thinks and acts more like our own culture's ideal. One has to ask where the inventing is more likely to be taking place, with the early Christians or with these scholars. James R. Edwards puts the question this way: "Did the early church freely invent stories and sayings and attribute them to Jesus, or did it preserve and guard a tradition that it considered inviolable?"[38] Was there not something about Jesus—about who he was and what he was like—that would have made *falsifying* his record detestable to his followers? Because their "good news" was so focused on what Jesus said and did, and because they were staking their lives on it, would they not have had a compelling interest in preserving the story accurately?

If we are willing to allow for the possibility that God might interact with human beings at key moments in ways that differ from our everyday experience, then we are in a position to read Matthew profitably on its own terms. As a source of historical information, particularly regarding Jesus' widely witnessed public ministry, we may be confident that Matthew gives us a substantially reliable portrait of the real Jesus. This Gospel, alongside the others in the New Testament, gives us enough information that is sufficiently accurate that we can draw responsible conclusions about who Jesus was and is, conclusions that the other New Testament documents bolster. We need not be disturbed if we see that Matthew reports events in a different sequence or if sayings appear in varied wording or in different contexts than in Mark or Luke. Such narrative practices accord with the standards of that era. By holding the Gospels side by side, we can see that the writers felt fairly free to sort and trim and rephrase what was written in their source documents, but still remained true to their content. A commentator may argue that a saying here or a narrated event there is inauthentic, but such an assertion, if hypothetically true, would not damage my basic argument. I would still respond that the overall thrust of Jesus' message and ministry is clear enough to enable us to make some valid decisions about Jesus.

The Gospel itself names no author. Tradition going back to the early second century attributes it to Matthew the tax collector, also known as Levi, one from Jesus' inner circle of twelve disciples. The best way to account for that tradition is to conclude that Matthew himself had at least some role in assembling the document we have in our Bibles, whether or not he is its final author. Whoever held the pen wrote so brilliantly and compellingly that this Gospel became the favorite of believers over the centuries. We who are Christians would go beyond saying that it is historically trustworthy (though that is enough for my current argument) and would assert that the entire process, from the remembering of eyewitnesses and the penning of written sources to the composing of our New Testament's first Gospel, all took place under God's oversight and guidance, so that the document we now have is divinely inspired.

This idea that God is at work leads to the question of worldview. Matthew has stories of God speaking and of Jesus performing miracles. Some readers of Matthew may hesitate, not because they doubt the honesty of the people who saw and told and remembered and wrote, but because they wonder whether these people were right about what they were seeing.

Some readers especially doubt reports connected with demonic activity. The ancients attributed to demons at least some maladies that we today would diagnose as standard medical problems, though by no means all of the stories of demons can be attributed to a primitive understanding of medicine. It seems clear from the narrative that Jesus himself believed that he was confronting real spiritual forces of evil and that overcoming them was a defining feature of his ministry (especially Matthew 12:28, "If it is by the Spirit of God that I drive out demons, then the kingdom of God has come upon you"). We in the West are prone to doubt the possibility that personal spiritual forces of evil (or of good—angels) exist in the world, but such doubts are likely more the result of our presuppositions than of weighing evidence. For what it is worth, few people of other cultures, from the first century to the twenty-first, have had such doubts about the existence of dark spiritual beings.

Regarding the Gospels' reports of Jesus as a miracle worker, most of the stories involve his healing known ailments or intervening into natural processes such as the multiplication of grain or the movement of wind on the sea. It is hard to account for the sheer number of miracle reports—most done in the presence of many witnesses—apart from Jesus having actually done miracles. As a whole, the miracles are inseparable from the Gospels' story and message: the miracles express Jesus' merciful purpose and are said to flow from individuals' trust that he could help them. In evaluating whether the Gospel is "true," the reader has to ask if the ancients were really more gullible than moderns when it comes to seeing what they previously thought was impossible. The Gospels repeatedly tell us that the people were astonished, just as we would be.

This goes especially for the stories of Jesus' resurrection. As we read the account in Matthew 28, we would have to think twice before suggesting that these stories were just made up. What first-century Middle Eastern male who was creating a resurrection legend would have said that the first witnesses to the resurrection were women (in a culture where a woman's word was commonly scorned as untrustworthy) or that some of Jesus' inner circle had doubts when they saw him risen (28:16)? No, what we have in Matthew and the other biblical resurrection narratives appears to be authentic testimony by people who were surprised and amazed as the events unfolded. Nor can the New Testament's claims of Jesus' victory over death be interpreted to mean only that Jesus had spiritually "gone to a better place" or that he was merely living on in the hearts and memories of his followers. To the contrary, from the beginning, both the empty tomb on the third day and Jesus' many bodily appearances to witnesses were cited as evidence of something unprecedented and tangible. Observe, for example, 1 Corinthians 15:1–20. Paul the Apostle writes in the mid-50s (just twenty-five years or so after the events) about what he insists had already been long established as the gospel message. He cites as "of first importance" that Jesus' burial ended on the third day with his resurrection, which was followed by a series of appearances by Jesus alive to hundreds of eyewitnesses, most of whom are still alive as Paul writes. He goes on to assert, "If Christ has not been raised, our preaching is useless and so is your faith." The early Christians' remarkable tenacity in proclaiming Jesus' resurrection even in the face of persecution is a stubborn fact.[39] In working out what we believe, we must be careful about our presuppositions regarding what is possible and what is not. The Gospel itself warns us against being so entrenched in long-standing intellectual tradition (in our case, naturalistic rationalism) that we rule out in advance what the Messiah actually turns out to be and do (Matthew 11:25; 16:6).

We do not need to resolve everything intellectually before deciding to follow Jesus. I remember my own hesitation, for example, about the story of the transfiguration in Matthew 17:1–8 when I was a college student beginning to work out seriously what it means to be a Christian. In my own case, once I became convinced that Jesus' resurrection from the dead was a real event, I was able to read other gospel stories that have supernatural elements with more openness. The point is: we can move forward with praying, entering church life, and working out discipleship to Jesus while we are still sorting through our attitudes toward particular stories.

The question of worldview is bigger than whether Jesus did this or that miracle. We are asking whether the true nature of reality is what Matthew's Gospel portrays: that the living God is fulfilling his long-term purposes for his people through Jesus, overcoming demonic forces to bring well-being and hope; that Jesus' death is God's decisive intervention to deliver humanity from spiritual bondage and guilt; that the risen Jesus is present "with us always" as we share in his ongoing work until the day when he will "come" in glory and judgment. As we read this Gospel's sweeping portrayal of reality, we are best advised simply to let it speak its own message. Matthew does not set out to "prove" what he announces; he just proclaims it as good news and beckons to us to decide about Jesus and respond. Jesus did the same to his audiences in the Gospel when he said repeatedly, "If you have ears to hear, then hear."

So as you read Matthew, if your ears and heart are open, if you will trust Jesus' words and do them, then you are in a position to confirm the truth of this "good news" by your own experience of it.

# NOTES

1 Millard Fuller and Diane Scott tell the whole story in *Love in the Mortar Joints: The Story of Habitat for Humanity* (Chicago: Association Press, 1980).

2. Regarding the reality of the devil and demons, see the discussion in the appendix, "Is Matthew True?" (esp. p. 312).

3. Matthew alone employs the expression "kingdom of heaven." He uses the New Testament's typical phrase, "kingdom of God," in 6:33; 12:28; 19:24; 21:31, 43. In 19:23–24, the two phrases are interchangeable.

4. Dallas Willard, *The Divine Conspiracy: Rediscovering Our Hidden Life in God* (San Francisco: HarperSanFrancisco, 1998), 100.

5. The helpful phrase "transforming initiatives" was coined by Glen H. Stassen and David P. Gushee in *Kingdom Ethics: Following Jesus in Contemporary Context* (Downers Grove, IL: InterVarsity Press, 2003), 298–301; Stassen, *Living the Sermon on the Mount: A Practical Hope for Grace and Deliverance* (San Francisco: Jossey-Bass, 2006), 76–81.

6 I will revisit the passage about divorce, verses 31–32, on Day 21.

7. In the Old Testament Law, Moses did not propose that any individual should attack an enemy's eye or tooth, and he never said to hate anyone. "Eye for eye, and tooth for tooth" was a law court limitation that criminal penalties could not be more severe than the crime that had been committed.

8. For the second time in the Sermon on the Mount, Jesus uses the phrase "*enter* the kingdom of heaven" (see 5:20; it recurs in 18:3; 19:23–24; and 23:13). Such a phrase could seem to suggest that we should think of the kingdom as a place, as our final destination. The phrase does refer to the final blessing, but it emphasizes inclusion rather than place. We could illustrate with the idea of being admitted to an Academy Awards ceremony, where the excitement comes not from being admitted into the place of the event, but from being included among the special people and from joy in the work they share and love; or of being admitted to a prince's wedding (22:2) where the joy comes from associating with royalty. In kingdom living now, we experience a foretaste of the inclusion, the joy of common endeavor, and the blessed closeness to the King that awaits us in the end. Jesus' alternative phrases

for "enter the kingdom" are "enter life" (7:13–14; 18:8–9; 19:17) and "enter into the joy" (25:21, 23 ESV).

9.   As a practical matter, governmental authorities sometimes grant access to poor and displaced people only on the condition that aid workers will not preach or try to convert them. In such cases, Jesus' messengers are limited to demonstrating the gospel rather than proclaiming it.

10.  Dallas Willard, *The Great Omission: Reclaiming Jesus' Essential Teachings on Discipleship* (San Francisco: HarperSanFrancisco, 2006), 62; italics mine.

11.  The illustrations are from Matthew 15:32, 35–36, 21–28; 20:29–34; 5:29–30, 39; 10:34–37, 39.

Because the Greek verb forms in Matthew 11:12 are ambiguous, and because two possible translations can fit well in the context, the verse is hard to translate with certainty. I have based my comments on the option reflected in the 1984 edition of the New International Version, which understands the kingdom and its people to be acting forcefully and effectively, but in a way that could be overlooked. The alternative presented in the latest New International Version understands Jesus to be saying that the kingdom of heaven has been subjected to physical violence and violent people are raiding it. That is, because people in power do not see and hear perceptively, John has been thrown in prison and will soon be executed, as will Jesus. The crowd should not deduce from such suffering that God has rejected either of them. Their kingdom work provokes violent resistance, and as we participate with Jesus, we too will experience suffering. His coming into the world brings a sword, and many of his loyalists will be pierced (10:34–36).

12.  For the story of God's rescue of Jonah, see Jonah 1:15–3:2, especially 1:17. For the Ninevites' repentance, see Jonah 3:3–10. The Queen of the South (Queen of Sheba) visits King Solomon in 1 Kings 10:1–10.

13.  In verse 4, when Jesus quotes Leviticus 20:9, he is unlikely to be endorsing the execution of children who mouth off to their parents. He does take seriously the obligation to honor father and mother. His point is that making excuses for not taking care of parents as they grow old is tantamount to cursing father and mother.

14.  Not all Pharisees rejected Jesus. Some supported and protected him; see Luke 13:31; John 3:1–2; 7:50–51; 19:39–40; also Acts 5:34–39. Some became his followers; see Acts 15:5; Philippians 3:4–7.

15.  Jesus' initial question is partly a claim: he is the "Son of Man." The phrase means "human being"—Jesus fully embodies our humanity, including our suffering. But as a title, the phrase points to the prophet's

vision of one who comes to rule eternally as sovereign king and to receive worship from the nations (Daniel 7:13–14). Suffering and glory are intertwined in the Son of Man.

16. The Greek word for "church" (*ekklēsia*) reflects a Hebrew word (*qāhāl*) representing the assembled people of Israel (Deuteronomy 4:10; 9:10). The church that Jesus is gathering fulfills God's plan for his people.

17. See p. 70 regarding the idea of "transforming initiatives" in the Sermon on the Mount.

18. Some early manuscripts of Matthew include two more words in 18:15: "If a brother or sister sins *against you*."

19. In Jesus' overwhelmingly male-dominant culture, the discarded woman, now regarded as used goods, was often forced into an exploitative man's arms in order to survive, so that she became a victim of adultery (5:32). We see the sad effects of this syndrome in the repeatedly discarded woman at the well in John 4:18.

20. The Apostle Paul specifically calls abandonment by one's partner permissible grounds for divorce in 1 Corinthians 7:15. In that same chapter (7:3–5), Paul cites traditional Jewish understanding of Moses' teaching (Exodus 21:10–11) that husbands are duty bound to provide bodily care (including food and clothing) and physical affection to their wives. See David Instone-Brewer's *Divorce and Remarriage in the Church: Biblical Solutions for Pastoral Realities* (Downers Grove, IL: InterVarsity Press, 2003), chaps. 8–9, and Instone-Brewer, *Divorce and Remarriage in the Bible: The Social and Literary Context* (Grand Rapids, MI: Wm. B. Eerdmans, 2002), chaps. 5 and 7.

21. This choice of singleness in response to God's special calling may be what Jesus has in mind when he speaks in 19:29 of "leaving . . . wife or children" for the sake of the kingdom—that is, relinquishing *in advance* the option of marriage and parenting. His strong advocacy of permanent marriage weighs against reading that verse (or Luke 18:29) to mean that Jesus calls some to abandon their spouse and children in order to serve him.

22. Jesus had intentionally selected a circle of twelve disciples, because they symbolize the fulfillment of God's grand plan to save humanity through the twelve-tribe family of Israel. Jesus may or may not be promising surpassing status to these twelve particular men; see Matthew 19:30 and 20:23. See also Jesus' statements that any and all faithful disciples will share his reign (24:47 and 25:23) and will possess the kingdom (5:3, 5, 10).

23. Regarding "leaving . . . wife or children," see note 21, above. I would add here another application. I remember several seminary friends

from Africa who endured being away from wife and children for periods of two or three years to come around the world to receive a seminary education so they could go home and become leaders in the cause of Christ.

24. Throughout Matthew, the author speaks as a Jew who is troubled that many of his fellow Jews have rejected Jesus and ultimately have sought his execution. It is because they are his own people that Matthew criticizes them and holds them accountable. In subsequent centuries, some non-Jews have used Matthew's criticism as a basis for anti-Jewish propaganda, saying especially that "the Jews killed Christ." Yet here in Jesus' third prediction of his crucifixion (20:18–19), he makes both Jews and Gentiles responsible for his execution. All of us, Jew and Gentile, have sinned against God, and all need the forgiveness of sins that his death obtains for us. Anti-Semitism, including "blaming the Jews," is an especially injurious form of supposing oneself to be superior over others, which these chapters repeatedly forbid. We do better to thank God humbly for his astonishing mercy toward us: because Jesus willingly subjected himself to his multiethnic killers, every human being has a full opportunity for life with God.

25. In a similar format to this book's month of devotional readings, Scot McKnight focuses on Jesus' affirmation of the two great commandments and draws out their implications for discipleship: *The Jesus Creed: Loving God, Loving Others* (Brewster, MA: Paraclete, 2004).

26. "If Jesus or his followers had practiced or countenanced homosexuality, it would have been profoundly scandalous within first-century Jewish culture. Such a controversy would surely have left traces in the tradition, as did Jesus' practice of having table fellowship with prostitutes and tax collectors. But there are no traces of such controversy." Richard B. Hays, *The Moral Vision of the New Testament: A Contemporary Introduction to New Testament Ethics* (San Francisco: HarperSanFrancisco, 1996), 395.

27. For more on Jesus' teaching about lust, see p. 72; on valuing singleness, p. 183; on a church member who continues in sinful behavior, p. 171; on not being judgmental, p. 90.

28. Edward W. Desmond, "Interview with Mother Teresa: A Pencil in the Hand of God," *Time* (December 4, 1989), 11.

29. The number three is a symbol of completeness in these chapters. Peter denies Jesus three times, completely disowning him. Jesus prays three times in Gethsemane, completely submitting his will to God. He is hung on one of three crosses, and so is thoroughly identified with lawless rebels. Darkness prevails for three hours as he fully bears the

world's sin. He remains in the tomb until the third day—he is fully dead before his resurrection.

30. Jesus' silence at the trials before the High Priest and Pilate fulfills the prophecy in Isaiah 53:7, "As a sheep before its shearers is silent, so he did not open his mouth." His silence will not necessarily be our model in every threatening situation. Sometimes we will negotiate, seeking reconciliation with our adversary (5:24–25). Sometimes we will speak boldly in dependence on the Holy Spirit, who will give us the right words to say (10:18–20, 32).

31. See note 24, above.

32. Donald A. Hagner, *Matthew 14–28*, Word Biblical Commentary 33B (Dallas: Word, 1995), 836.

33. Matthew 16:21; 17:23; 20:19; also 12:40; 26:32, 61.

34. Regarding some modern scholars' attempts to account for the resurrection stories on the theory that the earliest Christians were deceivers, see this book's appendix, "Is Matthew True?"

35. This is no exaggeration. See the statistics in Lamin Sanneh, *Disciples of All Nations: Pillars of World Christianity* (Oxford: Oxford University Press, 2008), 274–77, and the overview of global trends, xix–xxii.

36. On this matter of Mark's sources, oral and written, see the argument and bibliography in Robert A. Guelich, *Mark 1–8:26*, Word Biblical Commentary 34A (Dallas: Word Books, 1989), xxvii–xxxv.

37. See the useful chart of the material usually attributed to Q in Raymond E. Brown, *An Introduction to the New Testament* (New York: Doubleday, 1997), 118–19.

38. James R. Edwards, *Is Jesus the Only Savior?* (Grand Rapids: Wm. B. Eerdmans, 2005), 56. His first five chapters provide an excellent overview of the issues regarding historicity. In chapter 4, Edwards presents evidence against the thesis that Jesus' followers, in the period after his death, projected their own ideas and concerns back onto Jesus.

39. For a case that the resurrection of Jesus was a real event in the first century, see Craig Blomberg, *The Historical Reliability of the Gospels*, 2nd ed. (Downers Grove, IL: InterVarsity Press, 2007), 136–51; or N.T. Wright, *The Challenge of Jesus* (Downers Grove, IL: InterVarsity Press, 1999), 126–49. Wright expanded the latter into a major book, *The Resurrection of the Son of God* (Minneapolis: Fortress, 2003).

# ABOUT PARACLETE PRESS

### Who We Are

Paraclete Press is a publisher of books, recordings, and DVDs on Christian spirituality. Our publishing represents a full expression of Christian belief and practice—from Catholic to Evangelical, from Protestant to Orthodox.

We are the publishing arm of the Community of Jesus, an ecumenical monastic community in the Benedictine tradition. As such, we are uniquely positioned in the marketplace without connection to a large corporation and with informal relationships to many branches and denominations of faith.

### What We Are Doing

PARACLETE PRESS BOOKS | Paraclete publishes books that show the richness and depth of what it means to be Christian. Although Benedictine spirituality is at the heart of all that we do, we publish books that reflect the Christian experience across many cultures, time periods, and houses of worship. We publish books that nourish the vibrant life of the church and its people.

We have several different series, including the best-selling Paraclete Essentials and Paraclete Giants series of classic texts in contemporary English; Voices from the Monastery—men and women monastics writing about living a spiritual life today; award-winning poetry; best-selling gift books for children on the occasions of baptism and first communion; and the Active Prayer Series that brings creativity and liveliness to any life of prayer.

MOUNT TABOR BOOKS | Paraclete's newest series, Mount Tabor Books, focuses on liturgical worship, art and art history, ecumenism, and the first millennium church, and was created in conjunction with the Mount Tabor Ecumenical Centre for Art and Spirituality in Barga, Italy.

PARACLETE RECORDINGS | From Gregorian chant to contemporary American choral works, our recordings celebrate the best of sacred choral music composed through the centuries that create a space for heaven and earth to intersect. Paraclete Recordings is the record label representing the internationally acclaimed choir Gloriæ Dei Cantores, praised for their "rapt and fathomless spiritual intensity" by *American Record Guide*; the Gloriæ Dei Cantores Schola, specializing in the study and performance of Gregorian chant; and the other instrumental artists of the Gloriæ Dei Artes Foundation.

Paraclete Press is also privileged to be the exclusive North American distributor of the recordings of the Monastic Choir of St. Peter's Abbey in Solesmes, France, long considered to be a leading authority on Gregorian chant.

PARACLETE VIDEO | Our DVDs offer spiritual help, healing, and biblical guidance for a broad range of life issues including grief and loss, marriage, forgiveness, facing death, bullying, addictions, Alzheimer's, and spiritual formation.

Learn more about us at our website:
www.paracletepress.com or phone us
toll-free at 1.800.451.5006

SCAN
TO
READ
MORE

You may also be interested in . . .

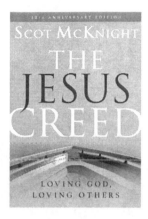

### The Jesus Creed
*Loving God, Loving Others*
Scot McKnight

Winner of the
2005 Christianity Today Book Award

Love God with all your heart, soul, mind, and strength, but also love others as yourselves. Discover how the Jesus Creed of love for God and others can transform your life.

ISBN: 978-1-61261-578-3 | Paperback
$15.99

### Fresh Air
*The Holy Spirit for an Inspired Life*
Jack Levison

"His scholarship is spot on, his human warmth and Christian compassion are everywhere. An unbeatable combination."
– N.T. Wright

"A rare and remarkable achievement."
– Eugene Peterson

The Holy Spirit is not just about speaking in tongues, or spiritual gifts, or "fruits"—but also about our deepest breath and our highest human aspirations.

ISBN: 978-1-61261-068-9 | Paperback
$15.99

CPSIA information can be obtained
at www.ICGtesting.com
Printed in the USA
FFOW03n1843110917
39847FF